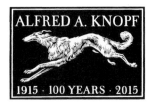

VEGETARIAN INDIA

VEGETARIAN INDIA

A JOURNEY THROUGH

THE BEST OF INDIAN HOME COOKING

Madhur Jaffrey

ALFRED A. KNOPF   NEW YORK   2015

Photography by Jonathan Gregson © Ebury Press 2014
Personal photographs by Sanford Allen on pages xiv, xv, xvii, xviii, xxi, xxiii, xxiv,
3, 16, 48, 61, 78, 79, 81, 82, 89, 100, 118, 131, 170, 188, 189, 216, 233, 269, 272,
291, 296, 302, 348, 361, 386, 398

Library of Congress Cataloging-in-Publication Data
Jaffrey, Madhur, [date] author.
Vegetarian India : a journey through the best of Indian home cooking /
Madhur Jaffrey. — First edition.
pages cm
Includes index.
ISBN 978–1-101–87486–8 (hardcover : alk. paper)—
ISBN 978–1-101–87487–5 (eBook)   1. Cooking, Indian.
2. Vegetarian cooking.   I. Title.
TX724.5.I4J314 2015
641.5954—dc23   2014048953
Front-of-jacket photograph © Jonathan Gregson
Jacket design by Kelly Blair

Manufactured in China
First American Edition

This Book Is Dedicated to Those in the Food World,
Alive or Departed,
Who Inspired Me,
Taught Me,
Encouraged Me,
Were Kind to Me,
And Helped Me
In a Variety of Thoughtful Ways:

JULIA CHILD

CRAIG CLAIBORNE

JUDITH JONES

JAMES BEARD

JANE GRIGSON

ELIZABETH DAVID

BILLY CROSS

MICHAEL JAMES

MARCELLA AND VICTOR HAZAN

ALICE WATERS

NILOUFER KING

CATHERINE BRANDEL

DONALD SLOAN

CONTENTS

ଓଓଓଓଓଓଓଓଓଓଓଓଓଓଓଓଓଓଓଓଓଓଓଓଓଓଓଓଓଓଓଓ

INTRODUCTION

ଓଓଓଓଓଓଓଓଓଓଓଓଓଓଓଓଓଓଓଓଓଓଓଓଓଓଓଓଓଓଓ

As many of us try to eat less meat and, instead, eat more of the natural grains, vegetables, and fruits that spring out of our good earth, people are turning to whole or partial vegetarianism as an answer.

Vegetarianism already exists in a widespread manner in several Eastern nations. But among them all, only India has a robust history of it that covers the different classes and regions of an entire subcontinent, from pauper to billionaire and from the mountainous Himalayan peaks in the north to the lush tropics of the south. Hundreds of millions of people in India eat traditional vegetarian cuisines. Indian vegetarian foods are perhaps the most flavorful and the most varied in the entire world. Many dishes are of ancient origin or inspiration, and they are seasoned with an array of spices carefully blended for both health and taste. Every housewife knows that turmeric is an antiseptic, ginger is good for colds and nausea, and asafetida is a digestive. This knowledge is used daily, almost automatically. What is more, Indian meals are always put together so they are nutritionally balanced: a grain is always served with a vegetable and a dairy product, not only because they taste good together but also because together they are nutritionally complete.

With this book, I want to take you on an adventurous ride through India, tasting the real vegetarian dishes that Indians eat in the privacy of their homes, in their local cafés and temples, at the parties they throw for each other, and at their wedding banquets and religious festivals.

Just imagine crisp okra fries dusted with chili powder, turmeric, and chickpea flour, or grilled portobello mushrooms flavored simply with green chilies, a couple of squeezes of lime juice, and salt, or a hot, sweet, and sour mash of eggplant on toast. You will find all these in the very first chapter, Soups, Appetizers, and Snacks.

The Vegetables chapter holds more good things. Some of you may, just may, have already had the sweet, sour, hot, salty, and coconut-enriched Kodava Mushroom Curry, which originated with the hunter-gatherers of the forested regions of Coorg in southern Karnataka—though I doubt it. Even Indians who live in North India are not familiar with this dish as it is a specialty of just one community, the Kodavas, who live in the heart of a specific wet, forested region in the hills that rise from the Arabian Sea in southern India. And it is never on any restaurant menu in the West. Yet it is so easy to make. You will find that recipe here. You will also find a sublime spinach stir-fried with garlic, cumin, and fenugreek seeds, and some potatoes from Goa studded with mustard seeds and refreshed with green chilies and cilantro.

Indians eat more dals—dried beans and legumes—than perhaps any other country. From black-eyed peas to chickpeas to mung beans and even soy granules, dals are eaten every day, and each time in a different manner. A dal might be boiled by itself and then brought to life with a tarka, a quick seasoning with whole spices dropped into hot oil. It could be cooked with other dals in a glorious mélange or cooked with vegetables. It could be transformed into a savory pancake for breakfast, or made into a flour and used in a batter for fritters. For Indians, dals are a protein-rich mainstay. They are cheap, highly nutritious, safe to eat, and an easy way to get a daily quota of protein. You will find dozens of recipes in these pages that might well change the look of your daily meals forever.

An American friend once told me that she had eaten an exquisite poha upma in a hotel in Madhya Pradesh. A *what*? She too was not familiar with the name, nor did she know exactly what she had eaten. She just knew that she has yearned for it ever since. You will find that recipe here in the Grains chapter. Poha is a version of rice that has been magically cooked, flattened, and dried in such a way that it retains all its nutrients. Because it is precooked, it can be combined with spices and vegetables to make poha upma, a spicy pilaf, with great speed. Indians need and love such recipes, as they too want to put food on the table as quickly and easily as possible. I want to help you get to know this ingredient, as I am sure you will want to use it frequently.

As I traveled around India for this book, I kept my eyes wide open for vegetarian dishes that are both delicious and easy to make. India has so many of them, and we all should have them in our repertoire.

In a way, I have been traveling for this book forever. I was born and raised in Delhi, and until I left India to study drama in London that was my world, in culinary matters and otherwise. It was when I was in America and not finding enough acting jobs that I turned to writing and to writing about food. My first book was on the food of Delhi. It was what I knew.

But I kept asking editors for assignments that would make me explore other parts of India. I needed to know my own country, which is really a continent. If a magazine asked for ten recipes, I came back with a few hundred. I wanted to understand the region. Recipes not required for the article went into my "bank," to be withdrawn as needed.

Over the years, I have developed my own system for collecting good recipes. I have learned that in India, these are always found in private homes, and that I cannot rely on generous offers of "written recipes." Well-meaning housewives who willingly part with them often leave out crucial ingredients that they take for granted, or use colloquial names and words I do not understand. I have to see the dish being cooked in front of my eyes. This way I know the exact amount of heat being used, the length of the cooking time, the amount of liquid required, and the exact cut of the vegetable.

When I decided to write this book, I knew that I could not collect all the material I needed in one trip. India is a vast nation, about the size of Europe, with as much variation between the cuisines of the different states as there is between the foods in the countries of Europe. And while I could fly between states, I preferred to rent a car and go from town to town and home to home, relying sometimes on connections I had already set up through emails and phone calls, and sometimes on the suggestions of people I happened to meet. My first trip was to my home region, including trips to Uttar Pradesh, Bihar, and Bengal, as well as to Bombay and the western state of Gujarat. I already knew all these areas quite well and could rely on friends and relatives to help me get the recipes I knew I wanted.

The next two trips were to areas that I knew less well, both in South India, Karnataka and Andhra Pradesh. This meant going right across India from the Arabian Sea to the Bay of Bengal, a good 645 miles as the crow flies, with many productive detours along the way. Driving on the roads, with every manner of traffic, from camels to bullock-carts to over-crowded, careening buses, was always painfully slow but also generous in allowing for many delicious food stops!

In Andhra alone, there were at least five distinct cuisines to be studied. I stayed in palace hotels to collect the recipes of the powerful former rulers, the Nizams; in private homes, watching dishes cooked by aristocratic Muslim housewives, I visited Kayastha women, who specialize in a mixed Hindu-Muslim cookery, and vegetarian weavers, who produce the finest natural-dyed ikats and whose wooden handlooms sit just a few feet away from their cooking stoves. Many brides dream of a red silk Pochampally ikat for their wedding saree, and only these weavers can make it. I spend a whole morning with D. Lalitha, just such a weaver, whose husband uses turmeric and indigo and annatto to dye the threads that she will weave later. As he dyes, she is kept busy making a lunch of a saaru (toovar dal with tamarind and the Indian vegetable known as a drumstick), rice, dosakai pacchadi (a special orange squash-like cucumber cooked with curry leaves, green chilies, cumin, mustard seeds, garlic, and ginger), and a wonderful green mango pickle.

Some dishes in this book were found quite serendipitously. The woman setting up my travels in Andhra mentioned a clothing designer in Hyderabad, Vinita Pittie, who lived in a 230-year-old family mansion in the heart of the old city. She was, I was told, a wonderful Marwari cook. I was immediately captivated: I love clothes, I love examining old mansions, and I love the vegetarian foods of the Marwari business community, which originated in Rajasthan but is now spread all over India. Her food turned out to be utterly delicious. And sure enough, I ended up buying a saree with fantastic embroidery! (For more on Vinita Pittie, see Potatoes in a Marwari Style, page 108.)

As we traveled along, I would call a halt at the sign of a good roadside food stand. "What, a pesarattu stand! Let us get out!" Pesarattus are mung bean pancakes (see page 250). I already knew that the recipe was going into the book, but I wanted to examine the technique of making the pancake yet again—and, let's face it, I wanted to eat one, too!

We traveled to chili fields and chili auctions, where I insisted on looking into everyone's lunch boxes and examining all the snacks being sold. How else could I understand the local palate? We went to the home of two sisters who made us Telengana-style food, rich in sesame seeds, and to the home of a lady from the Chowdhary business community who cooked an exquisite dish of spicy spinach.

In Karnataka, my routine was the same as in Andhra. Here I got in touch with Saras Ganapathy, the wife of a playwright I knew, and a very active social worker. She lives in Bangalore and knows everybody. I was going to be in Bangalore for just a week and then traveling through other parts of the state. I asked if she could please set up for me women from different communities who would do cooking sessions in the mornings and afternoons so I could watch and learn. It was a very tall order, but Saras managed it beautifully. She found me women from the Madhwa community who specialize in foods from the famous Udupi Temple area; Kodava women from the forests of Coorg whose mushroom and fern dishes are known only to them; women cooking foods from neighboring Tamil Nadu; women cooking the dishes of the Chitrapur Saraswat Brahmins; and women making the foods of the Palghat Iyers, who are Tamils living in Kerala.

In Bombay, I followed two very successful vegetarian jewelers to see what they ate for lunch and how they ate it. Both have shops at the Taj Mahal Palace. One, who comes from Varanasi in Uttar Pradesh, left his office every day around noon and went home to his family for lunch. This was the main meal of the day for the family. He spent about an hour and a half eating and then went back to his office. His father, who had replaced him in the shop for that time, then took his car and went back to the same home to have *his* lunch. They all live together. You will find the details of that meal, as well as the full menu, starting on page 158.

The second jeweler, whose shop had been shot at during the terrorist attack on the Taj Hotel in the winter of 2008, is a Punjabi from Delhi. His lunch setup, right in the shop, was entirely different. He and his two brothers, who work at their various Bombay shops, all ate together. The food, cooked by their wives, came from home at the last possible minute in a large tiffin carrier. The top of one of the larger jewelry cases was cleared off. Yes, the mirror to check out the earrings a customer might buy was removed, a tablecloth was spread out, and the "table" was laid properly. Then the tiffin carrier was opened and the brothers sat down to a full meal, right in the middle of the shop. For details, see page 168. The brothers pointed out a corner display case to me. On one shelf stood a statue of the elephant-headed god, Ganesh. When the terrorists' bullets had come flying in 2008—the men showed me the bullet holes—they went all around the statue but never touched it. Now, the brothers refuse to sell the statue.

I was also very curious about the hundreds of ashrams in India, as they all serve vegetarian food. What were they like, and what did they serve? Did they have certain culinary principles that they followed, or a certain style of cooking? I have friends, Virendra and Indira Dayal, who are familiar with the Aurobindo Ashram in Delhi and took me there. It is

located in a stunning modern building where the round, granite dining room, right at its heart, is open to the sky in the center. Anyone who is hungry is welcome to come in and eat—for free. The food, originating from all over India, is always made with very fresh ingredients, some grown on the premises, and is always mildly spiced and never too oily. I was taken around and shown where they grow, store, and cook their food. They even have a very good school on the premises. It is a whole way of life. (See more on the ashram on page 77.)

My friends also took me to the Chinmaya Mission in Delhi, which is connected to the famous Guruvayur Temple in Kerala. The priestess invited us in and, knowing of my interests, asked the head chef to join us. He came bearing food all so simple and delicious that two of the recipes found their way into this book, the Spicy Paneer Slices, page 9, and a dish of poha, the pressed dried rice that I mentioned earlier.

Ah, the poha! For this book I *am* going to make you go running to Indian shops to get a few new ingredients to store in your pantry. Poha will be one such new ingredient for many and, true, you will not find it in your local supermarket. At least not yet. Very few Indian ingredients were available when I first started writing cookbooks. But today cardamom and cilantro, which I could not find then, are in every supermarket. Even better, you can sit comfortably on your couch and order almost everything you need online. Poha is a great new ingredient to learn about. Indian vegetarians always have poha in their pantries to make a very quick snack if unexpected guests show up. You should too.

For this book I have collected recipes for potato salad from Nepal, which came from my "bank" and a quick trip to a Queens, New York, restaurant, page 344, the superb Eggs in a Hyderabadi Tomato Sauce, page 286, from one of the aristocratic families of Hyderabad, and a lovely potato dish, page 108, from the Marwari business community that originated in the deserts of Rajasthan.

This is the wonder of Indian food—its specificity to each state, each town, each community. It is these very regional foods that I wanted for this book, as that is where vegetarian India is at its most glorious. I am equally interested in *how* people in different Indian communities eat—their eating habits and their menus—as these offer true glimpses into the variety of vegetarian worlds within India. I hope, in the pages that follow, that you will get to know some of these people as I did. Food, as we all know, does not exist in a vacuum. I always like to know the background of the dishes I eat. I hope you do too, and I'll provide some context for the recipes as I go along.

I have also created quite a few "modern" dishes that use traditional Indian spices and techniques but have Western origins, such as the Pan-Grilled Zucchini with a Spicy Tomato Sauce, page 34, and Mangoes Mumtaz, a lovely, light, fluffy dessert.

Perhaps most important of all, none of the recipes in this book are overly complicated to prepare. They may have many ingredients and take a little time, but do not be put off by that, as the cooking process is usually quite simple. Indian dishes need their particular spices, and they need to cook at their own pace, but they do not require complicated cooking techniques. Vegetarians—and even non-vegetarians—will want them in their repertoires. In India's ancient Ayurvedic system of medicine, it is believed that the simple acts of cutting and chopping and stirring are graces that can bring you peace and calm. This is what I wish for you.

A restaurant kitchen in Vishakhapatnam, Telengana

ഇᢊഇᢊഇᢊഇᢊഇᢊഇᢊഇᢊഇᢊഇᢊഇᢊഇᢊഇᢊഇᢊഇᢊഇᢊഇᢊഇᢊഇᢊ

A NOTE ON INGREDIENTS

ഇᢊഇᢊഇᢊഇᢊഇᢊഇᢊഇᢊഇᢊഇᢊഇᢊഇᢊഇᢊഇᢊഇᢊഇᢊഇᢊഇᢊ

Here are some notes about a few of the common ingredients and techniques required in this book. More uncommon ingredients have notes within the chapters (see the index).

CHILIES, CHILI POWDER, AND THE MATTER OF HEAT How hot should a dish be? When is it too hot? Who decides? All these decisions are very personal. If chili heat were indicated by the color red, it would be true to say that Indian food comes in all shades, from a very pale pink to very deep crimson. You could also opt for no heat at all, as some Indians do. For every dish of Indian food you make, you will have to decide just how hot you want it. I have provided a guide by giving a sliding number to the chilies or chili powder in a recipe. Use more or less, as you desire. Practice and experience will have to be your guides.

To make matters more difficult, however, both green chilies and dried red chilies can have different amounts of heat, even if you buy the same variety each time. You have to leave a certain amount to chance. Use less to start off with, and if you want more heat later, increase it with chili powder.

GREEN CHILIES, FRESH Indian chilies are thin skinned, bright green, slim, and hot, but nowhere near as hot as the West Indian habañeros. Green chilies are an essential part of the taste of authentic Indian foods, so what kind should you buy? If you have access to an Indian grocer, buy your chilies there. They always carry the small, slim, bird's-eye chilies, and a longer chili somewhat like a cayenne pepper but milder. Buy any

FACING PAGE: The most common Indian green chili, found all over the country.

of them. If you have no access to an Indian grocer, get small serrano chilies. Their skin is thicker and they are fatter, but they will do. As serranos are larger, use fewer of them.

If whole green chilies are called for, quarter them lengthwise. Indians rarely remove the seeds.

RED CHILIES, DRIED India has many varieties of dried red chilies. The average is more like dried red Italian peperoncini, which you can use as a substitute. It is about 2 inches long and its heat can be medium or hot. In the north, these chilies are often used whole, whereas in the south, they are generally broken into two or three pieces. Another dried chili that I like very much is the byadgi, commonly used in the Indian state of Karnataka. It imparts a paprika-like red color and has a medium heat. Sadly, it is not easily found in the West. At my insistence, some stores (such as Kalustyan's in New York City) have started selling it. These chilies are long and slim, with a crinkly, uneven skin. I love them for the color they give. As they are milder, you can use several of them. In India you can also buy a powder made with these chilies. It gives both flavor and a lovely red color to the foods it is used with. Sometimes I combine red chili powder and a good red paprika to get the same effect.

CUMIN SEEDS, ROASTING AND GRINDING My Indian grocer now sells ground, roasted cumin seeds. Who would have thought it! Here is how you can do it yourself and make a very fresh, aromatic batch:

Put 3–4 tablespoons cumin seeds into a small cast-iron frying pan and set over medium heat. Stir the seeds around until they emit a lovely roasted aroma and turn a shade darker. Do not let them burn. Transfer to a sheet of paper towel to cool. Empty into a clean grinder or spice mill (I use a coffee grinder reserved for spices) and grind them as finely as possible. Store in a tightly closed jar.

CURRY LEAVES, FRESH These are essential for cooking foods from southern and western India. Either buy a plant online (the botanical name is *Murraya koenigii*—I keep two in my house) or find a source that sells the leaves. They are sold as sprays, and all Indian grocers have them. They last several weeks in the refrigerator.

GINGER, TO GRATE Peel as much of the ginger as you need (a 1-inch piece yields about 1 teaspoonful), then grate it on a Microplane. Micro-

FACING PAGE: Spices being ground in a mortar.

planes come in all sizes. I use the second-smallest size. You are aiming for a fine pulp.

TARKA An extra jolt of flavor given to a dish at the beginning, the middle, or the end of making it. This technique is common throughout India and may be used on a salad, in a yogurt relish, or in a cooked dish. It has different names in different places, including "chhownk," "baghaar," and "vaghaar." You heat a small amount of oil in a small pan, then drop spices into it in quick succession until they pop, caramelize, darken, or otherwise intensify in flavor. These spices and the oil are then tipped over the food, or the food is allowed to cook in the mixture. As tarkas take just a few seconds, it is important to have all the required ingredients close at hand. Many Indian grocers sell little pots, sometimes shaped like small woks, specifically for preparing tarkas. If you get one of them, make sure that it has good balance and a long handle. A small frying pan will also do. In South India, small quantities of dals (split peas) are frequently used as a spice in the tarka. As they darken, they add a very pleasant nutty flavor.

TOMATOES, TO PEEL I like to peel my tomatoes before chopping them as I do not like the little curls of skin that appear in cooked foods. Indians generally do not peel their tomatoes—but Indian tomato skins are not as tough as those grown elsewhere. I peel a firm tomato just like an apple, with a paring knife. If the tomato is soft, you can drop it into boiling water for a minute and then pull off the skin.

Tarka chilies

SOUPS, APPETIZERS, AND SNACKS

RED PEPPER AND TOMATO SOUP

LAL SHIMLA MIRCH AUR TAMATAR KA SOUP

cඑcඑcඑcඑcඑcඑcඑcඑcඑcඑcඑcඑcඑcඑcඑcඑcඑcඑcඑcඑcඑ

1 cup moong dal (skinned and
   split mung beans)
4 tablespoons olive or peanut
   oil
1 medium onion (about 5 oz),
   peeled and chopped
One 1 inch piece of fresh
   ginger, peeled and
   chopped
2 lbs red peppers, seeded and
   coarsely chopped
½ teaspoon whole fennel
   seeds
½ teaspoon ground turmeric
1 teaspoon ground cumin
1 teaspoon ground coriander
¼ teaspoon nice red chili
   powder
2 medium tomatoes (about
   10 oz in all), chopped
1½ teaspoons salt
6 tablespoons heavy cream
   (optional)

A very nutritious and delicious soup. If you leave out the cream, it is vegan.

As stock, I use the broth from cooking a dal, a trick commonly used in South India. In that area the leftover dal is used to make a curry (sambar), but I have used it later to make a risotto (see page 214).   SERVES 6

cඑcඑcඑcඑcඑcඑcඑcඑcඑcඑcඑcඑcඑcඑcඑcඑcඑcඑcඑcඑcඑ

1. Wash the dal in several changes of water. Drain. Put in a pan with 12 cups water and bring to a boil. Cover partially, then lower the heat and simmer gently for 45 minutes. Take the pan off the heat and let it sit for 15 minutes. Scoop off and reserve 5 cups of the liquid from the top of the pot. Discard the dal solids or use them to make a risotto.

2. Put the oil in a large pan over medium-high heat. When hot, add the onions, ginger, red peppers, and fennel seeds. Stir and fry for 5–6 minutes or until the vegetables just start to brown. Add the turmeric, cumin, coriander, chili powder, and tomatoes. Stir and cook for another 2 minutes. Now add 2 cups of the reserved liquid and bring to a simmer. Cover and simmer gently for about 25 minutes. Set aside to cool a little, then blend the soup and strain it through a coarse strainer.

3. Return the soup to the empty pan. Add the salt, 2 cups more of the reserved liquid, and the cream (if using). Stir to mix and see if the thickness is what you want. You can thin the soup further with some of the remaining liquid. Reheat, stirring, when you are ready to eat.

FACING PAGE: The gods protect a weaver's trade

RED LENTIL AND ZUCCHINI SOUP

MASOOR DAL AUR COURGETTE KA SOUP

2 tablespoons olive or peanut oil

4 cloves

1 medium onion (about 6 oz), peeled and chopped

2 teaspoons peeled and grated fresh ginger

1 teaspoon peeled and crushed garlic

1 teaspoon ground coriander

1 teaspoon ground cumin

¼–¾ teaspoon nice red chili powder

½ teaspoon ground turmeric

1 cup masoor dal (red lentils), picked over, washed, and drained

1 medium potato (about 4 oz), peeled and diced

Handful of fresh green cilantro tops

10–12 fresh curry leaves, lightly crushed in your hand

1½ cups chopped zucchini (or yellow squash)

About 1¾ teaspoons salt

FOR THE YOGURT SAUCE

1 cup plain yogurt

1 tablespoon lime or lemon juice

1 packed cup fresh cilantro, leaves and small stems only

2 fresh hot green chilies, chopped

¼ teaspoon salt

This delicious soup is a meal in itself, as it contains legumes and vegetables and is served with a yogurt sauce. Slices of whole-grain bread offered on the side would make the meal nutritionally complete.

The sauce that accompanies the soup is really a chutney, which may also be used to dress simply cooked vegetables, such as boiled potatoes, carrots, and peas, or diced and steamed zucchini.

SERVES 4–5

1. Put the oil in a good-sized pan and set over medium-high heat. When hot, add the cloves and let them sizzle for a few seconds. Add the onions and fry them, stirring, for about 6–7 minutes or until they just start to brown. Lower the heat to medium and stir in the ginger and garlic. Add the ground coriander, cumin, chili powder, and turmeric and stir for a minute. Now add 5 cups water, the masoor dal, potatoes, fresh cilantro, and curry leaves (take care, as these will splutter). Stir, turn up the heat, and bring to a boil. Turn the heat to very low, cover, and cook for 40 minutes.

2. Add the zucchini and salt. Stir and bring to a simmer. Cover, lower the heat again, and cook for another 10 minutes. Set aside to cool a little.

3. Blend the soup finely in two batches. Return it to the pan and add 1 cup water or more to thin it to your liking. Reheat as and when needed.

4. To make the yogurt sauce: Put all the ingredients in a blender in the order listed and whiz until smooth. This sauce should be refrigerated if not used soon. Serve it cold or at room temperature, drizzled generously over the very hot soup. More sauce should be offered on the side.

TOMATO RASAM SOUP

TAMATAR RASAM KA SOUP

৩৩৩৩৩৩৩৩৩৩৩৩৩৩৩৩৩৩৩৩৩৩৩৩৩৩৩৩৩৩৩৩৩

4 tablespoons plain toovar
    dal, well washed in several
    changes of water and
    drained

¼ teaspoon ground turmeric

1 tablespoon chickpea flour
    (besan or gram flour)

¾ teaspoon tamarind
    concentrate (sold in
    bottles)

1 tablespoon rasam powder

2 cups tomato puree

1½ teaspoons salt

2 teaspoons olive or peanut oil

Generous pinch of ground
    asafetida

¼ teaspoon urad dal

½ teaspoon whole brown
    mustard seeds

1 dried hot red chili

6–8 fresh curry leaves, lightly
    crushed in your hand

Rasams in South India are thin, watery drinks that are very hot, sour, and spicy. They are generally served with rice or just drunk on their own, but you can read more about them on page 359. For this particular recipe, I have thickened the drink so it can be served as a soup. Occasionally, I like to serve it with a little dollop of plain rice in the center. At other times, I serve it in small coffee cups even before my guests come to the dinner table. They just drink it from the cups.

Indian grocers sell rasam powder. Get a good South Indian brand, such as MTR. SERVES 4–5

৩৩৩৩৩৩৩৩৩৩৩৩৩৩৩৩৩৩৩৩৩৩৩৩৩৩৩৩৩৩৩৩৩

1. Put the dal and 3½ cups water in a good-sized pan and bring to a boil. Skim off the froth, then stir in the turmeric. Cover partially, lower the heat, and cook for 30–40 minutes or until the dal is soft.

2. Meanwhile, put the chickpea flour, tamarind concentrate, and rasam powder into a large bowl. Add 1 tablespoon of water and mix to a smooth paste. Add another tablespoon of water and mix again. Add the tomato puree, salt, and 1½ cups water and mix well.

3. When the dal is done, add the tomato puree mixture to the pan. Mix and bring to a boil. Cover partially, lower the heat, and simmer gently for 10 minutes. Let the soup cool a bit, then blend until smooth. Return it to the pan.

4. Put the oil in a small frying pan and set over medium-high heat. When hot, add the asafetida and let it sizzle for a few seconds. Add the urad dal. As soon as it starts to pick up color, add

the mustard seeds and chili. When the mustard seeds pop and the chili darkens, a matter of seconds, add the curry leaves (take care, as these will splutter). Stir once and pour the contents of the frying pan into the soup. Stir and cover.

5. Reheat the soup, removing the chili and curry leaves before serving.

CAULIFLOWER SOUP

GOBI KA SOUP

ღღღღღღღღღღღღღღღღღღღღღღღღღღღღ

3 tablespoons olive or peanut
oil

½ teaspoon whole cumin
seeds

¼ teaspoon whole fennel
seeds

1 medium onion (about 6½
oz), peeled and chopped

1 medium potato (about
6½ oz), peeled and
chopped

2 teaspoons peeled and grated
fresh ginger

2 cloves garlic, peeled and
chopped

1 fresh hot green chili,
chopped

2 teaspoons ground coriander

1 teaspoon ground cumin

¼ teaspoon ground turmeric

¼ teaspoon nice red chili
powder

About 3½ cups cauliflower
florets

2 medium tomatoes, peeled
and chopped

1½ teaspoons salt, or to taste

Generous handful of fresh
cilantro, chopped

Freshly ground black pepper

2 teaspoons lime juice
(optional)

4–5 tablespoons heavy cream

A simple soup that I loved as a child. It reminds me of Indian hotel soups in the waning years of the Raj. SERVES 4–6

ღღღღღღღღღღღღღღღღღღღღღღღღღღ

1. Put the oil in a good-sized pan and set over medium-high heat. When hot, add the cumin seeds, and a few seconds later the fennel seeds. Wait 2 seconds and add the onions and potatoes. Stir and sauté for 5 minutes. Add the ginger, garlic, and green chilies. Stir for 1 minute.

2. Turn the heat to medium low and add the ground coriander, cumin, turmeric, and chili powder. Stir for 1 minute. Now put in the cauliflower, tomatoes, salt, and fresh cilantro. Stir for 1 minute. Add 4 cups water, stir, and bring to a boil over medium-high heat. Cover, lower the heat, and simmer gently for 25 minutes.

3. Let the soup cool a bit, then blend it in two batches. Taste for seasoning, adding some black pepper, the lime juice if you want it, and the cream. You can push the soup through a sieve or food mill if you want a very smooth texture. Reheat to serve.

SPICY PANEER SLICES

TALA MASALEDAR PANEER

೧೮೧೮೧೮೧೮೧೮೧೮೧೮೧೮೧೮೧೮೧೮೧೮೧೮೧೮೧೮೧೮೧೮೧೮

12 oz fresh Indian cheese
(paneer), defrosted if
frozen

Scant ½ teaspoon salt

½–1 teaspoon nice red chili
powder

Scant ½ teaspoon ground
turmeric

1 tablespoon rice flour (also
called rice powder)

1 tablespoon chickpea flour
(besan or gram flour)

Oil, for frying

Sprinkling of chaat masala
(optional)

My friends Juji and Viru Dayal had told me that the food at the Chinmaya Mission in Delhi was very good and had taken me to sample some of it. I knew that the main branch was attached to the Guruvayur Temple in Kerala, so the food would be both northern and southern. The first dish I was offered was this spicy paneer from the north. It was superb.

You can make your own paneer (see note on page 292) or buy it ready-made from Indian grocers. It is generally frozen in rectangles, but does not take long to defrost. I just put the whole unopened packet in a bowl of warm water.   SERVES 4

೧೮೧೮೧೮೧೮೧೮೧೮೧೮೧೮೧೮೧೮೧೮೧೮೧೮೧೮೧೮೧೮೧೮೧೮

From the Chinmaya Mission in Delhi

1. Cut the paneer into slices about 1½ inches square and ½ inch thick. The shape of your slab of paneer will dictate the actual shape, but make the slices no thicker than ½ inch.

2. Lay the slices out in a single layer. Dust the first side with half the salt, half the chili powder, and half the turmeric. Rub these in as evenly as you can. Turn the slices over and do exactly the same on the other side with the remaining salt, chili powder, and turmeric.

3. Combine the rice flour and chickpea flour in a small bowl. Dip one paneer slice at a time into the bowl. Shake off the excess flour and put the slice on a board or plate. Repeat with the remaining slices. You can cover these slices and hold them for an hour.

4. Just before you are ready to eat, heat a ½ inch depth of oil in a medium frying pan over medium heat. When oil is hot, slide in half the slices and fry them for about a minute on each side or

until golden brown. Remove with a slotted spoon and transfer to a plate lined with a paper towel. Do a second batch the same way.

5. Lightly sprinkle the paneer with the chaat masala, if desired, and serve immediately.

CABBAGE FRITTERS

CABBAGE VEPADU

৶৶৶৶৶৶৶৶৶৶৶৶৶৶৶৶৶৶৶৶৶৶৶৶৶৶৶৶৶৶৶

½ head of cabbage (about 1 lb)

1 tablespoon cornstarch

3 tablespoons chickpea flour (besan or gram flour), plus more as needed

1 teaspoon salt

½–¾ teaspoon chili powder

2 teaspoons ground coriander

¼ teaspoon ground turmeric

Handful of raw peanuts, with or without skin (optional)

8–10 fresh curry leaves, shredded

Handful of fresh cilantro tops, well washed, dried, and chopped

Olive or peanut oil, for deep-frying

I was in Rajahmundry, a town on the banks of the mighty Godavari River—the widest river I have ever seen—in Andhra Pradesh. It was lunchtime, and I was desperately hungry. Someone thought I should try a mess. That suggested a military setup, but it turned out to be nothing of the kind, though the name may have originated there in British times.

Andhra messes are places to eat local food very cheaply. The one I went into was in a basement, dark and sad. But the food was vegetarian, clean, and excellent. For 50 rupees (about 80 cents) I got two types of rice, one plain and one Tomato Rice (see page 180), vegetables cooked in buttermilk, a jackfruit curry, two dals, including Sambar (see page 166) as well as Rasam (see page 359), a spicy drink, some chutneys and yogurt relishes, and this Cabbage Vepadu.

Vepadus are fried or stir-fried dishes. Crisp, fried foods are a basic part of every South Indian meal, as crunchy foods are considered an essential texture. Sometimes just a popadam will do, but here we actually had two such dishes—these cabbage fritters and crispy, mesh-like squares made with potato.

All this was served on what looked like metal "thalis," or platters, that were gold on the outside and silver on the inside. They were actually made out of a thin foil that initially had to be anchored to the table with a glass of water, because otherwise the fan just blew them away. At the end of the meal they were crumpled up and thrown away, just as banana leaves might have been in earlier times.

Serve these fritters as part of a meal, as a snack, or as a first course with a chutney.   MAKES 10–12

৶৶৶৶৶৶৶৶৶৶৶৶৶৶৶৶৶৶৶৶৶৶৶৶৶৶৶৶৶৶৶

1. The fritters have a spidery look when fried, with wild strands sticking out from a more solid center. To achieve this, the cab-

bage has to be cut by hand. Cut the cabbage in half lengthwise, then in half again. Remove the hard core. Now set a piece down on one of its flat sides and, using a bread knife, cut its other flat side lengthwise into the finest long shreds you can manage—the thinner, the better. Do the same with the other sections of the cabbage. Put all the cabbage shreds into a bowl. Add all the remaining ingredients, except the oil. Using your hands (you can wear plastic gloves if you wish), rub all the seasonings and flours into the cabbage. If you fry the fritters immediately (this is best), you will not need more chickpea flour. If you wait, the cabbage will weep and get watery, so you might need to rub in 1–2 more tablespoons of flour (making the fritters denser).

2. Put the oil for frying in a wok or medium frying pan and set over medium-low heat. When hot enough, a shred of cabbage placed in the oil should sizzle immediately. Using your hand and a light touch, pick up a tablespoon or so of the cabbage mixture, keeping it flat rather than ball-like. Carefully lower it into the oil. Repeat, adding as many fritters as the pan will hold easily. Fry, turning now and then, for 5–6 minutes or until golden red, crisp, and cooked all the way through. Remove with a slotted spoon and place on a tray lined with a paper towel.

3. Make all the fritters this way, adjusting the heat as needed. Serve immediately.

ONION FRITTERS

KANDA BHAJIA OR PYAZ KI PAKORI

curlicue separator

3 smallish onions (about 8 oz
in all), peeled and cut into
⅛ inch rounds (you could
use a mandoline here) and
the rounds cut into halves

⅛–¼ teaspoon nice red chili
powder

1 teaspoon peeled and finely
grated fresh ginger

3 tablespoons chopped fresh
cilantro

1 fresh hot green chili, cut into
fine rounds (optional)

½ teaspoon ground cumin

Generous pinch of ground
turmeric

4 tablespoons chickpea flour
(besan or gram flour)

⅓ teaspoon salt

Olive or peanut oil, for deep-
frying

It is Indian restaurants in the West, particularly Britain, that have popularized onion bhajias as a first course. That name comes from western India, where all varieties of fritters are called bhajias and eaten at teatime or as a snack with lots of hot chutney for dipping.

In most of northern India, fritters made with potatoes, green beans, eggplant, and other vegetables are known as "pakoras" or "pakoris" and eaten as a snack at teatime, and with drinks (both soft and alcoholic).

In Bengal, where fritters are known as "bhaja," they can, indeed, be a first course, eaten with rice and dal, the soft and the crunchy together considered a perfect balance. They may also be offered at *jalkhabar*, the midmorning snack. Bengalis prepare all manner of vegetable fritters, including those made with potato skins and dusted with kalonji, or nigella seeds.

In the south, where the fritters have a variety of names, including "vepadu," they are often an essential part of the meal, along with popadams, providing crunch and texture to the more soft and flowing rices and dals.

The flour used to bind the fritters is usually the nutritious chickpea flour, rice flour, or a combination of the two.

Serve piping hot with Green Chutney (see page 304) and/or Simple Tamarind Chutney (see page 308), diluting every tablespoon of the latter with a tablespoon of water.

MAKES 12 MEDIUM-SIZED FRITTERS

curlicue separator

1. Put the onions, chili powder, ginger, fresh cilantro, green chilies (if using), cumin, and turmeric into a bowl. Toss lightly to mix. Dust with the chickpea flour but do not mix it in yet. About 15 minutes before eating, add the salt. Now mix thoroughly with your hands, mashing the seasonings and flour into the onions. Do this for about 5 minutes or until you draw out enough water

from the onions to be able to hold the slices together in cohesive lumps.

2. Put a ½ inch depth of oil in a medium frying pan and set over medium heat.

3. Meanwhile, make 12 rough patties from the onion mixture, placing them in a single layer on a cutting board or plate as you make them. Onion pieces will stick out, but that is how it should be.

4. When the oil is hot, turn the heat to medium low and put in half the patties in a single layer. Fry for 1 minute on the first side. Turn the patties over and fry for another minute on the second side. Turn again and fry for another 30 seconds or so on each side. The patties should be reddish gold and crisp. Remove with a slotted spoon and drain on a paper towel. Make a second batch the same way.

5. Serve hot with chutney on the side, as suggested on the previous page.

Fried snacks from the streets of Vijaywada

Andhra Pradesh

SPINACH BHAJIAS

PALAG KI PAKORI

୧୨୧୨୧୨୧୨୧୨୧୨୧୨୧୨୧୨୧୨୧୨୧୨୧୨୧୨୧୨୧୨୧୨୧୨

4 cups chopped fresh
   spinach, washed and dried
   thoroughly (you can use a
   salad spinner if you like)
6 tablespoons chickpea flour
   (besan or gram flour)
2 tablespoons rice flour (also
   called rice powder)
1–3 generous pinches of nice
   red chili powder
½ teaspoon ground roasted
   cumin seeds (see page xx)
1 fresh hot green chili, finely
   chopped (optional)
2–3 tablespoons chopped
   fresh cilantro
⅓ teaspoon salt
Olive or peanut oil, for deep-
   frying
½ teaspoon kalonji (nigella
   seeds)

These are best served piping hot with some Green Chutney (see page 304) and/or Simple Tamarind Chutney (see page 308); dilute every tablespoon of the latter with a tablespoon of water.

For more on Indian fritters in general, see the introduction to Onion Fritters (see page 15).

MAKES 12 MEDIUM-SIZED FRITTERS

୧୨୧୨୧୨୧୨୧୨୧୨୧୨୧୨୧୨୧୨୧୨୧୨୧୨୧୨୧୨୧୨୧୨୧୨

1. Combine the spinach, chickpea flour, rice flour, chili powder, roasted cumin seeds, green chilies (if using), fresh cilantro, and salt in a bowl. Mix well, mashing the mixture with your hand. Slowly add about 6 tablespoons water, mashing and mixing until the mixture can hold together in small clumps. Do not add more water than necessary.

2. Put a ½ inch depth of oil in a medium frying pan and set over medium heat.

3. Meanwhile, make 12 rough patties from the spinach mixture, placing them in a single layer on a cutting board or plate as you make them. Sprinkle the kalonji evenly over the top of the patties.

4. When the oil is hot, turn the heat to medium low and put in half the patties in a single layer. Fry for 1 minute on the first side. Turn the patties over and fry for another minute on the second side. Turn again and fry for another 30 seconds or so on each side. The patties should be reddish gold and crisp. Remove with a slotted spoon and drain on a paper towel. Make a second batch the same way.

5. Serve hot with chutney on the side, as suggested above.

SPICED POTATO-BALL FRITTERS

BONDA OR BATATA VADA

1½ lbs unpeeled waxy potatoes (I use red ones), freshly boiled and cooled

2 tablespoons olive or peanut oil

Generous pinch of ground asafetida

¼ teaspoon whole brown or yellow mustard seeds

4 tablespoons finely chopped onions

2 teaspoons peeled and very finely chopped fresh ginger

1–2 fresh green chilies, finely chopped

1 teaspoon ground cumin

3 tablespoons chopped fresh cilantro

1½–2 teaspoons lime or lemon juice

1 teaspoon salt, or to taste

Olive or peanut oil, for deep-frying

FOR THE BATTER

1¼ cups chickpea flour (besan or gram flour)

¼ cup rice flour (also called rice powder)

½ teaspoon baking powder

½ teaspoon salt

¼ teaspoon ajowan seeds

Generous pinch of ground asafetida

½ teaspoon ground turmeric

Wherever Indian snack sellers congregate, such as Chowpatty Beach in Bombay, you are likely to find some version of these bondas. Round in shape, with a chickpea flour skin on the outside and spicy crushed potatoes inside, they are served still hot and crisp from the karhais (woks) in which they are fried. Very popular in western and southern India, they are eaten with chutneys, such as Simple Tamarind Chutney (see page 308), Green Chutney (see page 304), Fresh Cilantro, Ginger, and Coconut Chutney (see page 310), and Red Chutney from the Konkan Coast (see page 318).

MAKES 16 BONDAS

1. Peel the cooked and cooled potatoes and crush them. You are aiming for a very coarse version of mashed potatoes.

2. Put the 2 tablespoons of oil in a medium, preferably nonstick frying pan and set over medium heat. When hot, add the asafetida. A second later, add the mustard seeds. As soon as they pop, a matter of seconds, add the onions, ginger, green chilies, cumin, and fresh cilantro. Stir for a minute. Add the crushed potatoes, lime juice, and salt. Turn the heat to low and mix all the ingredients well. Taste for balance of flavors and make adjustments, if needed. Set aside until cool enough to handle, then make 16 balls, each about 1½ inches in diameter. Transfer to a plate and set aside.

3. Combine all the ingredients for the batter in a bowl. Slowly add water, about 2 tablespoons less than 1 cup, mixing and breaking up any lumps as you go. You should have a thick but flowing batter.

4. Put a 2 inch depth of oil in a deep frying pan, wok, or karhai and set over medium-low heat. Give it time to get hot.

5. Dip a potato ball in the batter, making sure it is well covered. Carefully lower it into the hot oil. Do this rapidly with half the balls. Fry, turning frequently for 5–6 minutes or until the outside batter looks crisp. It should not turn dark. Remove with a slotted spoon and drain on a paper towel. Make a second batch the same way.

6. Serve while still crisp and hot.

SPICY MATCHSTICK POTATOES

ALOO KA TALA HUA LACCHA

ಲ ಲ

2 teaspoons lemon juice

1 medium onion (about 5 oz),
   peeled and chopped

2 cloves garlic, peeled and
   chopped

A 1-inch piece of fresh ginger,
   peeled and chopped

1 hot dried red chili, crumbled

1 teaspoon ground cumin
   seeds

4 medium potatoes (about
   1¼ lbs in total)

Olive or peanut oil, for frying

1 tablespoon whole sesame
   seeds

¾–1 teaspoon salt

Freshly ground black pepper

1 teaspoon sugar

This is a wonderful snack to nibble on, especially when enjoying favorite TV programs and films at home. You could serve it with Simple South Indian Tomato Sauce (see page 345), plain old tomato ketchup, or nothing at all. It is good just by itself.

SERVES 4

ಲ ಲ

1. Put the lemon juice, onions, garlic, ginger, red chili, and cumin into a blender or food processor. Whiz, pushing down as necessary, until you have a smooth paste.

2. Peel the potatoes and cut them lengthwise into slices ⅛ inch thick. (You can use a mandoline if you wish.) Stacking a few slices together at a time, cut them into strips of the same thickness. If not frying immediately, put the potatoes into a bowl of water, then drain and pat dry before the next step.

3. Put a ½ inch depth of oil in a large frying pan and set over medium heat. When hot, put in as many potatoes as will fit easily. Stir and fry until they are golden and crisp. Remove with a slotted spoon and spread out on a paper towel to drain. Cook all the potatoes this way.

4. Remove all but 4 tablespoons of oil from the frying pan. Put the sesame seeds into the hot oil. Stir and fry until they begin to pop. Pour in the onion mixture, then stir and fry slowly until it has browned and is quite dry. This is important.

5. Now put in the fried potatoes, salt, pepper, and sugar. Mix, breaking up the spice clumps and spreading them about. Remove with a slotted spoon and serve hot or at room temperature.

SAVORY PASTRY STRIPS WITH AJOWAN SEEDS

NAMAKPARA

ഗഗഗഗഗഗഗഗഗഗഗഗഗഗഗഗഗഗഗഗഗഗഗഗഗഗഗഗഗ

1 cup flour

2 tablespoons sooji (see page 197)

¾ teaspoon salt

¼ teaspoon ajowan seeds

2 tablespoons olive or peanut oil, plus more for deep-frying

You can put a bowl of these snacks near the sofa, with a bowl of chutney to be used as a dipping sauce, and you are all set for an evening watching television. Namakparas, a great favorite in our family, are a savory nibbling food flavored with the thyme-like seeds known as ajowan (or ajwain). Among the chutneys you can use as a dip are Fresh Cilantro and Yogurt Chutney and Quick Yogurt and Pickle Chutney (see pages 307 and 316), or just plain old tomato ketchup.

Namakparas can be made ahead of time and stored in airtight tins, just like cookies.

SERVES 4–6

ഗഗഗഗഗഗഗഗഗഗഗഗഗഗഗഗഗഗഗഗഗഗഗഗഗഗഗഗഗ

1. Put the flour, sooji, salt, and ajowan seeds in a bowl and mix well with a fork. Dribble in the 2 tablespoons of oil and rub the mixture until you have a rough, breadcrumb-like texture. This must be turned into a very firm dough, so add some water a bit at a time. I used only 4½ tablespoons, but you might need a little more or a little less. Knead the dough for 2–3 minutes and shape into a ball. Set aside in the mixing bowl, covered by a damp dish towel, for 20 minutes or so. Knead the dough again for about a minute, then divide it into two equal balls. Set one aside, covered.

2. Take the other ball and flatten it, then roll it out into a 9 inch circle. You will need to push down hard, as the dough will be firm. (You will not need any extra flour to help with the rolling.) Using a sharp knife, cut the circle into long strips ½ inch wide. Now cut across the center, dividing each strip in half. Make similar strips with the second ball of dough. Keep both batches lightly covered.

3. Put a 1½ inch depth of oil into a wok, karhai, or frying pan and set over medium-low heat. When the oil is hot—a piece of dough dropped in should sink to the bottom, rise very slowly, and start sizzling—put in as many namakparas as will fit easily in a single layer. Fry, turning them over every minute or so, until they are golden. This should take about 5 minutes. If they are cooking too quickly, adjust the heat. Lift them out of the hot oil with a slotted spoon and spread them out on a baking sheet lined with a paper towel. Make all the namakparas this way. Allow them to cool completely, then store them in an airtight tin or a ziplock bag.

OKRA FRIES

TALI BHINDI

ᗭᗮᗭᗮᗭᗮᗭᗮᗭᗮᗭᗮᗭᗮᗭᗮᗭᗮᗭᗮᗭᗮᗭᗮᗭᗮᗭᗮᗭᗮᗭᗮᗭᗮᗭᗮ

½ lb fresh okra, wiped with a
damp cloth and air dried
(young tender okra is best)

¾ teaspoon chili powder

¼ teaspoon ground turmeric

¾ teaspoon chaat masala

3 tablespoons chickpea flour
(besan or gram flour)

Peanut or olive oil, for shallow
frying

About ⅓ teaspoon salt

½ teaspoon amchoor powder

Crisply fried okra is eaten all over India. I remember that in our family we cut the okra into thin rings, fried them until very crisp, then ate them with a sprinkling of salt, amchoor (sour green mango powder), and some chili powder. In Tamil Nadu, where crisp foods, such as popadams, are a basic part of every meal, they cut the okra into chunky rounds, dip them in a thick, well-seasoned chickpea flour batter, and serve this fritter-like vegetable dish with the main meal. This particular recipe comes from western India, where a mound of delicate crisp okra strands, cut on the vertical, may be eaten as a snack with drinks or as part of a meal.

SERVES 4

ᗭᗮᗭᗮᗭᗮᗭᗮᗭᗮᗭᗮᗭᗮᗭᗮᗭᗮᗭᗮᗭᗮᗭᗮᗭᗮᗭᗮᗭᗮᗭᗮᗭᗮᗭᗮ

1. Remove the very top cones on the okra pods, as well as the tips at the bottom. Cut each pod in half lengthwise, then cut each half into 3 lengthwise strips. Put in a bowl. Dust with ½ teaspoon chili powder, the turmeric, ¼ teaspoon of the chaat masala, and all the chickpea flour. Toss the okra gently with your hands to mix evenly. Set aside for 30–60 minutes.

2. Put a ½ inch depth of oil in a medium frying pan and set over medium heat until hot. Meanwhile, line a large plate or tray with a paper towel. Drop the okra rapidly, a piece at a time, into the hot oil so that you have a crowded single layer, and fry, turning now and then, for about 3 minutes. The okra should become golden and crisp. Adjust the heat if necessary. Remove okra with a slotted spoon and spread on the prepared tray. Do several batches, until all the okra has been fried. Dust immediately with salt, the amchoor powder, ¼ teaspoon chili powder, and ½ teaspoon of chaat masala. Serve immediately.

WILD MUSHROOM STEW WITH COCONUT SAUCE

KHUMBI KI TARKARI

೧೩೧೩೧೩೧೩೧೩೧೩೧೩೧೩೧೩೧೩೧೩೧೩೧೩೧೩೧೩೧೩

This makes a lovely first course, served plain or on toast. I make it with a mixture of the fresh mushrooms that are available to me—hon-shimeji (also called beech mushrooms, as they grow on beech trees), shiitake, and oyster mushrooms. Although all these mushrooms once grew wild in eastern Asia, they are now cultivated and may be procured fairly easily in the West as well. If you cannot get one of them, just get more of the other two, or add some other wild mushroom that you like. After trimming, I end up with about 1 lb of mushrooms.   SERVES 4–5

೧೩೧೩೧೩೧೩೧೩೧೩೧೩೧೩೧೩೧೩೧೩೧೩೧೩೧೩೧೩೧೩

About 1½ lbs mushrooms, including about 6 fresh shiitake mushrooms with thick caps about 3–3½ inches in diameter (use more if the caps are smaller), oyster mushrooms, and hon-shimeji (beech) mushrooms

3 tablespoons olive or peanut oil

½ teaspoon whole brown mustard seeds

½ teaspoon whole cumin seeds

6–7 fresh curry leaves, lightly crushed in your hand

3 medium shallots (about 2½ oz in all), peeled and finely chopped

1 fresh hot green chili, finely chopped

2 cloves garlic, peeled and finely chopped

Salt

1 teaspoon ground coriander

Generous pinch of nice red chili powder

Generous pinch of ground turmeric

¾ cup coconut milk, from a well-shaken can

2 teaspoons lime juice

1. Wipe the dirt off the mushrooms with a damp paper towel and trim them as follows: shiitake—break off and discard the stems; cut the caps into 4–8 wedges, depending on size; oyster—cut off the lower, hard part of the stems, separate the mushrooms, and cut larger caps into 1½ inch pieces; hon-shimeji—remove the bottom, hard part of the stems, and divide the larger bunches into smaller bunches.

2. Put the oil in a medium, preferably nonstick pan and set over medium-high heat. When hot, add the mustard seeds. As soon as they begin to pop, a matter of seconds, add the cumin seeds. Let them sizzle for a few seconds, then add the curry leaves (take care, as they will splutter), followed immediately by the shallots, green chilies, and garlic.

3. Stir for about 3 minutes, then put in all the mushrooms and ¼ teaspoon of salt. Stir gently for about 4 minutes or until the mushrooms appear wet. The pan will seem overcrowded at first, but the pile of mushrooms will soon settle down. Add the

ground coriander, chili powder, and turmeric. Stir and cook for another 2 minutes. Check for salt and add another ¼ teaspoon or so, as needed.

4. Pour in the coconut milk, bring to a simmer, then simmer gently for 2 minutes. Stir in the lime juice and taste again to check the balance of seasonings. Adjust as necessary.

5. If this dish sits around, the coconut milk can thicken up. In this case, add 1–2 tablespoons of water when reheating.

BROILED PORTOBELLO MUSHROOMS IN THE KODAGA STYLE

CHUTTA KUMME

໑໑໑໑໑໑໑໑໑໑໑໑໑໑໑໑໑໑໑໑໑໑໑໑໑໑໑໑໑໑໑

4 portobello mushrooms (12–13 oz), with large caps, each about 5–6 inches in diameter (use smaller mushrooms if large ones are not available)

2 tablespoons olive or peanut oil

¾ teaspoon salt, or to taste

4 teaspoons lime juice, or to taste

2 fresh hot green chilies, pounded to a paste in a mortar, or 1–2 generous pinches of nice red chili powder (such as Kashmiri)

During the four-month rainy season in the hills of Coorg (southern Karnataka), most people get their food by foraging in the dense forests that surround the rice fields and the massive coffee plantations. It is an age-old tradition followed by the rich and poor alike. It is at this time of year that delicacies such as wild mushrooms, young bamboo shoots, unfurled colocasia leaves, and ferns suddenly become available.

It is also a tradition, certainly among the landed gentry, to take some of the larger mushrooms, such as the *aalandi kumme* or the plate-sized *nethelé kumme*, and hold them over a wood fire with tongs until they are well singed. They then dress them with crushed green chilies, lime juice, and salt and serve them with drinks. Even the juice left behind in the serving plate is delicious.

Needless to say, I cannot get the mushrooms that grow in Coorg, so I buy large portobello mushrooms. You can also use large porcinis, if available. They can be cooked on a barbecue in the summer, but I use my oven all year round.

I sometimes serve these snacks with drinks, cutting the mushrooms into wedges and inserting a cocktail stick into each one. I also serve them as a first course—one large mushroom per person, with a small portion of Cherry Tomato Salad with Curry Leaves (see page 38), both on the same plate.   SERVES 4

໑໑໑໑໑໑໑໑໑໑໑໑໑໑໑໑໑໑໑໑໑໑໑໑໑໑໑໑໑໑໑

From Kaveri Ponnapa

1. Preheat the broiler until very hot, making sure the shelf is 4–5 inches away from the source of the heat.

2. Break off and discard the mushroom stems. Wipe the caps with a damp paper towel and leave to dry for 5 minutes. Put the

caps, gill side up, on a baking sheet. Brush all the mushrooms with 1 tablespoon of the oil. Place under the broiler for about 1½ minutes or until well singed. Turn the caps over. Brush with the remaining 1 tablespoon oil and broil for another 1½ minutes.

3. Transfer the mushrooms to a large plate, placing them gill side up again. Sprinkle with half the salt, half the lime juice, and half the chili paste or powder. Spread gently with your fingers. Turn the mushrooms over and sprinkle the remaining seasonings on the top in exactly the same way. Serve hot or at room temperature.

EGGPLANT "GOJJU" ON TOAST

SUTTID BADANKAI GOJJU

᷄᷄᷄᷄᷄᷄᷄᷄᷄᷄᷄᷄᷄᷄᷄᷄᷄᷄᷄᷄᷄᷄᷄᷄᷄᷄᷄᷄᷄᷄᷄᷄

1 medium eggplant (about 14 oz)

1½ teaspoons tamarind concentrate (sold in bottles)

½–¾ teaspoon salt

1½ tablespoons light or dark brown sugar

¼–½ teaspoon nice red chili powder

2 teaspoons olive or peanut oil

Generous pinch of ground asafetida

½ teaspoon whole brown mustard seeds

1 dried hot red chili

6–7 fresh curry leaves, lightly crushed in your hand

12 baguette slices, cut at a slight diagonal, and toasted lightly if you wish

Butter, for spreading

Gojjus, beloved by the Madhwa Brahmin community of Karnataka, are hot, sweet, and sour relishes, usually eaten with rice. This gojju, a kind of chutney, may be served as such with most Indian meals, but I love it as a dip with crackers or oatcakes, or, better still, spread out on lightly toasted baguette slices as a kind of Indian bruschetta.

Madhwa Brahmins worship at the Udipi Temple, famous for training the thousands of cooks who have later gone out into the world to start South Indian restaurants in distant parts. They eat mostly locally grown, traditional vegetables, such as eggplants, Indian gourds and squashes, and sweet potatoes. Their most important spice is asafetida—pure lump asafetida that can be crushed and put into water for kitchen use. If you go to the Udipi Temple, you can buy little bowls to do just that!   SERVES 4

᷄᷄᷄᷄᷄᷄᷄᷄᷄᷄᷄᷄᷄᷄᷄᷄᷄᷄᷄᷄᷄᷄᷄᷄᷄᷄᷄᷄᷄᷄᷄᷄

From Malathi Srinivasan

1. Preheat the oven to 450°F.

2. Prick the eggplant with a fork 12–15 times. Place in a roasting pan and bake for about 45 minutes, turning every 15 minutes. The eggplant should flatten out and get soft and pulpy inside. Set aside until cool enough to handle.

3. Peel the cooled eggplant, then chop the flesh and put in a bowl. Mash the pulp some more, adding and mixing in the tamarind concentrate, salt, sugar, and chili powder. Taste for balance and adjust the seasonings as necessary.

4. Put the oil in a small frying pan and set over medium heat. When hot, add the asafetida. Five seconds later, add the mustard seeds. As soon as they start to pop, a matter of seconds,

add the red chili. Let it turn dark. Now throw in the curry leaves (take care, as they will splutter), stir once or twice, then pour the oil and seasonings over the eggplant purée. Stir to mix, then remove the red chili and curry leaves.

5. Spread out all your baguette slices and butter them very lightly. Spread the gojju—warm or at room temperature—over the bread and serve immediately.

BOILED PEANUTS IN THEIR SHELLS

UBLI MOOMPHALI

~~~~~~

2 dried hot red chilies

1 teaspoon black peppercorns

1 teaspoon whole fennel seeds

1 teaspoon whole cumin seeds

1 teaspoon whole fenugreek
    seeds

2 teaspoons salt

10 oz fresh peanuts in their
    shells

India is the second-largest producer of peanuts in the world, after China, and vegetarians make ample use of the protein-rich product by adding it to their meals, either cooking it along with vegetables and legumes (peanuts are a legume too, of course), or by adding it to various snack foods, such as Bombay mix. These peanuts are fully mature and completely dried, but when peanuts are young and fresh, they are often just boiled in their shells, rather like soybeans, and people sit around peeling and eating them.

It is only in one season that fresh peanuts are available. I buy them as soon as I lay eyes on them in any country I happen to be in, and I cook them in the following way.

SERVES 6 AS A SNACK OR TO EAT WITH DRINKS

~~~~~~

1. Put 4 cups water in a pan. Add all the spices and the salt and bring to a simmer. Cover and simmer gently for 10 minutes. Strain the liquid and put it back in the pan.

2. Add the peanuts to the flavored water and bring to a boil. Cover, lower the heat, and simmer gently for about 10 minutes (15 if the peanuts are large). Strain thoroughly and serve lukewarm or cold. Shell and eat.

PAN-GRILLED ZUCCHINI WITH SPICY TOMATO SAUCE

TALA HUA ZUCCHINI

cⱷcⱷcⱷcⱷcⱷcⱷcⱷcⱷcⱷcⱷcⱷcⱷcⱷcⱷcⱷcⱷcⱷcⱷcⱷ

About 2 tablespoons olive or peanut oil

2 medium zucchini (about 6 oz in all), trimmed and cut into long diagonal slices ⅓ inch thick

Salt and freshly ground black pepper

Ground roasted cumin seeds (see page xx)

Nice red chili powder

About 8 fl oz Simple South Indian Tomato Sauce (see page 345)

You can grill the zucchini outdoors in the summer, but I usually fry them indoors in a heavy frying pan.

SERVES 6 AS A FIRST COURSE AND 4 AS A MAIN MEAL

cⱷcⱷcⱷcⱷcⱷcⱷcⱷcⱷcⱷcⱷcⱷcⱷcⱷcⱷcⱷcⱷcⱷcⱷcⱷ

1. Set a cast-iron frying pan over medium-high heat. When hot, spread 1 tablespoon of the oil over the bottom. Arrange a single layer of the zucchini in the pan and let them brown for about 2 minutes. You might need to move the slices around to brown them evenly. Turn the slices over and brown the opposite side, also for about 2 minutes. Transfer to a plate.

2. Add another tablespoon of oil to the pan and cook the remaining slices the same way.

3. Lay out all the zucchini in a single layer in a serving dish and sprinkle lightly with salt, pepper, the ground cumin seeds, and chili powder. Spoon the tomato sauce over their centers and serve.

CUCUMBER SPEARS

KHEERAY KI PHANKAY

ↄↄↄↄↄↄↄↄↄↄↄↄↄↄↄↄↄↄↄↄↄↄↄↄↄↄↄↄↄↄↄↄↄↄↄↄↄ

4 cucumbers, as described
  below, or the nearest
  substitutes
1 teaspoon lemon juice
¼ teaspoon salt, or to taste
⅛ teaspoon ground roasted
  cumin seeds (see page xx)
⅛ teaspoon chili powder
2 teaspoons olive or peanut oil
⅛ teaspoon whole brown
  mustard seeds
⅛ teaspoon whole cumin
  seeds
5–6 fresh curry leaves or small
  basil leaves

Whenever I am looking for a snack that is not too fattening, I turn to these cucumber spears. We used to eat a simpler version as children, cucumber halves or quarters just sprinkled with lime juice and dusted with spices, but now I have started giving the dish a final "tarka," which makes it even better. You can serve them with drinks (hand out napkins) or with all meals, Western or South Asian.

You need to use seedless cucumbers here. I like to use the ones that are labeled Armenian or Persian. They are about 6 inches long, about 1¼ inches wide, and are quite free of developed seeds. You can, of course, use other similar cucumbers.

Ideally, the cucumbers should be dressed shortly before you eat them, as salt makes them wilt.   SERVES 4

ↄↄↄↄↄↄↄↄↄↄↄↄↄↄↄↄↄↄↄↄↄↄↄↄↄↄↄↄↄↄↄↄↄↄↄↄↄ

1. Peel the cucumbers and halve them lengthwise. Arrange them on a plate, cut side up. Dribble the lemon juice over them as evenly as you can manage. Now sprinkle the salt, cumin seeds, and chili powder over them in the same even manner.

2. Put the oil in a small frying pan over medium-high heat. When hot, add the mustard seeds. As soon as they start to pop, a matter of seconds, add the cumin seeds and let them sizzle for a few seconds. Throw in the curry leaves and turn off the heat. Now tilt the frying pan and spoon the oil and spices evenly over the cucumbers. They are ready to be served.

CHERRY TOMATO SALAD WITH CURRY LEAVES

CHHOTE TAMATAR KA SALAAD

10 oz cherry or grape tomatoes, preferably in different colors and sizes

Salt and freshly ground black pepper

2 tablespoons olive or peanut oil

¼ teaspoon whole brown mustard seeds

1 dried hot red chili

7–8 fresh curry leaves or small basil leaves

Apart from being delicious, this is a very pretty salad that I often serve as a first course, sometimes combining it with Cucumber Spears (see page 37). It is prettiest when made with cherry tomatoes of different sizes and colors. Placed in a single layer on a white plate, they look like jewels.

If using small cherry tomatoes, cut them in half through their "equator." Larger ones may be quartered. If using grape tomatoes, cut them in half lengthwise.   SERVES 4

1. Arrange the tomatoes, cut side up, in a single layer on a plate. You can leave spaces between them.

2. Shortly before serving them, dust the tomatoes lightly with salt and pepper.

3. Put the oil in a small frying pan and set over medium-high heat. When hot, put in the mustard seeds. As soon as they start to pop, a matter of seconds, add the red chili, stirring until it darkens. Quickly add the curry leaves, then lift up the pan and spoon the oil and spices over the tomatoes. Serve as soon as you can, leaving the red chili on top as a garnish, but warn people not to eat it. It will have already done its job by flavoring the oil.

TOMATO SALAD

TAMATAR KA SALAAD

⌀⌀

FOR THE DRESSING

1 medium shallot, peeled and
finely chopped

1 tablespoon red wine vinegar

1 tablespoon Dijon mustard

Juice from 1 teaspoon peeled
and finely grated fresh
ginger

¼ teaspoon salt, or to taste

Freshly ground black pepper

½ teaspoon ground roasted
cumin seeds (see page xx)

4 tablespoons extra-virgin
olive oil

6 or more ripe summer
tomatoes, in shades of
pink, green, yellow, and
red, if you can get them
(the number depends on
size)

Salt

Ground roasted cumin seeds
(see page xx)

A few small fresh mint leaves
(optional)

During the winter months, the tomatoes in our garden in India bore endless fruit. Some were made into juice for us to have mid-morning, some were added to vegetable dishes and dals, and some were used to make salads. My father did not grow any heirloom tomatoes in shades of green, yellow, and pink, but I do, and I've had great success with them.

One day, when I was making lunch for four people, I thought we might start with our gorgeous tomatoes. I had been inspired by a tall salad I had eaten at my favorite tapas place in London, Barrafina, and by the shallot-filled dressing they used on another dish, their baby gem salad. I wanted to combine all this with the flavors of my mother's tomato salad. You can taste the result below.

This salad needs to be put together at the last moment, but the ingredients should all be gathered on the work surface before you start.

The dressing used for this salad is also very good on boiled and sliced beets (which you can combine with halved hard-boiled eggs for a delicious salad), boiled and diced potatoes, and par-boiled or steamed green beans (which you can mix with drained canned chickpeas).   SERVES 4

⌀⌀

1. First make the dressing: Put the shallots, vinegar, mustard, ginger juice, salt, pepper, and cumin into a bowl. Mix and set aside for 10 minutes or longer. Now slowly whisk in the oil, pouring in just a little at a time.

2. Just before you sit down to eat, slice the tomatoes about ⅓ inch thick. Put one slice each of the same color in the center of each serving plate. Dust it with a pinch of salt and a little cumin. Pick up slices of a second color and put them on top of

the first. Sprinkle with salt and cumin. Proceed this way until you have 5–6 rainbow slices, one on top of the other in a tower. If they slide and you end up with a mound, that is fine.

3. Whisk your dressing again and spoon a little over each tower, using only as much as you need. Scatter the mint around the plate and serve immediately.

ORANGE AND RADISH SALAD

NARANGI AUR LAL MOOLI KA SALAAD

⤳⤳⤳⤳⤳⤳⤳⤳⤳⤳⤳⤳⤳⤳⤳⤳⤳⤳⤳⤳⤳⤳⤳⤳⤳⤳⤳⤳

2 navel oranges

¼ packed cup radishes, very finely sliced (use a mandoline, if you have one)

⅛ teaspoon salt

Freshly ground black pepper

⅛ teaspoon ground roasted cumin seeds (see page xx)

¹⁄₁₆ teaspoon chili powder

2 small sprigs of fresh cilantro or mint

FOR THE RADISHES

½ teaspoon lemon juice

Freshly ground black pepper

Generous pinch of salt, or to taste

⅛ teaspoon ground roasted cumin seeds (see page xx)

A few sprinkles of chili powder

Here is another wonderful combination of fruit and raw vegetables that we often use to make our snack foods and salads. I find that it makes a light and delightful first course. This recipe may easily be doubled or tripled.

You can use different types of radishes here: thin white ones, known as mooli in India and the United Kingdom and as small daikon in the United States; red, pink, and white Chinese radishes; and the larger versions of plain red radishes.   SERVES 2

⤳⤳⤳⤳⤳⤳⤳⤳⤳⤳⤳⤳⤳⤳⤳⤳⤳⤳⤳⤳⤳⤳⤳⤳⤳⤳⤳⤳

1. Peel the oranges in such a way that you remove all the white pith. Slice off a good chunk of the top and bottom (I just eat these bits) and cut the remainder crosswise into circles ⅓ inch thick. Set aside in a single layer.

2. Put the sliced radishes into a bowl and set aside.

3. Half an hour before you eat, sprinkle the oranges with the salt, pepper, cumin, and chili powder as evenly as you can.

4. Just before you eat, sprinkle the radishes with the lemon juice, pepper, salt, cumin, and chili powder. Toss lightly.

5. Lay half the orange slices on a salad plate. Put half the sliced radishes to one side of them and garnish with a sprig of cilantro or mint. Serve immediately.

A NOTE ON PUFFED RICE

Puffed rice—fully cooked rice grains that are puffed up and crisp—is eaten in some form or another throughout India. It is generally added to snack foods, as illustrated in the two recipes that follow, but in eastern India it is so beloved that it is eaten for breakfast as well. Rather like Rice Krispies, it is combined with creamy milk, seasonal fruit such as mangoes and ripe jackfruit, and some liquid palm sugar.

In a mélange that is highly popular in West Bengal's countryside and in Bangladesh, puffed rice is tossed together with green chilies, chopped onions, and a drizzle of pungent mustard oil. Najmul Chaudhury, the gentleman from Dhaka from whom I buy my spices at Kalustyan's in New York, always keeps a stash of the basic ingredients under the counter in front of him. Whenever he feels peckish, he just tosses them together in a bowl that he also stores under the counter, and eats. If he feels like it, he adds some thin chickpea flour noodles called sev that he also sells in the store. If he wants to add a bit of sweetness to the pungency, he may, like his countrymen, suck on a piece of solid palm sugar as he nibbles.

Puffed rice has many names in India: murmura, kurmura, churmura, mumra, and moori are just a few of them. When you shop at an Indian store, you would be quite safe asking for murmura.

I like to crisp up my puffed rice before I prepare any snack, as this improves its texture and refreshes it. I have done this for the salad on page 46, where the puffed rice is used as is, straight from the packet without any toasting or frying. If you want to use it for your morning cereal—and why not?—you should follow this quick step first: Put a wok or medium frying pan over medium heat and let it get hot. Add the puffed rice and stir it about for 3–4 minutes or until it crisps up a bit. It should not change color. (Eat a grain each of the untoasted and toasted rice to check the difference.) Empty into a bowl and set aside to cool. Store leftovers in an airtight jar or tin.

SPICY, CRISP PUFFED RICE NIBBLES

MASALEDAR MURMURA

ෆ෨ෆ෨ෆ෨ෆ෨ෆ෨ෆ෨ෆ෨ෆ෨ෆ෨ෆ෨ෆ෨ෆ෨ෆ෨ෆ෨ෆ෨ෆ෨ෆ෨ෆ෨ෆ෨

3 tablespoons olive or peanut
oil

Generous pinch of ground
asafetida

½ teaspoon whole brown
mustard seeds

1–2 fresh hot green chilies, cut
into fine rings

6–7 fresh curry leaves, or Thai
basil or small basil leaves,
lightly crushed in your
hand

¼ cup raw cashews (this is a
good opportunity to buy
cashew halves or broken
cashews)

¼ cup raw peanuts (red skins
on or off)

4 cups puffed rice (murmura)

½ teaspoon salt

¼ teaspoon nice red chili
powder, if needed

1 teaspoon fine sugar

Many nations eat some sort of puffed rice. In the West it is generally used for breakfast cereal, to be eaten with milk and sugar. In India it is eaten in hundreds of different ways, some sweet but most others savory and spicy.

The recipe here is for a crunchy, nutty nibble, perfect with drinks. If I invite friends to watch television or a film at home, I hand them a drink and a homemade paper cone filled with this spicy murmura. That is the name for it in Delhi, and I find that most Indian stores in the West sell it by that name as well. Just ask for puffed rice or murmura and the grocer will get what you want.

This recipe cooks in 5 minutes or less, so have everything assembled before you start.

SERVES 4 AND FILLS A 1¾ PINT MEASURE

ෆ෨ෆ෨ෆ෨ෆ෨ෆ෨ෆ෨ෆ෨ෆ෨ෆ෨ෆ෨ෆ෨ෆ෨ෆ෨ෆ෨ෆ෨ෆ෨ෆ෨ෆ෨ෆ෨

1. Put the oil in a wok, karhai, or frying pan and set over medium heat. When hot, add the asafetida, quickly followed by the mustard seeds. As soon as the mustard seeds pop, a matter of seconds, add the green chilies and curry leaves (take care, as they will splutter). Stir and fry for a minute or less or until the last two ingredients dry out. Add the cashews and peanuts. Stir and fry briskly until they just turn golden.

2. Quickly add all the puffed rice. Stir and fry for a minute. Add the salt, chili powder, if needed, and the sugar. Stir well, then turn off the heat. Let the mixture cool completely, and transfer to an airtight jar or tin. It should stay fresh for at least a week.

SALAD OF PUFFED RICE, CUCUMBERS, ONIONS, AND TOMATOES

JHAL MOORI

About 3 seedless baby
cucumbers (1 cup or
4½ oz), cut into ⅓ inch
dice

½ cup onion, peeled and cut
into ¼ inch dice

1 cup firm tomatoes, cut into
⅓ inch dice

1 medium waxy potato (about
6 oz), freshly boiled,
cooled, peeled, and cut
into ¼ inch dice

½–1 fresh hot green chili,
finely sliced crosswise
(optional)

3 tablespoons chopped fresh
cilantro

¼ teaspoon ground roasted
cumin seeds (see page xx)

Freshly ground black pepper

¾ teaspoon salt

½ teaspoon chaat masala

1–3 generous pinches of nice
red chili powder

½ teaspoon Simple Tamarind
Chutney (see page 308,
optional)

½ teaspoon Green Chutney
(see page 304, optional)

1 teaspoon mustard oil (for a
true Bengali taste) or extra-
virgin olive oil

1 tablespoon lime juice, plus 1
teaspoon extra if not using
the chutneys

2 cups puffed rice

An inspired and variable mixture of vegetables, nuts, legumes, noodles, chutneys, and, most importantly, puffed rice, jhal moori is Calcutta street food par excellence, a kind of nutritious Bengali salad. It can be picked up from a vendor and eaten as a snack while on an evening stroll; office workers might have it in the afternoon with their tea, or even gobble some up for lunch.

I have eaten it at all these times, but now I find myself frequently making it as a first course at home when I am entertaining. I like to assemble all the parts in advance and put them together at the last minute. The salad holds well for 10–15 minutes but gradually begins to get soggy. It still tastes excellent 2 hours later, but loses all its crispness. This mixture is also very good on top of lightly dressed salad greens for lunch.

If you do not have the chutneys mentioned, just leave them out. The salad will still taste just fine.   SERVES 6

1. Put the cucumbers, onions, tomatoes, potatoes, chilies (if using), and fresh cilantro into a large bowl.

2. Put the cumin, pepper, salt, chaat masala, and chili powder into small bowl.

3. Have the chutneys, mustard oil, and lime juice at the ready.

4. Put a wok or medium frying pan over medium heat and let it get hot. Add the puffed rice and stir it about for 3–4 minutes or until it crisps up a bit. It should not change color. Empty into a bowl and set aside.

5. Now you need just a few minutes to throw the jhal moori together. Add the dry spices and puffed rice to the cucumber mixture. Also add the chutneys (if using), mustard oil, and lime juice. Toss well to mix. Taste for balance of seasonings and serve.

VEGETABLES

ROASTED EGGPLANT AND TOMATO

BAIGAN CHOKAH

ഔഔഔഔഔഔഔഔഔഔഔഔഔഔഔഔഔഔഔഔഔഔഔഔഔഔഔഔഔ

1 lb slim, tender eggplants (I used 4 of the Japanese variety, but Italian ones can be substituted)

2 medium (8 oz) plum tomatoes

⅓–½ teaspoon salt

Freshly ground black pepper

1–2 fresh green chilies, finely chopped

1½ tablespoons peeled and finely chopped shallots

2 teaspoons finely chopped mint

2 tablespoons chopped fresh cilantro

2–3 teaspoons lime juice

3 teaspoons mustard oil, or a fruity, good-quality extra-virgin olive oil

Chokah is eaten all over Bihar. In the villages there, it could be the only dish of the day, eaten with simple whole-grain flatbreads, such as Chapatis (see page 219), or rice. (Similar dishes, known as "bharta," exist all across North India.) It can also be served as part of a meal in small, individual bowls.

In India the eggplant is roasted over a simple wood fire, or sometimes buried in very hot embers. The tomatoes are simply held over a wood fire with chimta (tongs) until the skin blackens. Both vegetables are peeled, mashed together, and seasoned. That is all there is to it. The mustard oil used here gives it the true flavor of eastern India, but is not essential.

In my family, we sometimes mix this chokah with yogurt and serve it as a relish-like accompaniment.   SERVES 4

ഔഔഔഔഔഔഔഔഔഔഔഔഔഔഔഔഔഔഔഔഔഔഔഔഔഔഔഔഔ

From Jayanti Rajagopalan

1. Preheat the broiler until very hot. Line a baking sheet with foil.

2. Using a fork, prick the eggplants all over. Prick the tomatoes in just a few places. Place both vegetables on the prepared sheet and put it under the broiler, as close to the heat source as possible. Broil, turning the vegetables a little when one side is charred. This may not happen evenly, so keep checking. Slim, tender eggplants take 15–20 minutes, about the same as the tomatoes, but larger eggplants will take longer, up to 40 minutes. The vegetables need to get very brown or charred all over and become soft inside. Remove them as they get done and put in a sieve set over a bowl.

3. Set the vegetables aside until cool enough to handle, then peel them and remove their pulp.

4. Chop the vegetable pulp finely and put in a bowl. Add the salt, pepper, green chilies, shallots, mint, cilantro, lime juice, and 2 teaspoons of the mustard oil. Mix and taste for balance of seasonings, adjusting as necessary. Refrigerate until needed.

5. Put the chokah in a serving bowl and drizzle the remaining teaspoon of mustard oil over the top. Serve cold or at room temperature.

SIMPLE TWICE-COOKED EGGPLANT

BAIGAN BHARTA

ↄↄↄ

2 lbs eggplants (I used 3
   medium purple ones)
4 tablespoons olive, peanut, or
   mustard oil
½ teaspoon whole cumin
   seeds
½ teaspoon whole fennel
   seeds
¼ teaspoon nigella seeds
   (kalonji)
1 large onion (7–8 oz), peeled
   and finely chopped
One 3 inch piece of fresh
   ginger, peeled and very
   finely chopped
3 large cloves garlic, peeled
   and very finely chopped
1–2 fresh hot green chilies,
   finely chopped
2 good-sized tomatoes (about
   ¾ lb in all), peeled and
   finely chopped
1 teaspoon salt
3 tablespoons chopped fresh
   cilantro

When an Indian child fighting with another Indian child says, "I am going to make a bharta out of you," he or she means that the intention is to make a mash out of the other child. This is my way of explaining that bhartas are mashed vegetables, seasoned in a variety of ways.

We in the northern half of India (Punjab, Delhi, Uttar Pradesh) usually eat bhartas with flatbreads, while people in other areas (Bihar, Orissa, and West Bengal) eat them with rice. Here I have cooked the bharta partly in the Delhi way and partly in the Bengali way. If you want more of the Bengali flavor, cook this bharta in mustard oil.

Note that it really helps to use a large well-seasoned or non-stick wok, karhai, or frying pan here.   SERVES 3–4

ↄↄↄ

1. Preheat the oven to 400°F.

2. Using a fork, prick the eggplants all over. Place them in a roasting pan in the oven for 1¼ hours or until tender. Peel them and chop them finely.

3. Put the oil in a nonstick wok, karhai, or frying pan and place over medium-high heat. When hot, add the cumin seeds. Let them sizzle for 3–4 seconds, then add the fennel and nigella seeds. After 2 seconds, add the onions, stirring and sautéing for 5–6 minutes, until just starting to brown at the edges.

4. Now add the ginger, garlic, and green chilies. Stir and cook for 2 minutes. Add the tomatoes and keep cooking for 5–6 minutes or until the tomatoes soften.

5. Add the eggplant and salt and cook for 5 minutes. Stir in the cilantro and cook for another 3 minutes.

A NOTE ON PORIYALS

Poriyals, although technically from Tamil Nadu, are found all over South India. They are stir-fries, generally made in the wok-like karhai. The method is simple: you put a tiny amount of oil in your pan, add mustard seeds and one or two dals (which act as spices), then put in some broken dried red chilies and curry leaves. All this takes a few seconds. Then you add cooked or raw vegetables and stir-fry them, adding some salt. Cooked vegetables might include beets, cauliflower, potatoes, broad beans, and spinach, while uncooked vegetables would include cabbage and carrots. In the United States I have even eaten poriyals made with broccoli and asparagus. There are, of course, hundreds of possible variations and permutations. Coconut may be added, or onions, garlic, and ginger may be stir-fried before the vegetable is put in.

The poriyals you will find in this chapter are made with eggplant (see page 55), beets (see page 66), and carrot (see page 69). All have different flavorings. In the south, such stir-fried, unsauced dishes are referred to as "curries" by those speaking in English.

Poriyals serve as the vegetable that goes with the main dish, which in the south would be a combination of a rice, a dal, and a yogurt or buttermilk relish.

STIR-FRIED EGGPLANT COOKED IN A TAMIL NADU STYLE

KATHIRIKAI PORIYAL

ꚝꚝꚝꚝꚝꚝꚝꚝꚝꚝꚝꚝꚝꚝꚝꚝꚝꚝꚝꚝꚝꚝꚝꚝꚝꚝ

1 lb smallish purple eggplants
(I used 3 "baby" Italian
eggplants, but the long
Japanese variety is also
fine)

1 tablespoon chana dal

1 tablespoon whole coriander
seeds

2–5 dried hot red chilies

3 tablespoons olive or peanut
oil

½ teaspoon whole brown
mustard seeds

7–8 fresh curry leaves, lightly
crushed in your hand

1 medium onion (about 6 oz),
peeled and chopped

¾ teaspoon salt, or to taste

Here is a wonderfully delicious southern poriyal. (For more on the subject, see the note on page 54.) This is a dry stir-fry, so it does not have a sauce. It is eaten with rather flowing dishes, such as a sambar (see South Indian Dal with Vegetables, page 166), rice, and yogurt relishes. You can also serve it with flatbreads and a mixture of northern and southern dishes, such as Potatoes with Cumin and Asafetida (see page 104), a dal, and a simple yogurt relish. Add Stir-fried Spinach, Andhra-Style (see page 112) if you have company.

In India slim green eggplants are often used for this dish, but those are hard to find in the West. Small purple ones or the lighter pinkish Japanese eggplants work very well too.   SERVES 3–4

ꚝꚝꚝꚝꚝꚝꚝꚝꚝꚝꚝꚝꚝꚝꚝꚝꚝꚝꚝꚝꚝꚝꚝꚝꚝꚝ

1. Cut off the very top of each eggplant. Whatever kind you have, cut them into 1 x ¾ inch dice. (I quarter the baby Italian ones lengthwise, then cut them crosswise into ¾ inch pieces.) Put the cut pieces into a bowl of water until you are ready to start cooking. At that point, drain well and pat dry.

2. Place a small cast-iron frying pan over medium-high heat. Add the chana dal, coriander seeds, and red chilies, stirring and roasting them until they turn a few shades darker. Empty the mixture onto a piece of paper towel and set aside. When cool, place in a clean coffee grinder or spice mill and grind as fine as possible.

3. Pour the oil into a medium, preferably nonstick frying pan set over medium-high heat. When hot, add the mustard seeds. As soon as they start to pop, a matter of seconds, throw the

curry leaves into the frying pan (take care, as these will splutter). Quickly follow with the onions. Stir for about 2 minutes, then lower the heat to medium and stir-fry for another 2 minutes.

4. Now add the eggplant, which you have drained and dried, and stir for a minute. Add the salt and the ground spice mixture. Stir to mix. Sprinkle with about 3 tablespoons of water, stir, and cover. Cook 6–7 minutes, stirring now and then. Lift the cover, add another similar sprinkling of water, and stir gently. Cover again. Keep doing this—stirring, adding sprinklings of water, and covering again—every 6–7 minutes for 20–25 minutes, until the eggplant is tender, turning the heat down if necessary.

ᘁ

EGGPLANT IN A PEANUT AND SESAME SAUCE

BHAGARA BAIGAN

2 lbs medium Italian
  eggplants (I used 3)
8 tablespoons olive or peanut
  oil
1 tablespoon peanut butter
  (freshly ground is best)
1 tablespoon tahini (roasted
  sesame paste, sold in
  many supermarkets)
1 tablespoon tomato purée
2 tablespoons dark brown
  sugar
1½ teaspoons tamarind
  concentrate (sold in
  bottles)
½ teaspoon whole brown
  mustard seeds
½ teaspoon whole cumin
  seeds
6–8 fresh curry leaves, lightly
  crushed in your hand
1 large onion (8 oz), peeled
  and finely chopped
1 tablespoon peeled and finely
  grated fresh ginger
1 tablespoon peeled and finely
  chopped garlic
¼ teaspoon ground turmeric
1 teaspoon ground coriander
1 teaspoon ground cumin
¼–¾ teaspoon nice red chili
  powder
1¼ teaspoons salt, or to taste

Baghara baigan is one of Hyderabad's most famous and most luscious sweet-and-sour vegetarian dishes. It calls for small eggplants that are partially quartered lengthwise, stuffed, fried, and then put in a sauce filled with roasted and ground sesame seeds and nuts along with dozens of other roasted, fried, strained, or grated seasonings. It is delicious but complicated to make. I wanted to make a version that was much simpler but just as delicious, and here is the result.

I have cut down its numerous steps, which may be heretical, but it works beautifully. There are still a great many ingredients involved, but the cooking itself is simple.

This is a perfect dish for parties, served with a rich pilaf and other vegetable dishes.   SERVES 6

1. Cut the eggplants lengthwise into quarters, then crosswise into 1½ inch pieces.

2. Put 6 tablespoons of the oil in a large nonstick wok, karhai, or frying pan and set over medium-high heat. When hot, add the eggplant pieces and fry until lightly browned. They should be three-quarters cooked through. Using a slotted spoon, transfer them to a bowl.

3. Put the peanut butter and tahini in a separate small bowl. Slowly add 1 cup boiling water, stirring with a whisk as you do so, until you have a paste. Add the tomato purée, brown sugar, tamarind concentrate, and another 1 cup boiling water, stirring as you go. Mix well and set aside.

4. Most of the oil in the pan will have been absorbed by the eggplant. Add 2 tablespoons of oil to whatever is left and set over

medium-high heat. When hot, add the mustard seeds. As soon as they start to pop, a matter of seconds, add the cumin seeds and let them sizzle for a few seconds. Now add the curry leaves (take care, as these will splutter) and, a second later, the onions. Stir and fry for about 3 minutes or until the onions just start to brown. Turn the heat to medium low and stir-fry for another 2–3 minutes.

5. Add the ginger and garlic. Continue to stir and cook for 2 minutes. Add the turmeric, coriander, cumin, and chili powder. Stir for a minute, then add 1 cup water. Cook on low heat for 8–10 minutes.

6. Add the peanut sauce and cook gently, stirring all the time, for 5 minutes. Add the eggplant and the salt. Cook for another 10 minutes or so on lowish heat, stirring gently now and then, until the eggplant pieces are soft but still whole. If the sauce feels too thick, feel free to add water at any time, especially when you are reheating the dish. There should always be some thick sauce in the pan.

STEAMED GREEN BEANS WITH MUSTARD AND COCONUT

HURA LIKAYA PALLYA

2¼ cups green beans (round or flat), cut crosswise into ¼ inch pieces

1¼ teaspoons whole brown mustard seeds

1–2 hot dried red chilies, broken into small pieces

4 tablespoons fresh grated coconut, or defrosted if frozen

1 tablespoon olive or peanut oil

¼ teaspoon urad dal

About 10 fresh curry leaves, lightly crushed in your hand

½ teaspoon salt

༄༅༄༅༄༅༄༅༄༅༄༅༄༅༄༅༄༅༄༅༄༅༄༅༄༅༄༅༄༅

Meera Prasad is a very successful doctor in Bangalore. She belongs to a community of Shivalli Brahmins whose main temple, dedicated to Lord Krishna, is in Udupi, in northern Karnataka. Hundreds of people are fed at the temple daily, and it is here that young men come to study for two much admired futures—priesthood and the culinary arts.

The Udupi chefs have introduced South Indian food to the rest of India, and to much of the world, through chains with names like Udupi and Woodlands. The famous Mavalli Tiffin Rooms in Bangalore are also owned by Shivalli Brahmins.

Pallyas are dry dishes made with coconut, which makes them slightly sweet, and with ground mustard seeds, which gives them a touch of bitterness. Indians not only like the bitter flavor, they consider it healing.   SERVES 4

༄༅༄༅༄༅༄༅༄༅༄༅༄༅༄༅༄༅༄༅༄༅༄༅༄༅༄༅༄༅

From Meera Prasad

1. Put the green beans into a steamer and steam them for about 12 minutes or until they are tender.

2. Meanwhile, put 1 teaspoon of the mustard seeds into a small mortar and pound them until well crushed. Add the red chilies and pound until they too are well crushed. Now add the coconut and crush it as much as you can. (Alternatively, you could put the mustard seeds and red chilies in a clean coffee grinder or spice mill and whiz until they become a coarse powder. Add the coconut and whiz again.) Set aside.

3. When the beans are done, take them off the steaming water. Put the oil into a medium frying pan and set over medium-high heat. When hot, add the urad dal. As soon as it starts to change

color, add the remaining ¼ teaspoon of mustard seeds. When they pop, a matter of seconds, add the curry leaves (take care, as these will splutter). About 3 seconds after that, add all the green beans. Sprinkle with the salt and stir for about 2 minutes.

4. Take the pan off the heat and add the crushed mixture from the mortar. Stir a few times to mix thoroughly. Serve hot, warm, or, in the summer, at room temperature.

Coconuts in a Mysore market, South Karnataka

DELHI-STYLE GREEN BEANS WITH GINGER AND GREEN CHILIES

SEM KI SABZI

ↄⱺ

1 lb green beans, topped, tailed, and cut into 1 inch pieces

2 tablespoons olive or peanut oil

Generous pinch of ground asafetida

½ teaspoon whole cumin seeds

1–3 fresh hot green chilies, finely chopped

2 teaspoons peeled and finely chopped fresh ginger

¾ teaspoon salt, or to taste

1 teaspoon ground coriander

I love to eat this simple dish from North India with a dal, such as the Nepalese Black-eyed Peas with Potatoes and Bamboo Shoots (see page 126), rice, and a yogurt relish. It may also be served with a Western meal.

Beans in India are generally fully cooked and rarely crisp. They absorb the spices much better this way. If you wish to steam the beans instead of parboiling them, as I have done here, do so for about 12 minutes.   SERVES 4

ↄⱺ

1. Plunge the beans into a saucepan of rapidly boiling water and cook them for about 5 minutes or until crisply tender. Drain and set aside in a strainer or colander set over a bowl.

2. Put the oil in a medium frying pan set over medium-high heat. When hot, add the asafetida. A few seconds later, add the cumin seeds and let them sizzle for a few seconds. Take the pan off the heat and add the chilies and ginger. Stir a few times. Put the pan back on the heat, turning it down to medium low.

3. Add the beans, salt, and coriander, then stir and cook for 2–3 minutes. Add 2 tablespoons of water, cover, lower the heat, and cook very gently for another 5 minutes.

GREEN BEANS WITH POTATOES

SEM AUR ALOO KI SABZI

༄༄༄༄༄༄༄༄༄༄༄༄༄༄༄༄༄༄༄༄༄༄༄༄༄༄

2 tablespoons olive or peanut oil

Generous pinch of ground asafetida

½ teaspoon whole cumin seeds

¼ teaspoon nigella seeds (kalonji)

1 tablespoon peeled and finely chopped fresh ginger

1–2 fresh hot green chilies, cut into fine rounds

2 tablespoons tomato purée

12 oz green beans (flat or round), cut into 1 inch pieces

2 medium boiled, waxy potatoes (about 8 oz in all), cut into 1 inch dice

1¼ teaspoons salt, or to taste

¼ teaspoon nice red chili powder

½ teaspoon garam masala

Here is a simple green bean dish that I just love. It is good with any meal, but I also have it frequently as a snack. It can be rolled inside a Plain Delhi Paratha (see page 221), along with some Tomato, Onion, and Cucumber Koshambari (see page 341). If you do not have a leftover paratha, a pita bread will do instead. Just warm it and stuff the bean mixture and salad inside.

SERVES 4–5

1. Put the oil in a large frying pan and set over medium-high heat. When hot, add the asafetida. A few seconds later add the cumin and nigella seeds and let them sizzle for a few seconds. Add the ginger and green chilies, lower the heat to medium low, and stir for a minute. Add the tomato purée and stir until the paste turns thick and dark red.

2. Stir in 1 cup water, plus the beans, potatoes, salt, and chili powder. Mix well and bring to a simmer. Cover and cook on low heat until the beans are tender and the sauce has thickened, about 20 minutes. If there is too much sauce, raise the heat a bit and boil it off, stirring gently. Stir in the garam masala.

PUNJABI-STYLE BEETS WITH GINGER

PUNJABI CHUKANDAR KI SABZI

෴෴෴෴෴෴෴෴෴෴෴෴෴෴෴෴෴෴෴෴෴෴෴෴෴෴෴෴

2 tablespoons olive or peanut oil

⅛ teaspoon ground asafetida

½ teaspoon whole cumin seeds

¼ teaspoon whole fenugreek seeds

1½ lbs beets (I used 2 large ones), peeled and cut into ¾ inch dice

2 teaspoons peeled and finely grated fresh ginger

1 teaspoon ground coriander

½ teaspoon ground cumin

¼ teaspoon ground turmeric

¼–½ teaspoon chili powder

Salt

2 medium tomatoes (about 10 oz), peeled and finely chopped

North Indians nearly always start beet dishes with the raw vegetable, and generally cut it quite small so the pieces can be picked up easily with morsels of local flatbreads or rice. Save the stems and leaves, if you have them, for another dish.

Serve this sweet, sour, and hot dish with a dal of your choice and a green vegetable, such as Green Beans with Potatoes (see page 63). In the Punjab the meal would be eaten with a flatbread, but rice is fine too. At an Indian or Western meal, you could serve this dish cold, as a salad. You could also swirl some of it into beaten yogurt to make a raita.   SERVES 4

෴෴෴෴෴෴෴෴෴෴෴෴෴෴෴෴෴෴෴෴෴෴෴෴෴෴෴෴

1. Put the oil in a medium, preferably nonstick frying pan and set over medium-high heat. When hot, add the asafetida, quickly followed by the cumin seeds. Let them sizzle for a few seconds. Add the fenugreek seeds and, a second later, put in all the beets plus the ginger, coriander, and cumin. Stir for 2–3 minutes. Add the turmeric and chili powder and stir for a few seconds.

2. Stir in 1 cup water and ½ teaspoon of salt, then bring to a boil. Cover, lower the heat, and cook gently for 20 minutes or until the beets are tender. Add the tomatoes and cook, uncovered, stirring over a high heat, for another 2–3 minutes or until the tomatoes are tender and well combined and most of the liquid has been absorbed. Sprinkle in some more salt as needed.

MYSORE-STYLE STIR-FRIED BEETS

MULANGI PORIYAL

1 tablespoon olive or peanut
   oil

¼ teaspoon whole brown
   mustard seeds

¼ teaspoon urad dal

¼ teaspoon chana dal (if you
   do not have this, double
   the urad dal)

2 dried hot red chilies, broken
   into 2–3 pieces, depending
   on size

5–6 fresh curry leaves, lightly
   crushed in your hand

1 small onion (about 3½ oz),
   peeled and chopped

14 oz beets, boiled, peeled,
   and cut into ½ inch dice

½ teaspoon salt, or to taste

1–3 fresh hot green chilies,
   finely chopped

3 tablespoons fresh grated
   coconut, or defrosted if
   frozen

2 tablespoons chopped fresh
   cilantro

For more information about this dish, see the Note on Poriyals on page 54. SERVES 3–4

From the Windflower Resort and Spa, Chef Srinivasan

1. Put the oil in a wok or medium frying pan and set over medium heat. When very hot, add the mustard seeds, urad dal, and chana dal. As soon as the mustard seeds pop and the dals turn golden red, add the red chilies. They will darken in seconds. Add the curry leaves (take care, as these will splutter), quickly followed by the onions. Stir and fry until the onions have softened and just begun to brown, about 5 minutes.

2. Reduce the heat to medium low and add the beets, salt, green chilies, and coconut. Stir and toss for a minute. Add 4 tablespoons of water and cook gently on low heat for another 10 minutes, stirring now and then. The water should have evaporated. If it has not, boil it away. Add the cilantro and stir to mix.

EVERYDAY CARROTS AND PEAS

GAJAR MATAR KI SABZI

ๆๆๆๆๆๆๆๆๆๆๆๆๆๆๆๆๆๆๆๆๆๆๆๆๆๆๆๆๆ

1½ tablespoons olive or peanut oil

½ teaspoon whole cumin seeds

4 medium carrots (about 8 oz in all), peeled and cut into ½ inch dice

2 cups peas, defrosted if frozen, and parboiled if fresh

1 teaspoon ground coriander

¼ teaspoon ground turmeric

Generous pinch of nice red chili powder, or more as desired

½ teaspoon salt

A simple meal in North India might well consist of freshly made chapatis, a dal, these carrots and peas, and perhaps a second vegetable, as well as the usual complement of pickles, chutneys, and raita.   SERVES 4

ๆๆๆๆๆๆๆๆๆๆๆๆๆๆๆๆๆๆๆๆๆๆๆๆๆๆๆๆๆ

From Mehreen Khosla

1. Put the oil in a medium frying pan and set over medium heat. When hot, add the cumin seeds. Let them sizzle for a few seconds, then add the carrots and peas. Stir and fry for 2–3 minutes.

2. Add the ground coriander, turmeric, chili powder, and salt. Reduce the heat to medium low and stir a few times. Add 4–5 tablespoons of water, cover, and cook on low heat for 3–4 minutes or until the vegetables are tender.

STIR-FRIED CARROTS

CARROT PORIYAL

ᎭᏆᎭᏆᎭᏆᎭᏆᎭᏆᎭᏆᎭᏆᎭᏆᎭᏆᎭᏆᎭᏆᎭᏆᎭᏆᎭᏆᎭᏆᎭᏆᎭᏆᎭᏆ

5 medium carrots (about
    12 oz)

1 tablespoon olive or peanut
    oil

½ teaspoon urad dal

½ teaspoon whole brown
    mustard seeds

2 dried hot red chilies, broken
    in half

1 teaspoon peeled and finely
    grated fresh ginger

½ teaspoon salt

3 tablespoons finely grated
    fresh coconut, or defrosted
    frozen coconut

2 tablespoons roughly
    chopped fresh cilantro

This simple carrot dish can be served with most Indian meals. Leftovers may be added to salads. For more on South Indian poriyals, see the note on page 54. SERVES 3–4

ᎭᏆᎭᏆᎭᏆᎭᏆᎭᏆᎭᏆᎭᏆᎭᏆᎭᏆᎭᏆᎭᏆᎭᏆᎭᏆᎭᏆᎭᏆᎭᏆᎭᏆᎭᏆ

1. Peel the carrots and cut them into ⅓ inch rounds. Larger pieces from the top of the carrots should be halved.

2. Put the oil in a frying pan, wok, or karhai set over medium heat. When hot, add the urad dal. As soon as it begins to change color, add the mustard seeds and red chilies. When the mustard seeds pop and the chilies darken, a matter of seconds, add the carrots, ginger, and salt. Mix well, then add 4 tablespoons of water. Cover and cook on low heat for 3–4 minutes or until the carrots are tender. Add the coconut and cilantro and mix well.

STIR-FRIED CABBAGE

BANDH GOBI KI SABZI

I small green cabbage (about
  1½ lbs)

1–3 fresh hot green chilies,
  finely chopped

2½ tablespoons olive or
  peanut oil

¾ teaspoon whole brown
  mustard seeds

7–8 fresh curry leaves, lightly
  crushed in your hand

1–1¼ teaspoons salt

3–4 teaspoons lemon juice

Here the cabbage is finely shredded and barely cooked. It is delightfully light, part salad and part vegetable dish. It may be served hot, warm, at room temperature, or cold. You could put it on a plate with stuffed Indian pancakes or omelets, or serve it as part of any meal.

For shredding the cabbage, I prefer to use one of the newer, lighter mandolines. Some are made in Japan, but OXO makes an excellent one too. You could also use your food processor or just cut by hand. I like to use a bread knife for cutting cabbage.

SERVES 6

From Fatma Zakaria

1. Remove the damaged outer leaves of the cabbage. Quarter it lengthwise and remove the hard core. Now shred it or cut it into slivers ⅛ inch thick. You should have about 1¼ lbs. Place in a bowl and add the green chilies.

2. Put the oil in a wok or large, wide pan and set over medium heat. As soon as it is hot, add the mustard seeds. When they pop, a matter of seconds, add the curry leaves (take care, as they will splutter), quickly followed by the cabbage mixture. Stir and fry until the cabbage has just wilted, about 2–3 minutes.

3. Lower the heat and add the salt and lemon juice. Stir thoroughly, then turn off the heat. The cabbage should be wilted but still crunchy. Taste for balance of flavors and adjust as necessary.

ROASTED CAULIFLOWER WITH PUNJABI SEASONINGS

OVEN KI GOBI

ᕙᕗᕙᕗᕙᕗᕙᕗᕙᕗᕙᕗᕙᕗᕙᕗᕙᕗᕙᕗᕙᕗᕙᕗᕙᕗᕙᕗᕙᕗᕙᕗᕙᕗᕙᕗ

1 large head of cauliflower, broken into florets about 1½ inches wide and 2 inches long (about 1½ lbs of florets)

1½ tablespoons lemon juice

½ teaspoon ground turmeric

1 teaspoon peeled and finely grated fresh ginger

1 teaspoon salt

¼–½ teaspoon cayenne pepper

2 teaspoons ground cumin

2 teaspoons ground coriander

2 tablespoons chopped fresh cilantro leaves

4 tablespoons olive or rapeseed oil

1 teaspoon whole cumin seeds

I wanted to simplify a cauliflower dish that I love, where I fry the cauliflower until it is lightly browned and then sauté it with spices, such as ginger, coriander, and cumin. After many tries, here is the beautiful result. I marinate florets of cauliflower with all the seasonings and then just roast them in a hot oven.

Serve with a dish of chickpeas, or any other dal, a flatbread or rice, and a yogurt relish.   SERVES 4–5

ᕙᕗᕙᕗᕙᕗᕙᕗᕙᕗᕙᕗᕙᕗᕙᕗᕙᕗᕙᕗᕙᕗᕙᕗᕙᕗᕙᕗᕙᕗᕙᕗᕙᕗᕙᕗ

1. Put all the cauliflower florets in a large bowl. Combine the lemon juice, turmeric, and ginger in a small bowl, then pour the mixture over the cauliflower. Add the salt, cayenne, ground spices, and fresh cilantro and mix well, wearing plastic gloves if preferred. Set aside for 2 hours, tossing now and then.

2. Preheat the oven to 425°. Put the oil in a small frying pan and set over medium-high heat. When hot, add the cumin seeds, let them sizzle for a few seconds, then pour the spiced oil over the cauliflower. Toss well.

3. Spread out the cauliflower in a single layer in a large roasting pan. Place in the oven for 15 minutes, then turn the pieces and roast for another 10–15 minutes or until lightly browned and cooked through.

CAULIFLOWER WITH POTATOES

ALOO GOBI

This is an easy dish that I make frequently. A karhai or wok is ideal for cooking it, but a large frying pan will work as well. Serve with an Indian flatbread or rice, a dal, a raita such as Yogurt Raita with Tomatoes, Shallots, and Cucumbers (page 334), and perhaps a green vegetable. Day-old boiled and refrigerated potatoes work beautifully for this dish, but you could cook them that day and let them cool off before you dice them.   SERVES 4

FOR THE SPICE MIXTURE

2 teaspoons peeled and finely grated fresh ginger

1 teaspoon ground cumin

2 teaspoons ground coriander

¼ teaspoon ground turmeric

¼ teaspoon nice red chili powder, or to taste

½ teaspoon salt, plus more as needed

4 tablespoons olive or peanut oil

¼ teaspoon whole cumin seeds

4½–5 cups cauliflower florets, about 1 inch wide

2 medium waxy potatoes, boiled, cooled, and cut into ¾ inch dice

1. First, make the spice mixture. Simply combine all the ingredients for it in a bowl, add ¼ cup water, and mix thoroughly. Set aside.

2. Put the oil in a large karhai, wok, or frying pan and set over medium-high heat. When hot, add the cumin seeds, and a few seconds later add the cauliflower and potatoes. Stir and cook for about 10 minutes or until the vegetables are well browned in spots.

3. Add the spice mixture and stir-fry for 1 minute. Add another ¼ cup water, lower the heat, and cook gently, stirring now and then, for 2–5 minutes, until the vegetables are tender and the spices amalgamated. There should be no liquid left. Taste and adjust the salt. You will probably need a bit more.

CAULIFLOWER WITH PEAS

FLOWER VATANA NU SHAAK

ㄸㄸㄸㄸㄸㄸㄸㄸㄸㄸㄸㄸㄸㄸㄸㄸㄸㄸㄸㄸㄸㄸㄸㄸㄸㄸㄸㄸㄸㄸ

1 large head of cauliflower (about 1¾ lbs), broken into 2 inch florets (a little over 1 lb)

3 tablespoons olive or peanut oil

Generous pinch of ground asafetida

1 teaspoon whole brown mustard seeds

1–2 fresh hot green chilies, sliced crosswise into thin rounds

1 medium tomato (about 6 oz), peeled and finely chopped

1 teaspoon salt

¼ teaspoon ground turmeric

¼ teaspoon nice red chili powder (optional)

2 teaspoons ground coriander

1 teaspoon peeled and very finely grated fresh ginger

¾ cup shelled fresh peas or defrosted frozen peas

2–3 tablespoons chopped fresh cilantro, to serve

Rajul is a Jain from Palanpur in northern Gujarat, but she lives in Bombay. Under the British, Palanpur was a princely state with a Muslim nawab, but Jains prospered there, eventually becoming leaders of the diamond trade in Bombay and around the world. Jainism is about as old as Buddhism, and its adherents are not only complete vegetarians but also often refrain from eating garlic, onions, and many other root vegetables and bulbs that require the total destruction of plants when they are harvested.

This is a Palanpur Jain dish. It may be served with rice or Indian breads, along with a dal, a raita, and relishes. You could also serve it at a Western meal. I often mix it with cooked penne pasta and some grated Parmigiano Reggiano cheese.

I used fresh peas, as there was a profusion of them in my garden. If you use frozen peas, they should be defrosted thoroughly in warm water, drained, and added 3–4 minutes before the cooking is finished.   SERVES 4–6

ㄸㄸㄸㄸㄸㄸㄸㄸㄸㄸㄸㄸㄸㄸㄸㄸㄸㄸㄸㄸㄸㄸㄸㄸㄸㄸㄸㄸㄸㄸㄸ

From Rajul Gandhi

1. Wash the cauliflower and put the florets in a large bowl filled with water. Set aside for 10–30 minutes while you set out and prepare the other ingredients.

2. Put the oil in a large, preferably nonstick frying pan or sauté pan and set over medium-high heat. When hot, add the asafetida. A second later, add the mustard seeds, and as soon as they start to pop, a matter of minutes, add the green chilies and stir once. Now put in the tomatoes, salt, turmeric, chili powder (if using), ground coriander, and ginger. Stir and fry for a few minutes, until the tomatoes thicken into a paste.

3. Drain and add the cauliflower and the peas. Stir a few times, then lower the heat to medium low. Add ¼ cup water and bring to a simmer. Cover and cook gently, stirring now and then, for about 10 minutes or until the cauliflower is tender. Check the salt. If there is liquid left at the bottom of the pan, turn the heat up a bit and boil it away, stirring gently as you do this. Sprinkle the fresh cilantro over the top before serving.

CAULIFLOWER WITH AJOWAN AND GINGER

AJWAINWALI GOBI

౭౨౭౨౭౨౭౨౭౨౭౨౭౨౭౨౭౨౭౨౭౨౭౨౭౨౭౨౭౨౭౨

1 large head of cauliflower
(about 1¾ lbs), broken into
2 x 2 inch florets (about
1 lb florets)
4 tablespoons olive or peanut
oil
1 teaspoon ajowan seeds
One 2 inch piece of fresh
ginger, peeled and finely
chopped
4 cloves garlic, peeled and
finely chopped
½ teaspoon ground turmeric
½ teaspoon salt
1–3 fresh hot green chilies, cut
crosswise into very thin
slices

Ashrams in India cater to hundreds, if not thousands, of people at a time, so I was very interested in knowing just what they served and if they had any underlying principles to guide their chefs.

Ashram foods, as I should have expected, differ from ashram to ashram. The Aurobindo Ashram has its headquarters in Pondicherry, in South India. I went to the very modern, beautifully designed branch in Delhi, which boasted a vast, all-granite, circular dining area, open to the skies in the center. Food is served from large pots set on tables at opposite ends of the room. All who wish may eat, for free. There are signs, kindly reminders, everywhere: "Wasting Food is a Sin"; "Please Take Only as Much Food as You Need"; "Second Helpings Are Served with Pleasure."

Stainless steel metal trays with depressions for each dish are neatly stacked, as are the metal tumblers for water. Guests have to wash them up after the meal and restack them.

The kitchen posts its all-vegetarian menus for lunch, tiffin (in this case, tea and snacks), and dinner on the walls. The foods are neither too spicy nor too oily. Red chilies are never used in the cooking; fresh green chilies are allowed. Eggs may not be used in the baking. They have wonderful eggless coconut and chocolate cakes. The inspiration for the dishes comes from all over India. When I was there for lunch, there were chapatis, lemon rice and plain rice, as well as idlis (steamed rice cakes) for the starch; there were whole red lentils and yogurt for protein; potatoes, radishes, peas, cauliflower, and carrots were all cooked together, and there was a salad as well.

This cauliflower dish is based on an Aurobindo Ashram recipe. Ajowan seeds are rich in thymol, renowned for its medicinal properties, and impart a thyme-like flavor. All Indian grocers sell them.

SERVES 4

౭౨౭౨౭౨౭౨౭౨౭౨౭౨౭౨౭౨౭౨౭౨౭౨౭౨౭౨౭౨౭౨

1. Wash the cauliflower and put the florets in a large bowl filled with water. Set aside for 10–30 minutes while you set out and/or prepare the other ingredients.

2. Put the oil into a very large frying pan set over medium heat. When hot, add the ajowan seeds. Stir a few times, then add the ginger and garlic. Stir for a minute and add the turmeric. Stir once, then quickly add all the cauliflower, scooping it up with both hands from the water with open fingers. Add the salt and green chilies, stir a few times, and cover. Cook on low heat, stirring now and then, for about 6–10 minutes or until the cauliflower is tender enough to break with your fingers.

KITCHEN MENU

DAYS	BREAKFAST	LUNCH	TIFFIN	DINNER
MONDAY	a) DALIYA/CUSTARD b) FRUIT	a) RAJMA b) MILK ALOO/BAKED PATATOES c) SEASONAL VEG. d) SALAD & DAHI /*LASSI*	a) ROSE MILK (COLD) b) MURMURA c) BREAD JAM	a) CHANA DAL b) SEASONAL VEG. c) ACHAR
TUESDAY	a) IDLY b) SAMBER/CHATNEY	a) KALI MASOOR b) ALOO BHURJI/PANEER c) SEASONAL VEGETABLE d) DAHI/ LASSI	a) NIMBU PANI b) CHOCO CAKE c) BREAD JAM	a) MOONG CHILKA b) SEASONAL VEG/ PEAS c) ACHAR
WEDNESDAY	a) CHANA/NOODLES b) FRUIT	a) CHANA DAL b) ALOO SOYABIN/DUM ALOO c) BAKED VEG. d) SALAD & DAHI /*LASSI*	a) ROOHAFZA b) BISCUIT/CHEVDA c) BREAD JAM	a) ARHAR DAL b) SEASONAL VEG.
THURSDAY	a) VADA/SAMOSA/BURGER b) CHUTNEY	a) KARHI b) MASHED ALOO c) SEASONAL VEGETABLE d) DAHI/ LASSI	a) RASNA/TANG b) FRYUMS c) BREAD JAM	a) MOONG SABUT b) ALOO MATTAR c) ACHAR
FRIDAY	a) BREAD PATATO/BREAD PIZZA	a) CHANA DAL, b) TOMATO ALOO/DAHI ALOO c) STEW VEG. d) SALAD & DAHI /*LASSI*	a) NIMBU PANI b) ~~COCONUT CAKE~~ c) BREAD JAM	a) LAL MASSUR b) SEASONAL VEG. c) ACHAR
SATURDAY	a) CHIDWA/UPAMA	a) LOBIYA b) ALOO CURRY/ALOO VADI c) SEASONAL VEGETABLE d) DAHI/ LASSI	a) JAL JEERA b) NAMAK PARA c) BREAD JAM *COCONUTCAKE*	a) MOONG DHULI b) SEASONAL VEG. c) ACHAR
SUNDAY	a) PURI/PARATHA/CHHOLE BHATURE	a) CHANA DAL/URAD MIX b) FRIED ALOO c) SEASONAL VEGETABLE d) KHEER	a) NIMBU PANI b) FRYUMS c) BREAD JAM	a) KHICHRI OR PALAO b) DAHI c) PAPAD c) ACHAR

That day's menu, Aurobindo Ashram, Delhi

FACING PAGE: Stainless steel tumblers that diners use, wash, and return
Aurobindo Ashram, Delhi

QUICK STIR-FRY OF YOUNG ZUCCHINI AND YELLOW SQUASH

ZUCCHINI AUR SQUASH KI SABZI

໑ຕ໑ຕ໑ຕ໑ຕ໑ຕ໑ຕ໑ຕ໑ຕ໑ຕ໑ຕ໑ຕ໑ຕ໑ຕ໑ຕ໑ຕ໑ຕ໑ຕ໑ຕ

1 lb young zucchini and young yellow squash (I used 2 small zucchini and 2 small yellow squash, but just one or the other could be used if you prefer)

3 tablespoons plain yogurt

½ teaspoon ground turmeric

½ teaspoon ground coriander seeds

¾ teaspoon salt

Freshly ground black pepper

¼ teaspoon or more nice red chili powder

1 tablespoon olive or peanut oil

Pinch of ground asafetida

¼ teaspoon whole brown mustard seeds

¼ teaspoon whole cumin seeds

Many vegetarians in India, especially in the central desert region of Rajasthan, where there is a dearth of wood for fuel, stir-fry their vegetables quickly in a little yogurt. This gives them creaminess and tartness, as well as added protein. Here is one such quick-cooking and delicious dish. It is generally served with Indian flatbreads, such as chapatis, and a dal. You can also serve it with rice.

A nice, sour plain yogurt is best here. Indian stores sell it as "dahi," and health-food stores sell an acidophilus yogurt that is tart, but any plain yogurt will do. If it is not at all sour, just leave the required amount unrefrigerated in a warmish place for 24 hours.   SERVES 4

໑ຕ໑ຕ໑ຕ໑ຕ໑ຕ໑ຕ໑ຕ໑ຕ໑ຕ໑ຕ໑ຕ໑ຕ໑ຕ໑ຕ໑ຕ໑ຕ໑ຕ໑ຕ

1. Cut the zucchini and yellow squash in half lengthwise, then cut crosswise into ½ inch pieces. Combine the yogurt, turmeric, coriander, salt, pepper, and chili powder in a small bowl and mix well.

2. Heat the oil in a medium frying pan set over medium-high heat. When hot, add the asafetida, mustard seeds, and cumin seeds. As soon as the mustard seeds pop, a matter of seconds, add all the cut vegetables. Stir and fry for 3–4 minutes or until the vegetables just start to take on color.

3. Turn the heat down to medium and add 1 tablespoon of the yogurt mixture. Stir a few times, then add another tablespoon of the mixture. Do this again with the remaining mixture, stirring for a minute after each addition. Taste for salt. Add 1 tablespoon of water and stir a final time. Turn off the heat.

A Pochampally weaver prepares dosakai—

a South Indian cucumber—for lunch, Andhra Pradesh.

STIR-FRIED BABY KALE COOKED IN A BENGALI VILLAGE STYLE

KALE KI SABZI

ଔଔଔଔଔଔଔଔଔଔଔଔଔଔଔଔଔଔଔଔଔଔଔଔଔଔଔଔଔ

2–3 tablespoons mustard oil (use a good virgin olive oil as a substitute)

¾ teaspoon nigella seeds (kalonji)

2 fresh hot green chilies (such as bird's-eye), cut into thin rounds

10 oz young kale leaves, chopped

½ teaspoon salt

¼ teaspoon sugar

The style that I have used to cook this kale is the one used in some Bengali villages to prepare finely chopped stems of mixed green vegetables in a dish called "dahta." If, indeed, you have an assortment of stems from your garden, chop them into small pieces and generally follow this recipe. If you do not, use young kale or young collard greens. If the leaves are more mature, add more water and cook longer than specified, until the leaves are very tender.

Serve with any legume or dried-bean dish, rice, and a yogurt relish. Chutneys and pickles can be added to the meal as desired.

SERVES 3–4

ଔଔଔଔଔଔଔଔଔଔଔଔଔଔଔଔଔଔଔଔଔଔଔଔଔଔଔଔଔ

From Kaveri Kaul

Put the mustard oil in a medium pan and set over medium heat. When hot, add the nigella seeds and allow them to sizzle for a few seconds. Add the chilies, stir once, then add the kale, salt, and sugar. Stir a few times and add ½ cup water. Bring to a boil. Cover, lower the heat, and cook gently 5–10 minutes or until the kale is just tender.

FACING PAGE: Pochampally weavers' kitchen

WINTER KALE IN A KASHMIRI STYLE

KALE KI KASHMIRI SABZI

ৎৎৎৎৎৎৎৎৎৎৎৎৎৎৎৎৎৎৎৎৎৎৎৎৎৎৎৎৎৎ

2 tablespoons mustard or olive
   oil
⅛ teaspoon ground asafetida
1 dried hot red chili
½–1 fresh green chili, slit open
   lengthwise
½ small onion, peeled and
   thinly sliced
5½ cups winter/black kale,
   cut crosswise into ¼ inch
   strips
½ teaspoon salt

Kale can cook quickly or slowly, depending on its age. I picked some black kale in December and it took about 30 minutes to cook. In Kashmir it is always cooked in mustard oil and served with rice. I like to add a whole bean dish and a salad to the meal as well.   SERVES 4

ৎৎৎৎৎৎৎৎৎৎৎৎৎৎৎৎৎৎৎৎৎৎৎৎৎৎৎৎৎৎ

1. Put the oil in a medium saucepan and set over medium heat. When hot, add the asafetida. Let it sizzle for a few seconds, then add the red and green chilies. When the red chili darkens, add the onions and sauté until golden.

2. Add all the kale, 2 cups water, and the salt. Bring to a boil. Cover, lower the heat, and simmer gently for 30 minutes or until the kale is tender. Drain and serve.

KODAVA MUSHROOM CURRY WITH COCONUT

KUMME CURRY

~~~~~~

A 14-oz can coconut milk, left
    undisturbed for 24 hours
    to allow the cream to rise
    to the top

1 lb small button mushrooms

1 teaspoon salt, or to taste

½ teaspoon ground turmeric

4 tablespoons olive or peanut
    oil

6 tablespoons peeled and
    finely chopped shallots

2 teaspoons ground coriander

¼–½ teaspoon nice red chili
    powder

2–3 fresh hot green chilies, slit
    in half lengthwise or finely
    chopped

1 tablespoon lime juice

I cannot tell you how scrumptious—and simple—this curry is. I had never eaten it before until Kaveri made it for me in her large, beautiful modern home in Bangalore, replete with vaulted ceilings and two kitchens, one for Kaveri, who is a food writer, and one for the staff. She and her husband, Naresh, are both from Coorg in South Karnatka (Coorg is the British name, but it is now referred to frequently as Kodagu, its original name), where they have vast holdings that include coffee plantations and tracts of the forested, mountainous wilderness that this area is famous for.

Many of the Kodavas are of the Kshatriya or warrior caste and, perhaps not so strangely, have risen in the ranks of the Indian army to gain the highest positions. Kodavas are not vegetarians, but they have such unusual vegetarian dishes that I had to travel up and down Coorg to learn more.

Traditionally, the people here are farmers (rice grows in the valleys), but they are also hunter-gatherers because their misty land in the mountainous Western Ghats of southwestern India is filled with game and fish. The British called it India's Scotland. They grow cardamom, coffee, and black pepper, and some shops in Madikeri, the capital city, specialize in selling just those three items. They have wonderful honey, which is also sold in the Madikeri market. The forests provide wild mangoes and bitter oranges, and in the very wet, four-month rainy season, the wilderness provides the hunter-gatherers with most of their fresh produce. At this time it bursts over with bamboo shoots (which mysteriously disappear every sixty years and then slowly regenerate), wild greens such as ferns, colocasia (they cook the tender leaves while they are still uncurled), and many, many varieties of mushrooms.

The wild mushrooms, with names such nucchie kumme and aalandi kumme, range from tiny ones that carpet the forest floor to wood-ear types that grow on tree trunks and those that look like petalled flowers. The largest ones, nethelé kumme, can grow to the size of a large dinner plate, and are simply roasted over wood and seasoned with salt, lime juice, and crushed green chilies (see my version, Broiled Portobello Mushrooms in the Kodaga Style, page 28).

For this dish of curried mushrooms, the white cultivated variety works just as well, and that is what Kaveri uses when she is not on her Coorg estate or when local mushrooms are out of season.

Housewives in Coorg use a tiny amount of their thick, sticky local vinegar, called "kachampuli," when making this curry and many of their other dishes as well. Even though I was given a precious triple-wrapped bottle that I carried all the way back home, I did not use it when I tested this recipe as I know that it is found nowhere outside Coorg. I just used more of the lime juice. It still tasted wonderful.

Serve this creamy curry with rice. At one of my dinners I made Berry Pilaf (see page 185), Eggs in a Hyderabadi Tomato Sauce (see page 286), Toovar Dal with Spinach and Sorrel (see page 162), Cabbage Fritters (page 13), and this mushroom curry. It was a lovely combination.

This dish is also quite wonderful with rice noodles (see Note on Sevai, page 266) and superb when served on toast. SERVES 4

ʊʊʊʊʊʊʊʊʊʊʊʊʊʊʊʊʊʊʊʊʊʊʊʊʊʊʊʊʊʊʊʊʊʊ

From Kaveri Ponnapa

1. Open the can of coconut milk without disturbing it too much and spoon the thick cream at the top into a bowl. Leave the thin coconut milk in the can.

2. Halve the mushrooms. Any large ones may be quartered. Place them all in a bowl and sprinkle the salt and turmeric over them. Wearing plastic gloves if you wish, as the turmeric can stain, thoroughly rub these flavorings into the mushrooms. Set aside for about 10 minutes.

3. Put the oil in a medium frying pan and set over medium-high heat. When hot, add the shallots and stir-fry until they just start

to brown. Take the pan off the heat and add the coriander and chili powder. Stir a few times.

4. Put the pan back on the stove, turning the heat to medium low. Add the green chilies and stir a few times. Now add the mushrooms and their accumulated liquid. Stir and cook on medium-high heat for 2 minutes. Add ¾ cup of the thin coconut milk and bring to a simmer. Simmer, uncovered, for 10 minutes.

5. Add ¾ cup of the coconut cream and stir to mix. Bring to a simmer over medium-high heat, then reduce the heat to very low and simmer gently, uncovered, for about a minute, stirring now and then. Turn the heat off. Add the lime juice and stir it in.

Knives being sold in a Mysore Market, South Karnataka

SIMPLE KODAVA MUSHROOM CURRY

KUMME CURRY

ෛෛෛෛෛෛෛෛෛෛෛෛෛෛෛෛෛෛෛෛෛෛෛෛෛෛෛ

1 lb small button mushrooms

1 teaspoon salt, or to taste

½ teaspoon ground turmeric

½–¾ teaspoon nice red chili
    powder

2 tablespoons olive or peanut
    oil

¼ teaspoon whole brown
    mustard seeds

1–2 fresh hot green chilies,
    finely chopped

1 large onion (7–8 oz), peeled
    and cut into half rings
    ¼ inch thick

1½ teaspoons ground
    coriander

Another lovely mushroom curry from Coorg, this time made without coconut milk. Serve with rice, rice breads, rice noodles, or a poha dish, and (if you eat eggs) Eggs in a Hyderabadi Tomato Sauce (see page 286) and a green vegetable.

Mynah's house has fields along the front, where she keeps guinea fowl; around the back are forests, whence come her fiddlehead ferns, her still-curled colocasia leaves, her wild mushrooms and bamboo shoots. She provides lodging to paying guests and also gives cooking classes in her simple kitchen.

This dish can be made with chanterelles, shiitake, ceps, morels, and any other wild mushrooms you can access. Wipe them clean, remove the stems if they are hard, and cut them so they are about 1 inch at their widest. But I used button mushrooms and they were just fine. SERVES 4

ෛෛෛෛෛෛෛෛෛෛෛෛෛෛෛෛෛෛෛෛෛෛෛෛෛෛෛ

From Mynah Pemmaiah

1. Halve the mushrooms. Any large ones may be quartered. Place them all in a bowl and sprinkle the salt, turmeric, and chili powder over them. Wearing plastic gloves if you wish, as the turmeric can stain, thoroughly rub these flavorings into the mushrooms. Set aside for about 10 minutes.

2. Put the oil in a medium frying pan and set over medium-high heat. When hot, add the mustard seeds. As soon as the mustard seeds start to pop, a matter of seconds, add the green chilies and the onion slices. Stir and fry until the onions just start to brown, 3–4 minutes. Add the ground coriander and stir once.

3. Add the mushrooms and their accumulated liquid and stir over medium-high heat for about 3 minutes. Add ¾ cup water and bring to a simmer. Cover and simmer on low heat for 10 minutes.

OKRA COOKED IN A KONKAN STYLE

BHENDI BHAJI

ഒ‌ഒ

¾ lb okra (small tender pods are best)

3 tablespoons olive or peanut oil

I teaspoon urad dal

½ teaspoon whole brown mustard seeds

½ teaspoon whole cumin seeds

I small hot green chili, slit in half lengthwise, or ¼ teaspoon nice red chili powder

10–15 fresh curry leaves, lightly crushed in your hand

I medium onion (about 6½ oz), peeled and chopped

¼ teaspoon ground turmeric

½ teaspoon salt, or to taste

I tablespoon lemon juice

The Konkan region runs along the central west coast of India. Here is one of its simple everyday okra dishes that I just love.

Serve the okra with other vegetables and perhaps Whole Moong and Masoor Cooked with Meat Seasonings (see page 149), a rice dish or a flatbread, and a yogurt relish. SERVES 3

ഒ‌ഒ

1. Wipe each okra pod with a damp cloth, then spread them out to air-dry. Cut off and discard the very tops and tails of the okra, then cut the pods crosswise into ½ inch pieces.

2. Put the oil in a large frying pan or sauté pan and set over medium-high heat. When hot, add the urad dal. As soon as the dal begins to color, add the mustard and cumin seeds. When the mustard seeds begin to pop, a matter of seconds, add the green chilies or red chili powder, curry leaves, and onions (take care, as the curry leaves will splutter). Stir and fry until the onions just begin to brown at the edges, about 6 minutes.

3. Add the turmeric, stir once, and add the okra. Lower the heat to medium low and stir gently for 5–6 minutes. Add the salt and lemon juice and stir gently. Lower the heat again, then sprinkle in some water. Cover and cook on low heat for 5–6 minutes or until the okra is just tender, sprinkling in more water if it seems to be catching. Taste and add a little more salt if needed.

MY EVERYDAY OKRA

ROZ KI BHINDI

ひひひひひひひひひひひひひひひひひひひひひひひひひひひひひひ

1½ lbs okra

1 medium onion

4 tablespoons olive or peanut
    oil

1 teaspoon ground coriander

1 teaspoon ground cumin

Generous pinch of nice red
    chili powder

¾ teaspoon ground amchoor
    or 1 tablespoon lemon
    juice

1 teaspoon salt, or to taste

1 medium tomato, peeled and
    diced

**When buying okra, always look for young, tender pods, which tend
to be small as well.**

**Okra is cooked in dozens of ways throughout India. This
remains one of the simplest and most delicious North Indian
ways of preparing it. Here it is not at all glutinous—it turns nicely
brown and can be eaten with rice or flatbreads and a selection of
legumes and relishes.** SERVES 4–6

ひひひひひひひひひひひひひひひひひひひひひひひひひひひひひひ

1. Wipe off each okra pod with a damp cloth and leave it briefly
to air-dry. Cut off the tops and tails. Slice the pod crosswise into
⅓ inch pieces.

2. Peel and cut the onion into dice about the same size as the
okra.

3. Pour the oil into a large frying pan and set over medium-high
heat. When hot, add the okra and onions. Stir and fry until the
okra starts to brown, turning down the heat little by little and
stirring gently now and then. In about 15 minutes, the okra
should be almost done and the pan should be over very low heat.

4. Add the ground coriander and cumin, along with the chili
powder, amchoor or lemon juice, and salt. Stir for 2–3 minutes
more, then add the tomatoes and stir gently for another 3–4
minutes.

OKRA DRY-COOKED WITH YOGURT

SOOKHI DAHI WALI BHINDI

1 lb okra (small tender pods
    are best)

2 tablespoons olive or peanut
    oil

Generous pinch of ground
    asafetida

¼ teaspoon whole brown
    mustard seeds

¼ teaspoon whole cumin
    seeds

1 dried hot red chili

1 medium onion, peeled and
    chopped

¼ teaspoon garam masala

½–¾ teaspoon salt

½ teaspoon ground coriander

¼ teaspoon ground turmeric

3 tablespoons plain yogurt

Here the okra is cooked until it is quite dry, oozing none of the viscous juices normally associated with it. It can be served with most Indian meals, and goes particularly well with any black-eyed peas dish, a potato dish, and some flatbread. SERVES 4

1. Wipe off each okra pod with a damp cloth. Spread out the pods to let them air-dry. Cut off and discard the very tops and tails of the pods, then cut them crosswise into ½ inch pieces.

2. Put the oil into a large frying pan or sauté pan and set over medium-high heat. When hot, add the asafetida, then, a second later, the mustard seeds. As soon as the mustard seeds start to pop, a matter of seconds, add the cumin seeds and the red chili. Let them sizzle for a few seconds, then add the onions and okra. Stir and fry until they just start to brown. Cook, stirring, over medium heat for about 10 minutes, lowering the heat gradually, until the okra is almost cooked. By then it should be on medium-low heat.

3. Add the garam masala, salt, coriander, and turmeric. Stir for a minute, then add 1 tablespoon of the yogurt. Stir until it seems to vanish. Add a second and third tablespoon of yogurt the same way. Turn the heat to low and cook the okra, stirring, until it is cooked through. Check the salt and adjust as necessary.

PUNJABI-STYLE OKRA MASALA

PUNJABI BHINDI

ભૐஇபஜஐபஜஐபஜஐபஜஐபஜஐபஜஐபஜஐபஜஐபஜ

14 oz okra (small tender pods are best)

5 tablespoons peanut or olive oil

Salt and freshly ground black pepper

1 medium onion, peeled and very finely chopped

1 teaspoon peeled and very finely grated fresh ginger

1 teaspoon peeled and finely crushed garlic

2 medium tomatoes (about 10 oz in all), peeled and finely chopped

½ teaspoon ground coriander

½ teaspoon ground cumin

¼ teaspoon ground turmeric

¼–¾ teaspoon nice red chili powder

2 tablespoons dried fenugreek leaves (kasuri methi)

The day starts early in the villages of the Punjab, one of India's "granary" states. Cows have to be milked, breakfasts prepared (very often stuffed parathas served with buttermilk or tea), and lunches made for those who work in far-away wheat fields. These lunches could consist of simple whole-grain tandoori breads and a vegetable, perhaps this okra. There may be a small raw onion or a pickle to add an extra fillip. A majority of the villagers in the Punjab are vegetarian and basically wheat eaters, so no meal is really complete without the flatbreads of the area.

Okra ripens mostly in the summer or the monsoon season here, and it is a beloved vegetable that comes at a time when mostly summer squashes hold sway. It is prepared the way many Punjabi vegetables are prepared—with onion, garlic, ginger, tomatoes, and some basic spices, such as cumin and coriander. Very often dried fenugreek leaves are added as well for that special umami flavor.

SERVES 4

ભૐஇபஜஐபஜஐபஜஐபஜஐபஜஐபஜஐபஜஐபஜஐபஜ

1. Wipe each okra pod with a damp cloth, then spread them out to air-dry. Remove the very top cones on the pods as well as the tips at the bottom, then slice the pods crosswise into ½ inch pieces.

2. Put 3 tablespoons of the oil in a medium, preferably non-stick frying pan and set over medium-high heat. When hot, add all the okra. Stir and fry for about 5 minutes or until the okra begins to take on a little color. Turn the heat down to medium. Keep frying and lowering the heat as you go for about 15 minutes or until the okra is cooked through and lightly browned all over. Sprinkle in about ¼ teaspoon of salt and some pepper and mix well. Remove the okra with a slotted spoon and transfer to a bowl.

3. Add enough of the remaining oil to the pan to make 3 tablespoons. Turn the heat to medium high and add the onions. Stir and fry for about 5 minutes or until lightly browned. Add the ginger and garlic, lower the heat to medium, and stir-fry for a minute. Add the tomatoes, coriander, cumin, turmeric, chili powder, and fenugreek leaves. Stir and cook, breaking up the tomato pieces, until you have a thick sauce.

4. Fold in the cooked okra, adding ½ teaspoon of salt as you do so. Mix gently and cook on low heat for a minute. Check the salt.

OKRA WITH ONIONS AND GREEN CHILIES

PYAZ KAY SAATH BHUNI HUI BHINDI

ೞೞೞೞೞೞೞೞೞೞೞೞೞೞೞೞೞೞೞೞೞೞೞೞೞೞೞ

¾ lb okra (small tender pods are best)

3 tablespoons olive or peanut oil

1 medium onion (6–7 oz), peeled and chopped

1–2 fresh hot green chilies, chopped

1 teaspoon ground coriander

½ teaspoon salt

¼ teaspoon ground turmeric

¼ teaspoon nice red chili powder

Another dish from northern India, where okra is never covered as it cooks, to prevent it from releasing its viscous innards. The cooking starts on medium-high heat, which is slowly lowered as the ingredients start to brown. The process takes 15–20 minutes and produces an unctuous dish, where the onions brown perfectly and meld with the now much darker okra.

I like to eat this with an Indian flatbread or a whole-grain pita bread, a potato dish, a dal, and a yogurt relish.   SERVES 3–4

ೞೞೞೞೞೞೞೞೞೞೞೞೞೞೞೞೞೞೞೞೞೞೞೞೞೞೞ

1. Wipe the okra pods with a damp cloth, then spread them out to air-dry. Cut off their tops and tails, then cut the pods cross-wise into ⅓ inch pieces.

2. Put the oil into a medium, preferably nonstick frying pan and set over medium-high heat. When hot, add the onions, green chilies, and okra. Stir and cook for about 10 minutes or until the onions are lightly browned. Lower the heat to medium low and add the coriander, salt, turmeric, and chili powder. Mix gently, then cook, stirring, for another 4–5 minutes.

3. Lower the heat to low and continue to stir gently and cook for another 2–4 minutes or until the okra is tender.

POTATO AND ONION MÉLANGE

DOSA WALAY ALOO

 භභභභභභභභභභභභභභභභභභභභභභභභභභභභභභ

1¼ lbs waxy potatoes, peeled
and cut into ½ inch dice

2 tablespoons olive or peanut
oil

½ teaspoon chana dal

½ teaspoon urad dal

½ teaspoon whole brown
mustard seeds

6–7 fresh curry leaves, lightly
crushed in your hand

1 medium onion (about 6 oz),
peeled and cut into ⅓ inch
dice

1 teaspoon peeled and finely
chopped fresh ginger

1 fresh hot green chili, finely
chopped

1¼ teaspoons salt

½ teaspoon ground turmeric

2 tablespoons chopped fresh
cilantro

This is the very traditional stuffing for South Indian dosas (savory pancakes). It may also be served as a vegetable with any meal. It goes particularly well with Indian breads.

SERVES 4–5 AND MAKES ENOUGH FILLING FOR 6 DOSAS

භභභභභභභභභභභභභභභභභභභභභභභභභභභභභභ

From Swarnalatha and Rajalaxmi in Mysore

1. Boil the potatoes until tender, then drain, reserving about 1 cup of the cooking water in a jug. Crush the potatoes very coarsely.

2. Put the oil in a medium nonstick frying pan and set over medium heat. When hot, add the chana dal. Wait 15 seconds, then add the urad dal. As soon as the dals begin to take on any color, add the mustard seeds. Stir until the mustard seeds start to pop, then quickly add the curry leaves (take care, as these will splutter), followed a few seconds later by the onions, ginger, and green chilies. Stir for 3–4 minutes and then add 5 tablespoons of the potato water. Cover and cook on low heat for about 3 minutes or until the onions are soft.

3. Add the potatoes, salt, and turmeric. Stir and mix on low heat for 2–3 minutes. Add another 6 tablespoons of the potato water and stir for 2 more minutes. Finally, stir in the cilantro.

SIMPLE MARWARI-STYLE PEAS

MATAR KA SISUA

༁༊༁༊༁༊༁༊༁༊༁༊༁༊༁༊༁༊༁༊༁༊༁༊༁༊༁༊༁༊༁༊༁༊

2 tablespoons ghee (clarified
    butter), olive oil, or peanut
    oil, or a mixture of any oil
    and ghee
¼ teaspoon whole cumin
    seeds
1 tablespoon peeled and finely
    grated fresh ginger
1–2 fresh hot green chilies,
    finely chopped
2⅓ cups peas, parboiled and
    drained if fresh, defrosted
    under running water if
    frozen
¾ teaspoon salt
Freshly ground black pepper

Sometimes it is hard to fathom how a few carefully chosen seasonings can make a vegetable shine. In the case of peas, ginger, cumin, and green chilies will do just that—every time. This is Vinita Pittie's recipe. For more about her and her community, and her life in Hyderabad, see page 108.

The peas can be served with Potatoes in a Marwari Style (see page 108), a yogurt relish, a dal, and perhaps some Marwari Layered Griddle Breads (see page 232) or rice.   SERVES 4

༁༊༁༊༁༊༁༊༁༊༁༊༁༊༁༊༁༊༁༊༁༊༁༊༁༊༁༊༁༊༁༊༁༊

From Vinita Pittie

1. Put the ghee or oil in a medium, preferably nonstick pan and set over medium heat. When hot, add the cumin seeds. Let them sizzle for 10 seconds, then add the ginger and green chilies. Stir for a minute.

2. Add the peas, salt, and pepper and stir for 2–3 minutes, sprinkling with a little water if the peas get too dry.

FACING PAGE: A courtyard in Vinita Pittie's mansion in Old Hyderabad City

PEAS AND POTATOES COOKED IN A BIHARI STYLE

MATAR KI GHUGNI

ᕳᕲᕳᕲᕳᕲᕳᕲᕳᕲᕳᕲᕳᕲᕳᕲᕳᕲᕳᕲᕳᕲᕳᕲᕳᕲᕳᕲᕳᕲᕳᕲᕳᕲᕳᕲ

2 tablespoons olive, peanut, or mustard oil

½ teaspoon whole cumin seeds

1 medium onion, peeled and chopped

1 tablespoon peeled and finely grated fresh ginger

1–3 fresh hot green chilies, finely chopped

¼ teaspoon ground turmeric

2⅓ cups peas, parboiled and drained if fresh, defrosted under running water if frozen

1 medium waxy potato (about 4–5 oz), boiled, peeled, and cut into ¾ inch dice

1 teaspoon salt, or to taste

Freshly ground black pepper

This recipe is very similar to the previous one, but has a few additions and comes from Bihar. Ghugnis, made out of small red chickpeas, regular beige chickpeas, fresh green chickpeas, and fresh green peas, are breakfast food for many vegetarians in Uttar Pradesh and Bihar. They are eaten with flatbreads, such as Chapatis, Parathas, or Puffed Fried Breads (see pages 219–38). They can also be eaten as a snack. In Bihar they are sometimes served with crisped flattened rice.

If you have a boiled potato sitting in your refrigerator, this is the time to use it up. Otherwise, boil one and let it cool off before peeling and cutting it.   SERVES 4

ᕳᕲᕳᕲᕳᕲᕳᕲᕳᕲᕳᕲᕳᕲᕳᕲᕳᕲᕳᕲᕳᕲᕳᕲᕳᕲᕳᕲᕳᕲᕳᕲᕳᕲᕳᕲ

1. Put the oil in a medium, preferably nonstick pan and set over medium heat. When hot, add the cumin seeds and let them sizzle for 10 seconds. Add the onions, then stir and fry for about 5–6 minutes or until the onions are soft.

2. Add the ginger, green chilies, and turmeric and stir for a minute. Add the peas, potatoes, salt, and pepper and stir for 2–3 minutes, sprinkling with a little water if the peas get too dry.

POTATOES WITH CUMIN AND ASAFETIDA

HEENG ZEERAY KE ALOO

ଔଔଔଔଔଔଔଔଔଔଔଔଔଔଔଔଔଔଔଔଔଔଔଔଔଔଔଔଔଔ

¾ lb waxy potatoes, boiled and
    cooled (leftover potatoes
    are fine)

1 tablespoon olive or peanut
    oil

Generous pinch of ground
    asafetida

¼ teaspoon whole cumin
    seeds

1 dried hot red chili

1 fresh hot green chili, cut
    crosswise into fine slices

1 medium tomato (about 5 oz),
    chopped

½ teaspoon salt

This is a simplified version of the very first dish I learned to cook. I was in London, a student at the Royal Academy of Dramatic Art and desperate for family foods. I could not cook at all. I begged my mother in India to teach me and she answered with three-line recipes written on flimsy airmail paper. That was the cheapest way to communicate then. I devoured those letters with my eyes first, and then rushed off to the Indian shop near the college to buy the ingredients. My landlords, a kind young couple in north London, let me use their kitchen, and I was off and away.

I cook this potato dish in fifteen minutes, starting with boiled potatoes, which speeds up the process. Here I used fingerlings, but if you do not have access to them, any waxy potatoes will do. I like to eat this dish with flatbreads—Chapatis or Puffed Fried Breads are best (see pages 219 and 235), but you can choose any flatbread. You could also use whole-grain pita breads and heat them, one at a time, in the microwave for 20–30 seconds each. You should serve a dal, a green vegetable, such as spinach, and a yogurt relish with it as well.   SERVES 3–4

ଔଔଔଔଔଔଔଔଔଔଔଔଔଔଔଔଔଔଔଔଔଔଔଔଔଔଔଔଔଔ

1. Peel the potatoes and cut them into ½ inch dice. If they are fingerlings, just cut them crosswise into ½ inch rounds.

2. Pour the oil into a medium nonstick frying pan and set over medium-high heat. When hot, add the asafetida and, a second later, the cumin seeds. Allow to sizzle for a few seconds, then add the red chili. When it darkens, add the potatoes and green chilies. Stir for a minute or two, until the potatoes brown a little. Then add the tomatoes, salt, and ½ cup water. Bring to a boil, mashing up the tomatoes as you do so. Cover and simmer gently for 10 minutes.

STIR-FRIED POTATOES WITH CHAAT MASALA

CHAAT MASALAY WALAY ALOO

ʊʊʊʊʊʊʊʊʊʊʊʊʊʊʊʊʊʊʊʊʊʊʊʊʊʊʊʊʊʊ

5–6 medium waxy potatoes
    (about 1 lb in all), boiled,
    cooled, and peeled
1 teaspoon ground coriander
½–1 teaspoon nice red chili
    powder
1 teaspoon chaat masala
¾–1 teaspoon salt (start with
    the smaller amount)
¼ teaspoon ground black
    pepper
¼ teaspoon garam masala
1½ teaspoons whole cumin
    seeds
2 tablespoons chopped fresh
    cilantro
1 tablespoon lime juice
2 tablespoons olive or peanut
    oil

Here is another of Vinita's inspired dishes. Although it uses potatoes and might seem very similar to the previous recipe, it is actually very different. This is a "chaat," a spicy, hot, and sour snack food, which in India could be eaten by itself with a cup of tea. However, I often serve it as part of a lunch or dinner, along with Cauliflower with Ajowan and Ginger (see page 77), Chana Dal with Spinach and Tomato (see page 127), any Indian bread, and a yogurt relish. SERVES 4

ʊʊʊʊʊʊʊʊʊʊʊʊʊʊʊʊʊʊʊʊʊʊʊʊʊʊʊʊʊʊ

From Vinita Pittie

1. Cut the potatoes lengthwise into fat fries and put them in a bowl.

2. Put the ground coriander in a small bowl with the lower amount of chili powder, the chaat masala, the lower amount of salt, the black pepper, and the garam masala.

3. Put a small, heavy-based frying pan over medium heat. When hot, add the cumin seeds and stir them around until you get a roasted aroma and they turn a shade darker. Add all the ground spices in the small bowl. Stir for 5 seconds, then tip onto a piece of paper towel. Once cool, put the spice mixture into a clean coffee grinder or spice mill and grind as finely as you can.

4. Sprinkle the spice mixture, fresh cilantro, and lime juice over the potatoes and mix well with a gentle hand.

5. Put the oil in a well-seasoned wok, karhai, or nonstick frying pan and set over medium heat. When hot, add the potatoes and stir for a minute. Taste for salt and chili powder, adding more if you wish.

POTATOES COOKED IN A BANARASI STYLE

BANARASI ALOO

ぐぅぐぅぐぅぐぅぐぅぐぅぐぅぐぅぐぅぐぅぐぅぐぅぐぅぐぅぐぅぐぅぐぅ

4 tablespoons olive or peanut
oil

Generous pinch of ground
asafetida

1 teaspoon whole brown
mustard seeds

½ teaspoon whole cumin
seeds

A ½-inch piece of fresh ginger,
peeled and cut into minute
dice

1–2 fresh hot green chilies,
very finely chopped

1½ teaspoons ground
coriander

¼ teaspoon ground turmeric

½ teaspoon nice red chili
powder

1½ lbs waxy potatoes, boiled,
peeled, and cut or broken
into small pieces, none
larger on any side than
⅓ inch

1–1½ teaspoons ground
amchoor or lemon juice

1–1½ teaspoons salt

¾ teaspoon garam masala

A very typical dish from the bazaars of the old city of Banaras (I and many others still use the old name for Varanasi). Serve with Puffed Fried Breads (see page 235) or any other Indian flatbreads, as well as other vegetables, chutneys, and raita. SERVES 4

1. Put the oil in a large nonstick frying pan or wok and set over medium heat. When hot, add the asafetida and, a second later, the mustard seeds. As soon as the seeds start to pop, a matter of seconds, add the cumin seeds. Two seconds later add the ginger and green chilies. Stir for a few seconds. Add the coriander, turmeric, and chili powder. Stir once, then quickly add all the broken potatoes. Stir and fry for a minute.

2. Add ½ cup of water, lower the heat, and mix until well incorporated. Add the amchoor, salt, and garam masala. Stir gently and cook for another minute.

POTATOES IN A MARWARI STYLE

ALOO SABZI

ৎৡ

5–6 medium waxy potatoes (about 1 lb), boiled, cooled, and peeled

¾ teaspoon salt, or to taste

¼ teaspoon ground turmeric

⅛–½ teaspoon nice red chili powder

1 teaspoon ground coriander

2 tablespoons olive or peanut oil

Generous pinch of ground asafetida

½ teaspoon whole cumin seeds

1 dried hot red chili, broken in half

½ medium onion, peeled and thinly sliced

1½ teaspoons peeled fresh ginger, grated to a pulp

1 fresh hot green chili, thinly sliced

2 tablespoons chopped fresh cilantro

Marwaris are a highly successful business community that originated in Marwar, in the deserts of Rajasthan. Many left their hometowns to create large businesses elsewhere in India. They are completely vegetarian, with a distinct and much-admired cuisine.

Vinita has married into a family long settled in Hyderabad. They still live in the 230-year-old *haveli* (mansion) that fills an entire block in the heart of the city. The inner city is crumbling, and so is the mansion, but Vinita, with her great sense of style, has taken up a corner of it and filled it with antique furniture and family paintings that match the half-lost frescoes on some of the walls.

Vinita is a very popular dress designer. She has given part of the mansion over to the tailors and embroiderers she works with. She also cooks, the kitchen being right next to the room with the disappearing frescoes. She made these delicious potatoes for me as part of a dinner that included Simple Marwari-Style Peas, Mixed Dal in a Marwari Style, Marwari Layered Griddle Breads, and a yogurt dish (see pages 101, 154, 232).   SERVES 4

ৎৡ

From Vinita Pittie

1. Cut the potatoes lengthwise into fat chips and put them in a bowl. Add the salt, turmeric, chili powder, and ground coriander, then (wearing plastic gloves if you wish, as turmeric can stain) mix gently so that the spices cling to the potatoes.

2. Put the oil in a well-seasoned wok, karhai, or nonstick frying pan and set over medium-high heat. When hot, add the asafet-

ida. Two seconds later add the cumin seeds and let them sizzle for a few seconds. Throw in the broken red chili and stir for a second or two. Now add the onions and stir for a minute. Stir in the ginger and green chilies. Still on medium-high heat, add the potatoes and stir gently, lifting them from the bottom, for 4–5 minutes. The potatoes should get lightly browned. Check the salt, toss in the fresh cilantro, and mix.

GOAN POTATOES

BATATA BHAJI

ᘓᘐᘓᘐᘓᘐᘓᘐᘓᘐᘓᘐᘓᘐᘓᘐᘓᘐᘓᘐᘓᘐᘓᘐᘓᘐᘓᘐᘓᘐᘓᘐ

1¼ lbs waxy potatoes, boiled,
    peeled, and cut into ½ inch
    dice

½ teaspoon salt, plus a little
    extra

5 tablespoons olive or peanut
    oil

Generous pinch of ground
    asafetida

¼ teaspoon urad dal

¼ teaspoon whole brown
    mustard seeds

¼ teaspoon whole cumin
    seeds

Generous pinch of whole
    fenugreek seeds

15 fresh curry leaves, lightly
    crushed in your hand

2 fresh hot green chilies (such
    as bird's-eye), sliced into
    thin half rings

1 medium onion (5–6 oz),
    peeled and cut in half
    lengthwise and then into
    fine half rings

¼ teaspoon sugar

2 tablespoons chopped fresh
    cilantro

This dish, from a Hindu Goan restaurant in Bombay, tastes best if made with waxy potatoes. It is generally eaten with rice or rice breads, but can also be rolled up in a chapati, along with some chopped tomatoes and cucumber, and eaten as a snack or for lunch.

Urad dal is a split legume, often used as a seasoning as well. All Indian grocers sell it.   SERVES 4

ᘓᘐᘓᘐᘓᘐᘓᘐᘓᘐᘓᘐᘓᘐᘓᘐᘓᘐᘓᘐᘓᘐᘓᘐᘓᘐᘓᘐᘓᘐᘓᘐ

From the Highway Gomatak restaurant in Bombay

1. Put the potatoes in a bowl. Add the ½ teaspoon of salt and mix well, separating the pieces. Set out and/or prepare all the remaining ingredients, as the dish will cook quite fast.

2. Put the oil into a medium nonstick frying pan and set over medium-high heat. When hot, add the asafetida and, a second later, the urad dal. As soon as the dal starts to color, add the mustard seeds and cumin seeds. As soon as the mustard seeds start to pop, a matter of seconds, add the fenugreek seeds and, a second later, the curry leaves and green chilies (take care, as the curry leaves will splutter). Stir once or twice and add the onions. As soon as you see a hint of browning in the onions, add a tablespoon of water. Do this three times, cooking the onions for about 7–8 minutes.

3. Add a dash of salt and the sugar to the pan. Tip in all the potatoes and add about ½ cup water. Stir and cook on very low heat for 10 minutes, mixing every now and then. Some of the potatoes should melt into the water. Scatter the fresh cilantro over the top.

SPINACH WITH DILL

DAKHINI SAAG

∽∽∽∽∽∽∽∽∽∽∽∽∽∽∽∽∽∽∽∽∽∽∽∽∽∽∽∽∽∽

1 lb 3 oz spinach, well washed
and drained

2 tablespoons olive oil

2 tablespoons unsalted butter

¼ teaspoon whole cumin
seeds

1 medium onion, peeled and
cut into fine half rings

3 good-sized cloves garlic,
peeled and finely chopped

2 tablespoons very finely
chopped fresh dill

¾ teaspoon salt

¼ teaspoon ground turmeric

¼–½ teaspoon nice red chili
powder

2 tablespoons finely sliced
scallions (white parts only)

4 tablespoons peeled and
finely diced tomatoes

A simple but very flavorful spinach dish from the royal palaces of Hyderabad. Serve it at meals with either breads or pilafs, along with a dal, such as Hyderabadi "Sour" Dal (see page 164). At the Falaknuma Palace Hotel, where I first ate this, the spinach had been blended into a smooth purée. I just chop mine, as I like the texture. SERVES 3–4

∽∽∽∽∽∽∽∽∽∽∽∽∽∽∽∽∽∽∽∽∽∽∽∽∽∽∽∽∽∽

From the Taj Falaknuma Palace hotel in Hyderabad

1. Bring a large pan of water to a rolling boil. Drop all the spinach into it. As soon as the leaves have wilted, drain them in a colander and run cold water over them until cool enough to handle. Squeeze out most, but not all, of the water, then chop finely and set aside.

2. Put the oil and butter into a medium, preferably nonstick frying pan and set over medium heat. When hot, add the cumin seeds and let them sizzle for 10 seconds. Add the onions and sauté for 3–4 minutes. Add the garlic and sauté for another 2 minutes. Lower the heat to medium low, then add the chopped spinach, dill, salt, turmeric, and chili powder. Mix well, then stir and cook on low heat for 2 minutes. Add the scallions and diced tomatoes. Stir and cook for another 2 minutes.

STIR-FRIED SPINACH, ANDHRA-STYLE

PALAKOORA VEPADU

༄ཅ༔

1 lb 2 oz spinach, well washed

2 tablespoons olive or peanut oil

¼ teaspoon whole cumin seeds

3 cloves garlic, peeled, 1 halved lengthwise and 2 finely chopped

4–5 whole fenugreek seeds

6–7 fresh curry leaves, lightly crushed in your hand

1 medium onion (about 4½ oz), peeled and finely chopped

1 teaspoon peeled and very finely grated fresh ginger

Generous pinch of ground turmeric

½ teaspoon ground coriander

¼–1 teaspoon nice red chili powder

½ teaspoon salt

In Andhra, the term "vepadu" refers to dishes that are either stir-fried or deep-fried until they are crisp (see page 13 for vepadus and more on Andhra meals). In the south this delicious spicy spinach is generally served on the side, along with rice, thin dals, and yogurt dishes. I love it that way. I also love to eat it with North Indian chapatis, a potato dish, and a dal, such as those on pages 104 and 122.   SERVES 3–4

༄ཅ༔

1. Bring a large pan of water to a rolling boil. Drop all the spinach into it. As soon as the leaves have wilted, drain them in a colander and run cold water over them until cool enough to handle. Squeeze out most, but not all, of the water by picking up balls of spinach and gently pressing them between your palms. Chop the spinach coarsely and place in a bowl.

2. Put the oil in a medium, preferably nonstick pan and set over medium-high heat. When hot, add the cumin seeds. Let them sizzle for 3–4 seconds, then add the halved garlic clove. Stir once or twice. Add the fenugreek seeds and, a second later, the curry leaves (take care, as these will splutter). Quickly add the onions and reduce the heat to medium low. Stir and sauté for 5–6 minutes or until the onions become soft and begin to pick up a little color at the edges.

3. Add the ginger and chopped garlic. Sauté for another minute, then add the turmeric, coriander, and chili powder. Stir for a minute. Now add the chopped spinach, any accumulated liquid in the bowl, and the salt. Stir and sauté gently for another 8–10 minutes to allow all flavors to meld.

STIR-FRIED ORANGE PUMPKIN OR BUTTERNUT SQUASH

LAL KADDU KI SABZI

~~~~~~

2 tablespoons olive or peanut oil

¼ teaspoon urad dal

¼ teaspoon whole brown mustard seeds

1–2 dried hot red chilies

1 small onion (about 3 oz), peeled and chopped

1 lb orange pumpkin or butternut squash (see note below), cut into ½ inch dice

¾–1 teaspoon salt

1 tablespoon dark brown sugar

1 teaspoon ground cumin

Freshly ground black pepper

I have combined northern and southern Indian seasonings to make this dish, a great favorite in our household. Indians often add jaggery, a raw brown sugar, to pumpkin dishes, which, when combined with hot spices, makes the dish most addictive. I have used dark brown sugar instead.

India does not really have butternut squash, but it is so similar to orange pumpkin that it makes a perfect substitute. These days they can be found everywhere, all peeled, cut, and ready to cook, making our lives much easier. Whether you use orange pumpkin or butternut squash, the net weight after peeling and removing the seeds should be about 1 lb.

Serve in a meal that also has a spinach dish, a dal, and a yogurt relish or a salad of some sort. Eat with Indian breads or rice.

SERVES 4

~~~~~~

1. Put the oil into a medium nonstick frying pan and set over medium heat. When hot, add the urad dal. As soon as it starts to change color, add the mustard seeds and the red chilies. When the mustard seeds start to pop and the chilies darken, a matter of seconds, add the onions. Stir and fry for 2 minutes. Add the pumpkin or squash, then stir and fry for about 4 minutes or until the pumpkin and the onions start to brown.

2. Add ¾ cup of water, the salt, brown sugar, cumin, and black pepper. Mix well and bring to a boil. Cover, lower the heat, and simmer gently for about 10 minutes or until the pumpkin is soft enough to pierce easily with a knife. Taste for seasoning and make adjustments if needed.

3. When you are getting ready to serve, boil away any water that remains, stirring as you do so.

TURNIP BHARTA

SHALJUM BHARTA

ↄↄ

For more on bhartas (mashed vegetables), see page 53. The seasonings here are very North Indian.

Serve with any Indian bread or warmed whole-grain pita, perhaps a paneer dish, and a cauliflower dish. SERVES 5–6

ↄↄ

From Yasmin Tayebbhoy

6 medium turnips (about 1 lb 10 oz in all)

4 tablespoons olive or peanut oil

½ teaspoon whole cumin seeds

1 large onion (7 oz), peeled and chopped

1 tablespoon peeled and finely grated fresh ginger

3–4 cloves garlic, peeled and finely chopped

1–3 fresh hot green chilies, finely chopped

2 medium tomatoes (10 oz in all), peeled and finely chopped

¾–1 teaspoon salt

Freshly ground black pepper

4 tablespoons chopped fresh cilantro

1. Peel the turnips and cut each into 8 pieces. Put them in a pan, cover generously with water, and bring to a boil. Cover, lower the heat, and cook gently until tender. Drain thoroughly and mash well.

2. Put the oil in a medium nonstick frying pan and set over medium-high heat. When hot, add the cumin seeds and let them sizzle for 10 seconds. Add the onions and fry for 2 minutes. Stir and sauté over medium heat for another 3–4 minutes.

3. Add the ginger, garlic, and green chilies and stir for a minute. Add the tomatoes and cook over medium heat for 5–6 minutes or until they are paste-like and the oil begins to show at the edges.

4. Add the mashed turnips and salt, then cook for 20–25 minutes, turning the heat down as needed, until the turnips are well sautéed. Check the salt, then add the pepper and 3 tablespoons of the fresh cilantro. Stir well.

5. Sprinkle the remaining chopped fresh cilantro over the top when serving.

1 teaspoon black peppercorns

Seeds from 5 cardamom pods

4 cloves

A 1-inch piece of cinnamon
stick

1 bay leaf

2 tablespoons olive or peanut
oil

½ teaspoon whole brown
mustard seeds

1 dried hot red chili

15 or so fresh curry leaves,
lightly crushed in your
hand

2 medium shallots, peeled and
chopped

2 fresh hot green chilies, slit
in half lengthwise

2 cloves garlic, peeled and cut
into fine slivers

1 teaspoon fresh ginger, peeled
and finely grated

1 medium potato, cut into
¾ inch dice

1 teaspoon salt, or to taste

1½ cups cauliflower florets of
medium size

1 cup green beans (round or
flat), cut into ¾ inch pieces

1 medium carrot, peeled and
cut into ¾ inch dice or
rounds

¾ cup peas, defrosted if frozen

A 14-oz can coconut milk, well
shaken

1 teaspoon vinegar (rice
vinegar is ideal, but white
wine or red wine vinegar
is fine)

KERALA VEGETABLE STEW

KERALA ESHTEW

There are probably as many recipes for this in Kerala as there are families. Locally called "eshtew"—a charming mispronunciation of the English word—it is generally eaten with appam (rice pancakes) or idi appam (rice noodles) or plain rice. There are many ingredients involved, but the dish cooks quite quickly.

SERVES 3–4

1. Put the peppercorns, cardamom seeds, cloves, cinnamon stick, and bay leaf into a grinder and grind to a powder.

2. Put the oil in a wok or frying pan and set over medium-high heat. When hot, add the mustard seeds. As soon as they start to pop, a matter of seconds, add the red chili, then, a few seconds later, the curry leaves (take care, as these will splutter). Stir once and add the shallots, green chilies, and garlic. Stir for about 2 minutes, then add the ginger. Stir once or twice and add the potatoes. Stir a few times and add 1 cup water and ¼ teaspoon salt. Bring to a boil. Cover, lower the heat, and cook gently for about 10 minutes or until the potatoes are almost done.

3. Add the cauliflower, green beans, carrots, and peas followed by the ground spices and ¾ teaspoon of salt. Pour in just enough water to cover the vegetables, then stir and bring to a boil. Cover, lower the heat, and cook for about 6–8 minutes or until the vegetables are tender.

4. Add the coconut milk and bring to a simmer. Stir in the vinegar and turn off the heat. Taste for salt, adding more if needed.

DALS:

DRIED BEANS AND LEGUMES

A NOTE ON DALS

Pronounced "daal" (with a soft Spanish *d*), the word *dal* in India stands for the whole family of dried beans, pulses, legumes, and split peas. Indian grocers generally have a large section devoted just to dals. This includes various versions of the same dal—whole with skin, whole without skin, split with skin, split without skin—as well as dal flours and combinations of dal flours for specific dishes.

In China and much of the Far East, only the soybean and, to a much lesser extent, the mung bean and the red aduki bean have been explored to reveal the bounty they can offer. Only India has taken almost all the legumes it grows (other than the soybean), as well as those it has received in the past from other continents, and revealed all their potential.

Dals are a very important part of every Indian's food world. For Indian vegetarians this is doubly true, as legumes are a major source of protein. Each dal has its own taste and texture. For variety, not only can different dals be cooked every day, but the seasonings can be varied, as can the vegetables the dal is cooked with. Dals may also be combined in various ways not only for the somewhat soupy or porridge-like dishes we eat with our rice and breads, but to make savory cakes, pancakes, pastas, snacks, starters, dry chutneys, and sweet desserts. Chickpea flour alone can account for foods in all these categories. Indians are hard put to understand why the Americas, which grow so many wonderful varieties of legumes, do so little with them, other than boiling them up whole.

There are further minute distinctions in the dal dishes cooked in various parts of India. For example, in the south, an "usali" is a somewhat dry combination of a dal and a vegetable, a "kootu" is a slightly wetter combination, and a "sambar" is a very soupy one. In the north you could have a very rich creamy dish of the black whole urad dal one day, the very light moong dal with crisply browned onions the next, and a dish of sprouted mung beans on the third day. (If you want to learn how to sprout your own mung beans the easy Indian way, see page 143.) Eating dal every day is never boring for an Indian, any more than eating meat every day is boring for meat eaters. It is a matter of what meat or dal you eat and how it is cooked. In both cases, the variety is endless.

Whole beans need to be soaked overnight before they are cooked. If the split dals are going to be made into savory pancakes, they too need to be soaked and then blended into a batter. Recipes for pancakes are in "Grains: Breads, Pancakes, Savories, and Noodles."

The dals used in this book are discussed here in alphabetical order, but the list does not, by any means, cover all the dals cooked in India.

BLACK-EYED PEAS I have seen the fresh version of this bean only in India, but I am sure it is available in that form wherever it is grown. Most of the time it is sold in its dried form, or cooked and canned. I have used only the dried peas in my recipes. They need to be soaked overnight.

CHANA DAL This is really the split, skinned version of a smaller yellow chickpea. It makes for a meaty dal. It is also used as a spice in the south.

CHICKPEAS In India, chickpeas come in many sizes and colors. In the spring, markets sell fresh green ones on the bush in large bunches. The only kind of chickpeas I have used in this book are canned because they are so easy to prepare. Try to get organic ones—both they and the liquid they come in taste better than nonorganic ones.

CHICKPEA FLOUR Also called "besan" or "gram" flour, this is used to make fritters, to thicken soupy dishes, and to make pancakes.

GREEN LENTILS These are just the ordinary lentils that are sold in most supermarkets.

MASOOR Sabut masoor is whole red lentils, unsplit and with skin. Masoor dal is split red lentils, generally hulled.

MUNG Sabut moong or mung beans are whole and dark green, often used for sprouting. Indian sprouts have very short tails and the sprouting process takes just twenty-four hours. They are also soaked and ground into a rough batter to make delicious pancakes. Moong dal is the split version of mung beans, and can be bought with or without skin. Anything with skin has much more fiber, but takes longer to cook.

SOYA GRANULES Very popular with Indian vegetarians, these are used to make meat-like dishes.

TOOVAR Also called "arhar" and "toor," this dal is nearly always used in its hulled and split form in India. It is very popular in southern and western parts of India, though northerners love it as well. Apart from what I call "plain" toovar, there is also an oily form, which just means that it has been rubbed with castor oil to protect it from insects. This oil needs to be washed off before the dal is cooked.

URAD DAL This pulse has a dark skin and is used in both whole and split forms. It has a slightly glutinous texture, which has always endeared it to me. It is frequently used as a spice in the south, and for this purpose it is always hulled and split.

BLACK-EYED PEAS WITH CILANTRO AND GREEN CHILIES

LOBHIA AUR HARI CHUTNEY

࿓࿓࿓࿓࿓࿓࿓࿓࿓࿓࿓࿓࿓࿓࿓࿓࿓࿓࿓࿓࿓࿓࿓࿓

A simple, everyday dish from the north that goes well with both rice and flatbreads.   SERVES 4

࿓࿓࿓࿓࿓࿓࿓࿓࿓࿓࿓࿓࿓࿓࿓࿓࿓࿓࿓࿓࿓࿓࿓࿓

1 cup dried black-eyed peas, washed and soaked overnight

¾ teaspoon salt, or to taste

1 well-packed cup fresh cilantro tops, chopped

2–4 fresh hot green chilies, chopped

1 tablespoon tomato purée

2 teaspoons olive or peanut oil

Generous pinch of ground asafetida

½ teaspoon whole cumin seeds

1 dried hot red chili

½ medium onion, peeled and cut into fine half rings

1. Drain the peas, place in a pan with 4 cups water, and bring to a boil. Skim off the froth, lower the heat, and simmer very gently, partially covered, for 1¼ hours. Mash a few tablespoons of the beans against the sides of the pan, then mix in the salt.

2. Put 4 tablespoons of water in a blender. Add the cilantro, green chilies, and tomato purée. Blend thoroughly. You might need to push the ingredients down with a rubber spatula or add a tiny bit more water.

3. Put the oil in a small frying pan set over medium heat. When hot, add the asafetida and, a few seconds later, the cumin seeds. Let the cumin sizzle for a few seconds, then add the red chili and let it darken all over. Add the onions and fry until reddish brown.

4. Tip in the paste from the blender and fry until it is thick. Pour the contents of the pan into the beans and mix thoroughly. You can make the dal as thin or as thick as you like.

GOAN BLACK-EYED PEAS WITH COCONUT
CHAWLI USAL

᪥᪥᪥᪥᪥᪥᪥᪥᪥᪥᪥᪥᪥᪥᪥᪥᪥᪥᪥᪥᪥᪥᪥᪥᪥᪥᪥᪥᪥

2¼ cups dried black-eyed peas, washed and soaked overnight

3 medium onions, peeled

1 well-packed cup fresh grated coconut, or defrosted if frozen

5 tablespoons olive or peanut oil

4–5 medium tomatoes (about 1½ lbs), peeled and finely chopped

¾–1 teaspoon nice red chili powder

2 tablespoons ground coriander

¾ teaspoon ground turmeric

2 teaspoons salt, or to taste

2 teaspoons garam masala

Shashikala Potnis, the wife of the owner and head chef of the Highway Gomatak restaurant, together with her main assistant and daughter-in-law Sanjali, were extremely kind and generous when I visited. They patiently taught me many of the exquisite Hindu Goan-style dishes they cook and serve in their rather rough-and-ready, though highly successful, restaurant. This dish was one of them. It is generally served with rice or rice breads and other vegetable and fish dishes (yes, they eat fish).   SERVES 6

᪥᪥᪥᪥᪥᪥᪥᪥᪥᪥᪥᪥᪥᪥᪥᪥᪥᪥᪥᪥᪥᪥᪥᪥᪥᪥᪥᪥᪥

From the Highway Gomatak restaurant in Bombay

1. Drain the peas, put them into a pan with 6 cups water, and bring to a boil. Skim off the froth, then partially cover, lower the heat, and simmer gently for 45–60 minutes, until the peas are tender. Transfer them to a bowl and wash the pan.

2. While the peas are cooking, chop one of the onions and place in a blender with the coconut and ¾ cup water. Blend until you have as fine a paste as your blender can manage, pushing down with a rubber spatula if needed. Set aside.

3. Finely chop the remaining onions. Put the oil in the clean pan and set over medium-high heat. When hot, add the onions and fry until they brown at the edges. Add the tomatoes and fry until they soften and turn into a dark mush. The oil should show at the edges.

4. Tip in the paste from the blender and stir a few times, scraping up all the good bits stuck at the bottom. Add the chili pow-

der, coriander, and turmeric and fry over medium heat for 7–8 minutes or until the mixture browns lightly. Add all the cooked beans and their liquid, plus another 4–8 tablespoons of water, depending on how thick you want the beans to be. Stir in the salt and garam masala and bring to a simmer. Cook, uncovered, for 15–20 minutes or until the beans are very tender, stirring now and then.

NEPALESE BLACK-EYED PEAS WITH POTATOES AND BAMBOO SHOOTS

ALOO TAMA BODI

ๆๆๆๆๆๆๆๆๆๆๆๆๆๆๆๆๆๆๆๆๆๆๆๆๆๆๆๆๆๆๆๆๆๆ

1 cup dried black-eyed peas, washed and soaked overnight

An 8-oz can thinly sliced bamboo shoots (1 cup drained weight), cut into ¾ inch pieces

2 medium waxy potatoes (about 9 oz in all), peeled and cut into ¾ inch dice

2 tablespoons olive or peanut oil

1 medium onion (5 oz), peeled and chopped

1½ teaspoons peeled and finely grated fresh ginger

2 cloves garlic, peeled and finely chopped

1 medium tomato (5 oz), finely chopped

1 teaspoon ground cumin

¼ teaspoon ground turmeric

¼–1 teaspoon nice red chili powder

1 teaspoon salt

A simple and very nutritious dish from Nepal, where it is made with the bamboo shoots that grow in the southern Himalayan forests. (I use canned thinly sliced bamboo shoots instead.) While it is sometimes described as a soup, it is really a main dish, eaten with rice. You can also serve it with crusty bread and a salad.

SERVES 4

ๆๆๆๆๆๆๆๆๆๆๆๆๆๆๆๆๆๆๆๆๆๆๆๆๆๆๆๆๆๆๆๆๆๆ

From the Thakali Kitchen

1. Drain the peas and place in a pan with the bamboo shoots, potatoes, and 4 cups water. Bring to a boil. Skim off the froth, lower the heat, and simmer very gently for 40 minutes.

2. Meanwhile, heat the oil in a medium frying pan set over medium-high heat. When hot, add the onions and fry for about 5 minutes or until they just start to brown. Add the ginger and garlic and stir for a minute. Add the tomatoes and lower the heat to medium. Stir in the cumin, turmeric, and chili powder and cook on medium heat until the sauce is thick.

3. When the peas are done, mix in the salt. Add the tomato mixture and mix well. Continue to cook the beans for another 20 minutes or until all the seasonings and beans have unified.

CHANA DAL WITH SPINACH AND TOMATO

SAAG-TAMATAR WALI CHANA DAL

ᘓᘔᘓᘔᘓᘔᘓᘔᘓᘔᘓᘔᘓᘔᘓᘔᘓᘔᘓᘔᘓᘔᘓᘔᘓᘔᘓᘔᘓᘔᘓᘔᘓᘔᘓᘔ

1½ cups chana dal, washed in several changes of water and drained

½ teaspoon ground turmeric

1½ teaspoons salt

3 tablespoons ghee (clarified butter) or olive or peanut oil, or a mixture of ghee and any oil

⅛ teaspoon ground asafetida

½ teaspoon whole brown mustard seeds

½ teaspoon whole cumin seeds

1–2 dried hot red chilies

7–8 fresh curry leaves

1 large onion (about 8 oz), peeled and chopped

2 cloves garlic, peeled and finely chopped

1½ teaspoons peeled and finely grated fresh ginger

2 good-sized tomatoes (about 10 oz in all), peeled and chopped

5–6 oz well-washed spinach, chopped (see introduction)

¼–½ teaspoon nice red chili powder (optional)

Freshly ground black pepper

This dish, from no specific region of India, but with a lovely mixture of northern and southern seasonings, could also be made with moong dal or toovar dal. I often make it for dinner for my husband and me, accompanying it with rice, a dish of green beans or cauliflower, and plain yogurt. I also love to make it for large groups. Just recently, I was going to have a dozen people come back with us after one of my husband's concerts. I had prepared everything beforehand for a grand meal. The spread included this dal (I doubled the recipe), the Berry Pilaf (see page 185), and the Eggplants in a Peanut and Sesame Sauce (see page 58). A yogurt relish, Quick Yogurt and Pickle Chutney (see page 316), was already in the refrigerator. All I had to do was heat up the food.

I like to use fresh spinach for this dish. You do not need very much. Cut the stems crosswise into tiny dice and chop the leaves into small pieces.   SERVES 6

ᘓᘔᘓᘔᘓᘔᘓᘔᘓᘔᘓᘔᘓᘔᘓᘔᘓᘔᘓᘔᘓᘔᘓᘔᘓᘔᘓᘔᘓᘔᘓᘔᘓᘔᘓᘔ

1. Put the dal in a medium pan along with 5 cups water. Bring to a boil, skimming off the froth as it rises to the top. Do not let it boil over. Stir in the turmeric, cover partially, lower the heat, and cook for 1¼ hours. When done, mix in the salt.

2. While the dal cooks, heat the ghee and/or oil in a small, preferably nonstick frying pan and set over medium-high heat. When hot, add the asafetida and, a second later, the mustard seeds. As soon as the seeds start to pop, a matter of seconds, add the cumin seeds. Stir for 5–6 seconds, then add the red chilies and fry until they darken. Throw in the curry leaves, stir once, then add the onions. Sauté for about 7–10 minutes or until the onions start to brown.

3. Add the garlic and ginger and stir for another 1–2 minutes. Now add the tomatoes and stir for 5–6 minutes, until they

soften, mashing them down with the back of a wooden spoon as you do so. Add the spinach and ½ cup water. Stir and bring to a simmer. Cover and cook gently for 10–12 minutes or until the spinach wilts and is very soft.

4. When the dal has finished cooking, add the spinach mixture and stir well. Check the seasoning and add the chili powder if you need it. Grind black pepper over the top. If the dal feels too thick, you can stir in a little water.

CHANA DAL WITH YELLOW SQUASH, CHAYOTE, OR DOODHI

DOODHI AUR CHANA DAL

ᘖᘖᘖᘖᘖᘖᘖᘖᘖᘖᘖᘖᘖᘖᘖᘖᘖᘖᘖᘖᘖᘖᘖᘖᘖᘖᘖᘖᘖᘖᘖᘖ

1½ cups chana dal, washed in several changes of water and drained

1 lb piece of doodhi (ghiya) or 1 chayote or 1 medium yellow squash

½ teaspoon ground turmeric

1 teaspoon salt, or to taste

2 or more teaspoons jaggery (see note on page 366) or brown sugar, according to taste

3 tablespoons ghee (clarified butter) or olive or peanut oil

Generous pinch of ground asafetida

½ teaspoon whole brown mustard seeds

½ teaspoon whole cumin seeds

3 cloves

1 teaspoon peeled and finely grated fresh ginger

¼–¾ teaspoon nice red chili powder

This is a Gujarati dish usually made with the very long, pale green Indian squash known as "doodhi" or "ghiya." Many Indian grocers sell it, but I find that chayote or sayote, the South American pear-shaped vegetable (also known as "cho cho," "chow chow," and "christophene"), or yellow squash make good substitutes. Gujaratis like their dal slightly sweet, which is how I have cooked it here. This may be a no-no in the north, but it is quite delicious! I love the Gujarati combination of sweet and hot. Gujaratis also like to use ghee to finish off their dals. All Indian stores sell it.

Serve this with Chapatis (see page 219), whole-grain pita bread, or plain rice, and a vegetable and yogurt dish. SERVES 6

ᘖᘖᘖᘖᘖᘖᘖᘖᘖᘖᘖᘖᘖᘖᘖᘖᘖᘖᘖᘖᘖᘖᘖᘖᘖᘖᘖᘖᘖᘖᘖᘖ

1. Put the dal in a medium pan along with 5 cups water. Bring to a boil, skimming off the froth as it rises to the top. Do not let it boil over.

2. Meanwhile, prepare your chosen vegetable. If using doodhi or chayote, peel and quarter it lengthwise, remove the seeds, and cut the flesh into 1 x ½ inch pieces. If using squash, cut it in half lengthwise, then cut crosswise into ½ inch pieces.

3. Stir the turmeric into the boiling dal, then partially cover and cook for 1 hour. Add the salt, jaggery or brown sugar, and your chosen vegetable. Stir and bring to a gentle simmer, then cover fully. Cook the doodhi and chayote for another 20 minutes, but the squash for just another 15 minutes. Uncover the pan while you complete the final step.

4. Heat the ghee or oil in a small, preferably nonstick frying pan and set over medium-high heat. When hot, add the asafetida and, a second later, the mustard seeds. As soon as the

seeds start to pop, a matter of seconds, add the cumin seeds and cloves. Three seconds later add the grated ginger, stir for 10–15 seconds, then mix in the chili powder. Tip the mixture immediately over the dal and cover quickly to trap the aromas. Stir and remove the cloves before serving.

Powdered colors for decorating

CHICKPEAS IN A SIMPLE NORTHERN STYLE

ROZ KAY CHANEY

જા

Two 15-oz cans chickpeas, preferably organic

3 tablespoons olive or peanut oil

1 medium onion (about 5½ oz), peeled and finely chopped

1 tablespoon peeled and very finely grated fresh ginger

3 cloves garlic, peeled and crushed

1–3 fresh hot green chilies, finely chopped

2 teaspoons ground coriander

1 teaspoon ground cumin

¼ teaspoon ground turmeric

3 tablespoons tomato puree

1 teaspoon salt, or to taste

For this recipe I used two cans of organic low-salt chickpeas only because that is what I was able to find. I prefer to use organic chickpeas because I can use all the liquid in the can. If your chickpeas are not organic, throw away the liquid in the can and use fresh water instead. The salt is a matter of preference. I add salt later in the recipe anyway, so if you start out with a can of ready-salted chickpeas, just taste and add less salt.

I love to eat this dish with Indian flatbreads. It is particularly good with Bhaturas (see page 237), but any other Indian bread would do. The chickpeas also combine well with tortillas. Just roll them inside with some raw onion slivers, chopped radishes, and cucumbers, or the Tomato, Onion, and Cucumber Koshambari or Green Chutney (see pages 341 and 304), and eat!   SERVES 4–6

જા

1. Drain the chickpeas, saving the liquid (only if organic). Set both aside.

2. Pour the oil into a medium nonstick frying pan and set over medium heat. When hot, add the onions and fry for 7–8 minutes, until soft and golden. Add the ginger, garlic, and green chilies. Continue to stir and fry for another 2–3 minutes, until the onions have picked up a little color. Add the coriander, cumin, and turmeric. Stir a few times, then add the tomato puree and stir again.

3. Add the drained chickpeas, the salt, and 2¼ cups of the (organic) chickpea liquid or water or a combination of the two. Bring to a simmer, then cover and simmer very gently for 30 minutes. Check the salt, adding a bit more if needed.

CHICKPEAS IN A FRESH CILANTRO SAUCE

HARI CHUTNEY WALAY CHANAY

꧁꧂꧁꧂꧁꧂꧁꧂꧁꧂꧁꧂꧁꧂꧁꧂꧁꧂꧁꧂꧁꧂꧁꧂꧁꧂꧁꧂

1 tablespoon lime or lemon
   juice

½ medium tomato, chopped

1½ well-packed cups fresh
   cilantro leaves and tender
   stems

1–2 fresh hot green chilies,
   chopped

A 1-inch piece of fresh ginger,
   peeled and very finely
   chopped

Salt

Two 15 oz cans chickpeas,
   preferably organic

3 tablespoons olive or peanut
   oil

Generous pinch of ground
   asafetida

¼ teaspoon whole cumin
   seeds

1 medium onion (about
   5½ oz), peeled and
   chopped

1 teaspoon ground coriander

¼–1 teaspoon chaat masala
   (optional)

Everything said in the introduction to the preceding recipe applies here as well, so please read that before you begin.

If you want this dish to be hot and pungent, sprinkle the chaat masala over the top just before serving and stir it in. SERVES 4–6

꧁꧂꧁꧂꧁꧂꧁꧂꧁꧂꧁꧂꧁꧂꧁꧂꧁꧂꧁꧂꧁꧂꧁꧂꧁꧂꧁꧂

1. Put (in this order) the lime juice, tomatoes, fresh cilantro, green chilies, ginger, and ¼ teaspoon of salt in a blender. Add 4–6 tablespoons water (as needed) and blend until smooth.

2. Drain the chickpeas, saving the liquid (only if organic). Set both aside.

3. Pour the oil into a medium nonstick frying pan and set over medium heat. When hot, add the asafetida and, a few seconds later, the cumin seeds. Let them sizzle for a few seconds, then add the onions. Stir-fry for 7–8 minutes, until the onions are slightly browned at the edges. Add the ground coriander and stir for 30 seconds. Add the drained chickpeas, ½ teaspoon of salt, and 1½ cups (organic) chickpea liquid or water or a combination of the two. Stir and bring to a simmer. Cover and simmer very gently for 20 minutes.

4. Stir in the paste from the blender and bring to a simmer again. Cover and cook gently for another 20 minutes. Check the salt, adding a bit more if needed, and stir in the chaat masala (if using).

HOT YOGURT SAUCE FROM THE KONKAN COAST

TAKKA KARHI

ೞೞೞೞೞೞೞೞೞೞೞೞೞೞೞೞೞೞೞೞೞೞೞೞೞೞೞೞೞೞ

2 cups plain yogurt (do not use Greek yogurt here)

2 teaspoons chickpea flour (besan or gram flour)

⅓–½ teaspoon salt, or to taste

1 teaspoon olive or peanut oil

Generous pinch of ground asafetida

¼ teaspoon whole cumin seeds

1 dried red chili or 1 fresh hot green chili, split in half lengthwise

2 cloves garlic, peeled and crushed

A "karhi" is just heated and flavored yogurt. Since yogurt curdles when it is boiled, it has to be stabilized with a starch. That starch in India is usually chickpea flour (though it could be rice flour), which adds its own nutrients to the dish. All Indians eat karhis, but they vary considerably from region to region. Delhi's karhis are very thick, colored yellow with turmeric, and filled with bobbing dumplings. Gujarati karhis can be sweet and flavored with cloves. This takka karhi, from the Saraswat Brahmins of the western Indian Konkan Coast, is thin, unsweetened, and almost white. It is generally eaten with rice, but it can also be served in individual bowls and either just drunk with the meal or eaten with flatbreads, along with other vegetables and dals.

It is best to make this dish with sour yogurt. Simply leave it out of the refrigerator in a warm spot for 24 hours or longer, until it has soured a bit, or use an acidophilus yogurt, which is already sour.

This recipe may easily be doubled.   SERVES 2–3

ೞೞೞೞೞೞೞೞೞೞೞೞೞೞೞೞೞೞೞೞೞೞೞೞೞೞೞೞೞೞ

1. Put the yogurt in a bowl and whisk until smooth. Slowly add 2 cups water, whisking as you go.

2. In a separate bowl, mix the chickpea flour with a tablespoon or so of water to make a smooth paste. Add to the yogurt along with the salt and whisk again.

3. Put the oil in a small pan and set over medium heat. When hot, add the asafetida and the cumin seeds. Let the seeds sizzle for a few seconds, then add the chilies. Stir once, add the garlic, and stir a few more times.

4. Pour in the yogurt sauce, stirring constantly while it comes to a gentle simmer. Allow to simmer on a low heat for 2–3 minutes, stirring all the time.

HOT YOGURT SAUCE FROM SOUTHERN INDIA

MOR KOZHAMBU

〜〜〜〜〜〜〜〜〜〜〜〜〜〜〜〜〜〜〜〜〜〜〜〜〜〜〜〜〜

2 cups plain yogurt (do not use Greek yogurt here)

2 teaspoons rice flour (also called rice powder) or chickpea flour (besan or gram flour)

¼ teaspoon ground turmeric

¾ teaspoon sambar powder (get a good South Indian brand, like MTR)

⅓–½ teaspoon salt, or to taste

1 teaspoon olive or peanut oil

Generous pinch of ground asafetida

½ teaspoon whole brown mustard seeds

¼ teaspoon whole fenugreek seeds

1 tablespoon chopped fresh cilantro

1 fresh hot green chili, finely chopped (optional)

In India, rice is always served with something wet and flowing because it is considered too dry on its own. The exception is a rich biryani, but even that is offered with a raita and salads. The wetness deemed necessary could come from a curry with a sauce, a dal, or maybe just some melted ghee. Of course, it could also come from this thin yogurt sauce, known in the south as "mor kozhambu." The thickening, slight as it is, is provided by either chickpea flour or rice flour. Quite often in the south it is eaten last, with rice and pickles. (This always reminds me of how the Japanese like to end their meals—with rice, pickles, and tea!)

There are hundreds of variations to this recipe. I find this one delicious and easy to make. I like to serve it with Stir-fried Eggplant Cooked in a Tamil Nadu Style (see page 55), Plain Rice (see pages 172 and 173), and a dal. It is best to pour it into small individual bowls.

As with the preceding recipe, the yogurt here needs to be fairly sour. You can leave it in a warm spot for 24 hours or longer until it has soured a bit, or use an acidophilus yogurt, which is already sour.

This recipe may easily be doubled.   SERVES 2–3

〜〜〜〜〜〜〜〜〜〜〜〜〜〜〜〜〜〜〜〜〜〜〜〜〜〜〜〜〜

1. Put the yogurt in a bowl and whisk until smooth. Slowly add 2 cups water, whisking as you go.

2. In a separate bowl, mix the rice or chickpea flour with a tablespoon or so of water to make a smooth paste. Add to the yogurt, along with the turmeric, sambar powder, and salt, and whisk again.

3. Put the oil in a small pan and set over medium heat. When hot, add the asafetida and then the mustard seeds. When the

seeds pop, a matter of seconds, add the fenugreek seeds. Stir once, then pour in the yogurt sauce. Keep stirring and bring the mixture to a gentle simmer. Let the sauce simmer on a low heat for 2–3 minutes, stirring all the time.

4. Add the fresh cilantro and green chilies (if using) and stir once.

OKRA IN A YOGURT AND CHICKPEA FLOUR SAUCE

VENDEKAYA MAJJIGA PULUSU

꒜꒜꒜꒜꒜꒜꒜꒜꒜꒜꒜꒜꒜꒜꒜꒜꒜꒜꒜꒜꒜꒜꒜꒜꒜꒜

¾ lb fresh okra

3 tablespoons olive or peanut
oil

Salt

2 tablespoons chickpea flour
(besan or gram flour)

1½ cups plain yogurt

¼ teaspoon urad dal

¼ teaspoon chana dal

¼ teaspoon whole brown
mustard seeds

2 dried hot red chilies

2 tablespoons peeled and
chopped onion

1 fresh hot green chili,
partially split in half
lengthwise

¼ teaspoon ground turmeric

You will find this Andhra dish only in South Indian homes and local restaurants. I have yet to come across it in any Indian eatery in the West. It is a simple dish, very much like the karhis of northern India. It is soupy, the yogurt in it held together with a little binding of chickpea flour. This one has sautéed okra floating around in it. It is normally eaten with rice and generally served in individual bowls. It may also be poured directly over the rice. Other vegetables can be served on the side.

If you do not have chana dal, double the urad dal.   SERVES 4

꒜꒜꒜꒜꒜꒜꒜꒜꒜꒜꒜꒜꒜꒜꒜꒜꒜꒜꒜꒜꒜꒜꒜꒜꒜꒜

From the Taj Gateway Hotel in Vishakapatnam, Andhra Pradesh

1. Wipe the okra pods with a damp cloth, then allow to air-dry. Trim off the tops and tails, then cut the pods crosswise into 1 inch pieces.

2. Put 2 tablespoons of the oil in a medium frying pan and set over medium-high heat. When hot, add the okra and fry for 5–6 minutes, until just starting to brown. Reduce the heat to medium and fry for another 3–4 minutes, until the okra is almost cooked. Using a slotted spoon, transfer it to a plate lined with a paper towel. Sprinkle a generous pinch of salt over the top and toss.

3. Put the chickpea flour in a bowl. Slowly add 2 tablespoons of water, mixing with a wooden spoon as you go. Once you have a smooth paste, whisk it into the yogurt along with another ½ cup water.

4. Put the remaining 1 tablespoon of oil in a medium pan and set over medium heat. When hot, add the urad and chana dal.

As soon as they start to pick up some color, add the mustard seeds and red chilies. As soon as the seeds start to pop, a matter of seconds, add the onions, green chilies, and turmeric and sauté for a minute. Stir the yogurt mixture and pour it into the pan. Stir and bring to a simmer, and keep stirring until the mixture thickens. Add ½ teaspoon of salt and the okra and stir until you are back at a simmer. Lower the heat and simmer gently for 2–3 minutes.

5. As this dish sits, it can thicken up, so add a little water to thin it as you wish.

GREEN LENTIL CURRY WITH KALE

HARAY LENTILS AUR KALE

ↄฬ

1⅓ cups green lentils

¼ teaspoon ground turmeric

½ teaspoon cayenne pepper

4 oz green beans cut into
    ¾ inch segments

3 oz kale, thick stems and
    veins discarded, finely
    chopped

3 tablespoons finely chopped
    fresh cilantro

1 medium carrot, peeled and
    cut into ¼ inch rounds

1¼ teaspoons salt

FOR THE CURRY PASTE

1 teaspoon peeled and finely
    grated ginger

1 clove garlic, peeled and
    crushed

1 teaspoon ground cumin
    seeds

2 teaspoons ground coriander
    seeds

3 tablespoons olive or
    rapeseed oil

¼ teaspoon whole cumin
    seeds

1 tablespoon peeled and finely
    chopped shallots

2 tablespoons tomato puree

This is almost a meal in itself, nutritionally complete if you add some whole-grain pita bread (or rice) and yogurt on the side. You could also convert it into a soup by adding a mugful of water or stock toward the end of the cooking time.   SERVES 4–6

ↄฬ

1. Put the lentils, turmeric, and 2 pints water into a medium pan and bring to a boil. Cover partially and simmer gently for 20 minutes. Add the cayenne, beans, kale, cilantro, carrots, and salt. Stir and bring to a boil again. Cover partially and cook gently for another 20 minutes.

2. Meanwhile, make the curry paste: combine the ginger, garlic, ground cumin, and coriander in a small bowl, then mix in 2 fl oz water.

3. Pour the oil into a medium frying pan and set over medium-high heat. When hot, add the whole cumin seeds. Let them sizzle for 5 seconds, then add the shallots. Stir and fry until lightly browned. Add the curry paste and fry until you can see the oil along the edges, about 1½ minutes. Add the tomato puree and fry for about another minute, until you see the oil along the edges.

4. When the lentils have finished cooking, add the contents of the frying pan. Stir and cook gently for another 5 minutes.

A NOTE ON INDIAN-STYLE MUNG BEAN SPROUTS

PHUTI MOONG

Mung beans, or whole moong, as Indians call them, are native to India. The country has been eating them in hundreds of ways, including sprouting them, as far back as can be remembered. The sprouts are not like Chinese bean sprouts; they are smaller, less watery, and much more delicate, yet with ample body. Chinese sprouts take three or four days to develop their long "tails," while Indian sprouts develop their short, thin tails within twenty-four hours.

Mung sprouts are very popular in India, especially among vegetarians, as breakfast foods and snack foods, because they have all the nutrients of dried beans but are easier to digest. They may be strewn raw onto salads (see page 342), cooked in breakfast dishes (see page 204), or cooked as main dishes (see page 146).

Ideally, you should get your mung beans from a reliable Indian or Chinese source, where the beans are sold rapidly and replaced constantly with fresh supplies.

HOW TO MAKE INDIAN-STYLE MUNG BEAN SPROUTS

ৎ৴ৎ৴ৎ৴ৎ৴ৎ৴ৎ৴ৎ৴ৎ৴ৎ৴ৎ৴ৎ৴ৎ৴ৎ৴ৎ৴ৎ৴ৎ৴ৎ৴ৎ৴ৎ

1 cup mung beans will yield about 1 lb bean sprouts, roughly 3 to 5 cups, depending on their freshness

1. Pick over and wash 1 cup whole mung beans. (Throw away any broken ones.) Put them in a large bowl, cover with 3½–4 inches tepid water, and leave to soak for 12 hours. Drain the beans in a colander and let some fresh, tepid water flow over them. Leave them to drain.

2. Wash out your soaking bowl and line it with a triple layer of thick paper towels in such a way that there will be some left to fold over the beans. (You can use dish cloths or towels if you wish, but they will discolor.) Dampen the paper towels or cloths and put all the beans in the bowl. Cover with the overhanging paper, or use extra dampened paper towel if you need to.

3. Put the bowl in a dark, warm place (I use my unheated oven) for 12 hours. The beans should sprout. Rinse them in cool water, then cover and store in the refrigerator, making sure to rinse them in cool water every day. They should keep for 3–4 days.

MUNG BEAN SPROUTS WITH SWISS CHARD

PHUTI MOONG AUR SWISS CHARD

ભ્ર૦ભ્ર૦ભ્ર૦ભ્ર૦ભ્ર૦ભ્ર૦ભ્ર૦ભ્ર૦ભ્ર૦ભ્ર૦ભ્ર૦ભ્ર૦ભ્ર૦ભ્ર૦ભ્ર૦

We do not really have Swiss chard in India, but this recipe serves to illustrate that Indian sprouts can be combined with most vegetables. Serve with a yogurt relish and a flatbread. SERVES 4

ભ્ર૦ભ્ર૦ભ્ર૦ભ્ર૦ભ્ર૦ભ્ર૦ભ્ર૦ભ્ર૦ભ્ર૦ભ્ર૦ભ્ર૦ભ્ર૦ભ્ર૦ભ્ર૦ભ્ર૦

2 large stalks of Swiss chard (about 6 oz in all)

1 tablespoon olive or peanut oil

Generous pinch of ground asafetida

1 teaspoon whole brown mustard seeds

3 cloves garlic, peeled and finely chopped

1–2 fresh hot green chilies, finely chopped

½ teaspoon ground turmeric

3 cups Indian-style mung bean sprouts (see page 142)

3 tablespoons chopped fresh cilantro

¾–1 teaspoon salt

2 tablespoons lime juice

1 teaspoon sugar

1. Cut the chard stems into ¼ inch dice and the leaves into ½ inch dice.

2. Put the oil in a medium frying pan and set over medium-high heat. When hot, add the asafetida and, a second later, the mustard seeds. As soon as the seeds start to pop, a matter of seconds, take the pan off the heat and stir in the garlic and green chilies. Put the pan back on medium heat, add the chopped chard stems, and stir for 2 minutes. Mix in the turmeric, then add the bean sprouts, fresh cilantro, chard leaves, 6 tablespoons of water, and the salt. Stir and bring to a simmer on medium-high heat. Cover and cook very gently for 20 minutes.

3. Finally, stir in the lime juice and sugar, then taste to check for balance of seasonings.

MUNG BEAN SPROUT, POTATO, AND MUSHROOM CURRY

PHUTI MOONG, ALOO AUR KHUMBI KI SABZI

ʊʊʊʊʊʊʊʊʊʊʊʊʊʊʊʊʊʊʊʊʊʊʊʊʊʊʊʊʊʊʊʊ

Full of nutrients and flavor, this dish can be served with any type of Indian bread and a yogurt relish. For a more Western-style meal, serve it with a simple green salad. SERVES 4–5

ʊʊʊʊʊʊʊʊʊʊʊʊʊʊʊʊʊʊʊʊʊʊʊʊʊʊʊʊʊʊʊʊ

3 tablespoons olive or peanut
    oil

½ teaspoon whole cumin
    seeds

1 medium onion, peeled and
    chopped

1 teaspoon peeled and finely
    grated fresh ginger

3 cloves garlic, peeled and
    crushed

2 tablespoons tomato purée

¼ teaspoon ground turmeric

3 cups Indian-style mung bean
    sprouts (see page 142)

2 medium potatoes (about
    8 oz in all), peeled and
    chopped into ½ inch dice

2 large mushrooms (I
    like cremini here), cut
    lengthwise into ¼ inch
    slices

1 teaspoon salt

¼–¾ teaspoon nice red chili
    powder

1½–2 tablespoons lime or
    lemon juice

1. Put the oil into a large frying pan and set over medium-high heat. When hot, add the cumin seeds and let them sizzle for 5 seconds. Add the onions and fry for 6–7 minutes or until just starting to brown at the edges. Add the ginger and garlic and stir for a minute. Now add the tomato purée and turmeric and stir for another minute.

2. Pour 2 cups water into the pan and mix well. Add the bean sprouts, potatoes, mushrooms, salt, and chili powder, stir, and bring to a boil. Cover and cook very gently for 25 minutes. Stir in the lime or lemon juice.

INDIAN-STYLE BEAN SPROUTS WITH ONIONS, GINGER, AND GARLIC

MATKI

⋍⋍⋍⋍⋍⋍⋍⋍⋍⋍⋍⋍⋍⋍⋍⋍⋍⋍⋍⋍⋍⋍⋍⋍⋍⋍⋍⋍⋍⋍⋍⋍⋍⋍

2 tablespoons olive or peanut oil

1 medium onion (about 6 oz), peeled and chopped

4 cloves garlic, peeled and very finely chopped

A 1½-inch piece of fresh ginger, peeled and very finely chopped

½–1 fresh hot green chili, finely chopped

1½ teaspoons ground coriander

¼ teaspoon ground turmeric

⅛–¼ teaspoon nice red chili powder

3 cups Indian-style mung bean sprouts (see page 142)

1 teaspoon salt

3–4 cherry tomatoes, cut into ½ inch dice

1 tablespoon chopped fresh cilantro

Anita is a successful businesswoman who owns ten branches of a very popular store named Good Earth. It specializes in hand-crafted goods. On the day we met, she, with her daughter Simran and her grandson, were entertaining on the landscaped terrace of their stylish Bombay flat. They are from the Punjab, but their food has taken on a few hints of Bombay as well. Nothing is too hot or too spicy or too oily, which is typical of North Indian home cooking.

The menu for lunch consisted of this bean sprout dish, which is eaten all over India, some fried fish, toovar dal, stir-fried cabbage with mustard seeds, green beans, a yogurt and spinach raita, a turnip dish, and some custard apple ice cream. It was a perfect meal for a lovely sunny winter afternoon.

In Bombay, a common method for cooking vegetables is to put very little water in the pan. Instead, the vegetable is covered with a flat lid that has an indentation in it. Water is put in that indentation, and condensation from it keeps the vegetable moist. That was the method used to cook these bean sprouts.

I find that most of my flat lids have indentations, so I use those. If you cannot find anything but a domed lid, put 5–6 tablespoons of water in the pan, cover tightly, and cook on very low heat for 20 minutes. Take a peek inside once or twice and sprinkle in some more water if needed.

SERVES 3

⋍⋍⋍⋍⋍⋍⋍⋍⋍⋍⋍⋍⋍⋍⋍⋍⋍⋍⋍⋍⋍⋍⋍⋍⋍⋍⋍⋍⋍⋍⋍⋍⋍⋍

From the home of Anita Lal

1. Put the oil into a medium pan and set over medium-high heat. When hot, add the onions and fry for 6–7 minutes or until they brown a bit. Now add the garlic, ginger, and green chilies. Stir for 2–3 minutes. Take the pan off the heat and add the

ground coriander, turmeric, and chili powder. Put the pan back on the heat and stir for a minute. Add the bean sprouts, 4 tablespoons water, and the salt. Stir a few times, going all the way to the bottom, then cover and reduce the heat to very low. If you have a flat lid with an indentation in it, pour water into the indentation, replacing the water as needed. If you do not have such a lid, keep an eye on the sprouts, sprinkling in a little water when the bottom seems to have dried out. Cook, covered, for about 20 minutes or until the bean sprouts are tender.

2. Transfer to a serving dish when ready to eat, and garnish with the tomatoes and fresh cilantro.

SIMPLE MOONG AND MASOOR DAL COOKED IN THE STYLE OF UTTAR PRADESH MUSLIMS

SAADI MUSSALMANI MOONG AUR MASOOR DAL

1 cup mung beans

¼ cup masoor dal (red lentils)

½ teaspoon ground turmeric

1–2 fresh hot green chilies, finely chopped

1 clove garlic, peeled and lightly crushed

1–1½ teaspoons salt, or to taste

2 tablespoons olive or peanut oil

½ teaspoon whole cumin seeds

1 dried hot red chili

½ medium shallot, peeled and cut into very fine slivers

Muslims in India rarely use asafetida in their cooking. They use garlic instead. Here is a simple, everyday dal that I cook frequently. All that is needed with it is rice or a flatbread, some yogurt raita, and a vegetable dish made with okra, cauliflower, or eggplant.

1. Combine the mung beans and masoor dal in a bowl and wash in several changes of water. Drain, then place in a heavy-based pan with 4½ cups water. Bring to a boil, skimming off the froth that rises to the top. Stir in the turmeric, green chilies, and garlic. Cover partially and simmer very gently for 45 minutes or until the dal is tender. Mash down with a potato masher, then mix in the salt.

2. Put the oil in a small frying pan set over medium-high heat. When hot, add the cumin seeds and let them sizzle for 3 seconds. Add the red chili and stir until it darkens. Add the shallots and fry until they turn a reddish brown.

3. Tip the contents of the pan over the dal. Cover to entrap the aromas, and stir before serving.

WHOLE MOONG AND MASOOR COOKED WITH MEAT SEASONINGS

SABUT MOONG AUR MASOOR

ᴄᴜ

¾ cup mung beans

¾ cup whole red lentils (sabut masoor)

1 teaspoon salt, or more to taste

5 tablespoons olive or peanut oil

A 2-inch cinnamon stick

2 bay leaves

5 cardamom pods (you can put these in a small muslin bag for easy removal)

1 medium onion (about 7 oz), peeled and finely chopped

A 3-inch piece of fresh ginger, peeled and finely grated

5 cloves garlic, peeled and crushed

3 tablespoons tomato purée

1 tablespoon ground coriander

2 teaspoons ground cumin

1 teaspoon ground turmeric

½–1 teaspoon nice red chili powder, according to taste

1 teaspoon garam masala

Dollop of ghee (clarified butter) or ordinary butter (optional)

Here is a combination of two old and beloved legumes—whole mung beans, which originated in India, and whole red lentils, which came to India from the Arab world in ancient times—cooked together with seasonings used in North India today for meat dishes. Strangely enough, I came across this dish on an Indian airline. Who would have thought!

For a festive dinner, serve the dal with a vegetable or two of your choice and rice or a flatbread, and any salad or chutney you desire. A yogurt relish is definitely required. For a family meal, just one other vegetable, rice or bread, and plain yogurt would be fine.

Remember that a dal may be as thick or thin as you like. Generally, dals should be thicker when eaten with breads and thinner when eaten with rice. Indian cooks tend to thin the latter a bit more by adding extra water at the end. SERVES 6–8

ᴄᴜ

1. Combine the mung beans and red lentils in a sieve, then pick over and wash them. Place them in a heavy-based pan, add 7 cups water, and bring to a boil. Boil for 2 minutes, then cover and set aside, off the heat, for 1 hour. Bring to a boil again, lower the heat, cover, and simmer gently (there should always be a few bubbles rising) for 1½ hours. The beans will be very, very tender. Mix in the salt and set aside.

2. Put the oil in a medium, preferably nonstick frying pan and set over medium-high heat. When hot, add the cinnamon stick, bay leaves, and cardamom pods. Stir once or twice, then quickly add the onions and fry for 7–8 minutes or until they begin to brown at the edges. Add the ginger and garlic and stir for another 2 minutes. Stir in the tomato purée a tablespoon

at a time, then add the coriander, cumin, turmeric, and chili powder. Stir for 2 minutes. Now add 1 cup water, stir well, and simmer gently for 5 minutes. Pick out all the whole spices—the cinnamon, bay leaves, and cardamom—and discard them. Mix in the garam masala.

3. When the beans have finished cooking, stir the spice paste into the dal. Taste and add more salt if you wish. The dal should be as thick as you like, so add more hot water if you want it thinner. Just before eating, ladle it into a serving dish and drop in a knob of ghee or butter (if using).

MIXED DAL, DELHI-STYLE

DILLI KI MILI JHULI DAL

½ cup mung beans

¼ cup masoor dal (red lentils)

¼ cup plain toovar dal

½ teaspoon ground turmeric

1 teaspoon salt

1 tablespoon olive or peanut oil

Generous pinch of asafetida

½ teaspoon whole cumin seeds

1–2 dried hot red chilies

PICTURED ON PAGES 152–153

As dals are eaten every day by most Indians, not just vegetarians, they are varied and sometimes mixed in different combinations. This is a simple northern combination, found in Delhi, Uttar Pradesh, Madhya Pradesh, and Bihar. The north has its own variety of toovar dal called arhar dal. Either will suffice for this recipe.

SERVES 4

1. Put the three dals in a bowl and wash in several changes of water. Drain thoroughly, then place in a heavy-based pan. Add 4 cups water and bring to a boil. Skim off the froth, reduce the heat to low, and stir in the turmeric. Cover partially and cook for 45–60 minutes or until the dals are very soft. Mash coarsely with a potato masher. Mix in the salt.

2. Put the oil in a small frying pan set over medium-high heat. When hot, add the asafetida and, a few seconds later, the cumin seeds. Let the seeds sizzle for a few seconds, then add the chilies and fry until darkened on all sides.

3. Quickly tip the contents of the frying pan over the cooked dal and cover to entrap the aromas. Stir before serving.

MIXED DAL, MARWARI-STYLE

MARWARI MILI JHULI DAL

ഗ്ര

¼ cup chana dal

¼ cup plain toovar dal

¼ cup split urad with skin
(sold as chilkewali urad
dal)

¼ cup split mung beans with
skin (sold as chilkewali
moong dal)

2 bay leaves

2 cloves

4 cardamom pods

¼ teaspoon ground turmeric

¾ teaspoon salt, or to taste

2 tablespoons ghee (clarified
butter) or olive or peanut
oil

Generous pinch of ground
asafetida

¼ teaspoon whole cumin
seeds

1 dried hot red chili, broken
in half

¼ teaspoon nice red chili
powder

1 teaspoon ground coriander

1 teaspoon peeled and grated
fresh ginger

1–2 fresh hot green chilies,
finely sliced crosswise

2 tablespoons chopped fresh
cilantro

For information about the Marwari community, see the introduction on page 108. I will add here that Marwaris love their ghee. To do a final tarka (see page xxii) for the dal without using ghee is to invite a look of astonishment in the eyes of a Marwari, and pity too.

This dal dish combines four dals, two with skin and two without, so it is nutritious and full of natural fiber. Generally, it is cooked to a thickish consistency, all the better to eat it with flatbreads, such as Chapatis or Puffed Fried Breads (see pages 219 and 235). You can also eat it with rice, in which case it should be thinned with about 4 oz boiling water. A yogurt relish and a vegetable dish added to the meal would make it just perfect. This is among my favorite dal dishes.   SERVES 4

ഗ്ര

From Vinita Pittie

1. Combine all the dals in a bowl and wash them thoroughly in several changes of water. Drain, then leave to soak in a generous covering of water for 2 hours.

2. Drain the dals and place in a heavy-based pan with 4 cups water. Bring to a boil, skimming off the froth that rises to the surface. Add the bay leaves, cloves, cardamom pods, and turmeric, tied in a small muslin bag if you like. Stir and cover partially, then cook very gently for 1¼ hours or until the dal is tender. (Remove the muslin bag now, if using.) Add the salt, then mash the dal with a potato masher.

3. Put the ghee in a small frying pan and set it over medium-high heat. When hot, add the asafetida and, a few seconds later, the cumin seeds and red chili. After 2 seconds, add the chili powder and ground coriander. Stir once and quickly add the ginger and green chilies. Stir once, then quickly tip the contents of the frying pan over the dal. Cover immediately to entrap the aromas.

4. Stir before serving and sprinkle the fresh cilantro over the top.

WHOLE RED LENTILS WITH CUMIN AND SHALLOTS

SABUT MASOOR

༺ໆໆໆໆໆໆໆໆໆໆໆໆໆໆໆໆໆໆໆໆໆໆ༻

1 cup whole red lentils (sabut masoor)

¼ teaspoon ground turmeric

1 teaspoon salt

1½ tablespoons olive or peanut oil

Generous pinch of ground asafetida

¼ teaspoon whole cumin seeds

2–3 dried hot red chilies

1 good-sized shallot, peeled and cut into fine slivers

Butter (optional)

Lime or lemon wedges (optional)

A lovely, nutritious dish, full of fiber and protein. I love it with Tomato Rice (see page 180), a yogurt relish, and a leafy vegetable. You could also serve it with Indian flatbread, pickles, relishes, and a potato dish.

Indian grocers sell this dal as whole masoor or sabut masoor. The red lentil is whole, not split, and still has its brownish skin.

SERVES 4

༺ໆໆໆໆໆໆໆໆໆໆໆໆໆໆໆໆໆໆໆໆໆໆ༻

1. Wash and drain the lentils. Place them in a medium saucepan, add 4½ cups water, and bring to a boil. Skim off the froth from the surface and add the turmeric. Stir, cover partially, and simmer gently for 1 hour. Mix in the salt.

2. Put the oil in a small frying pan and set over medium heat. When hot, add the asafetida. After a few seconds, add the cumin seeds and let them sizzle for a few seconds. Add the red chilies and fry until they darken, then quickly stir in the shallots. Fry until the slivers turn a rich reddish color and become crisp.

3. Tip the contents of the frying pan over the lentils and cover immediately to entrap the aromas. Stir before serving, adding about 2 pats of butter if you wish. Serve with the lime wedges on the side (if using).

SIMPLE TOOVAR DAL

SAADI TOOVAR DAL

ᕙᕗᕙᕗᕙᕗᕙᕗᕙᕗᕙᕗᕙᕗᕙᕗᕙᕗᕙᕗᕙᕗᕙᕗᕙᕗᕙᕗᕙᕗᕙᕗ

1 cup oily or plain toovar dal, picked over

¾–1 teaspoon salt

½ teaspoon ground turmeric

½–2 fresh hot green chilies, cut crosswise into thin slices

10–12 fresh curry leaves, lightly crushed in your hand

1 tablespoon ghee (clarified butter) or oil

¼ teaspoon whole brown mustard seeds

¼ teaspoon whole cumin seeds

Generous pinch of ground asafetida

¼–½ teaspoon nice red chili powder

Lime wedges, to serve

The Taj Mahal Palace in Bombay, built at the start of the twentieth century, is a jewel, a beautifully carved, rock-like structure that sits guard by the Indian Ocean. Attacked by terrorists a few years ago for being exactly that, a symbol of beauty and power, it has several elegant shops within it. I know some of them intimately, as I have been visiting them since the 1940s, when my father took me and my siblings to the hotel. One of them is the jewelry shop Gazdar, which opened its doors in the 1980s. I stare in its windows every time I am there. I have even bought a few small things.

When collecting material for this book, I wanted to go into the homes of people I meet in life casually and briefly—shopkeepers, farmers, doctors, lawyers, weavers—to see what they actually eat and how they eat it. I approached the owner of Gazdar, Ravi Gandhi, and he very kindly and generously opened up the doors to his seaside flat for me.

Ravi is a Marwari (of the merchant class whose origins lie in Rajasthan) from a Varanasi family, and a vegetarian. He consciously eats healthy meals, and starts his day with raw fruit and vegetables, plus some cooked food that could take the form of light, steamed, savory cakes called "dhoklas."

Lunch is at 12:30 p.m., and he always goes home for it. His father replaces him at the shop. This is the main meal of the day. Dinner is usually a light vegetable soup.

Perhaps because I was there, as was the whole family, there was a large spread that appeared in two courses. It was served on individual thalis (silver platters). The first course has two sweetmeats bought from a Bengali halvai, or candymaker: the milk-based sandesh and the crispy, thready sohan papri. You are meant to start with them.

There was also a simple toovar dal that I just loved and give the recipe for here, potatoes with cumin, some chickpeas, paneer, long beans with green chilies, and a salad with cucumbers, water chestnuts, tomatoes, and zucchini. Other than the sweets, everything was eaten with rice.

For the second course, the rice disappeared and warm, fresh phulkas (flatbreads like delicate, small chapatis) were offered, fresh and hot from the kitchen. There were also steamed sooji cakes and a glorious green chutney with cilantro and mint. The toovar dal was served again, this time with squeezes of lime, and more of the vegetables were offered.

We ended the meal with chaas, a kind of lassi with curry leaves (see page 355).

The dal that was used in this Gandhi family recipe is sold as oily toovar dal—most of western India prefers that version—and the oil needs to be washed off.   SERVES 4

ೞೞೞೞೞೞೞೞೞೞೞೞೞೞೞೞೞೞೞೞೞೞೞೞೞೞೞೞ

From Ravi Gandhi's home

1. Put the dal in a bowl, cover generously with water, and rub with your hands to remove the oil. Drain, then repeat this step 5 or 6 times. When clean, cover generously with water again and leave to soak for 30 minutes.

2. Drain the dal and place in a heavy-based pan. Add 2½ cups water and bring to a boil, skimming off the froth that rises to the surface. Add the salt, turmeric, and green chilies, cover partially, lower the heat, and cook very gently for 30–45 minutes or until soft. Mash the dal coarsely with a potato masher. Taste for salt and adjust as necessary. If the dal is too thick, which it probably will be, add 4–5 tablespoons of water. Stir in the curry leaves.

3. Just before you sit down to eat, heat the dal, stirring as you do so, then empty it into a serving bowl. Put the ghee or oil in a very small pan and set over medium-high heat. When hot, add the mustard seeds. As soon as they pop, a matter of seconds, add the cumin seeds and asafetida. After 3–4 seconds, add the chili powder, then immediately tip the contents of the pan over as much of the surface of the dal as you can. Serve immediately, with lime wedges if you wish.

SIMPLE TOOVAR DAL FROM THE CHITRAPUR SARASWAT BRAHMINS OF COASTAL KANNADA

DALI SAAR

ຆຆຆຆຆຆຆຆຆຆຆຆຆຆຆຆຆຆຆຆຆຆຆຆຆຆຆຆຆຆ

1 cup plain or oily toovar dal, picked over

½ teaspoon ground turmeric

¾ teaspoon salt, or to taste

2 tablespoons olive or peanut oil

Generous pinch of ground asafetida

1 teaspoon whole mustard seeds

1–3 fresh hot green chilies, cut in half lengthwise

1 dried hot red chili

3–4 cloves garlic, peeled and cut in half lengthwise

10–12 fresh curry leaves, lightly crushed in your hand

Dali saar is comfort food for the Saraswat Brahmins of Chitrapur, who are mainly professionals from the Konkan Coast. Some are academics, others lawyers. I ate with one family where every member was some kind of doctor. Most of their women are educated. Their food, which includes fish, is unique and utterly delicious.

Why these Brahmins eat fish is part legend now. Between 3000 and 2000 BC, there was a tectonic shift, and the mighty Saraswat River flowing down from the Himalaya Mountains started drying up. The vegetarian Brahmins living along its shores had to flee. They were starving when a holy man they met got fish from the drying river and fed it to them. Since then, they have eaten fish. They continued their journey south and ended up in Goa, where they built their temples. After the Portuguese invasion in the sixteenth century, they fled further south into what is now Karnataka.

Saar means juice or juice-like, so this dal tends to be very thin, meant to be eaten with rice. Those who are lucky get to eat it with the very nutritious red rice that is local to the area. The cooking talents of brides used to be judged by their ability to make a simple dali saar. I have had many dali saars that are highly flavored with garlic, and I like them very much. Santha does not use any garlic in hers, but you can add some in your tarka (see page xxii) if you wish. I do.

SERVES 4

ຆຆຆຆຆຆຆຆຆຆຆຆຆຆຆຆຆຆຆຆຆຆຆຆຆຆຆຆຆຆ

From Santha Gersappe

1. Put the dal in a bowl and cover generously with water. If using oily dal, rub it with your hands to remove the oil; if using plain dal, just wash it. Pour out the water. Do this 5 or 6 times.

Now cover generously with water again and leave to soak for 30 minutes.

2. Drain the dal, place it in a heavy-based pan, and add 3 cups water. Bring to a boil, skimming off the froth that rises to the surface. Stir in the turmeric, then partially cover the pan and cook for 35–40 minutes or until the dal is tender. Mash the dal coarsely with a potato masher. Mix in the salt, then slowly add about 1 cup water, stirring as you go, until the dal reaches the thinness you desire. Cook it over medium-low heat for another 5 minutes.

3. Put the oil in a very small pan and set over medium-high heat. When hot, add the asafetida. A few seconds later, add the mustard seeds. As soon as they pop, a matter of seconds, add all the chilies and the garlic. Stir until the garlic pieces turn a light brown on both sides. Throw in the curry leaves (take care, as they will splutter), stir once, then immediately tip the contents of the pan over the dal. Cover to entrap the aromas. Stir before serving.

TOOVAR DAL WITH SPINACH AND SORREL

PALAKOORA CHUKKAKOORA PAPPU

꣑꣑꣑꣑꣑꣑꣑꣑꣑꣑꣑꣑꣑꣑꣑꣑꣑꣑꣑꣑꣑꣑꣑꣑꣑꣑꣑꣑꣑꣑꣑

1 cup plain toovar dal, picked over and washed in several changes of water

1 well-packed cup spinach, finely chopped

1 well-packed cup sorrel, finely chopped

1 medium tomato, peeled and chopped

1 tablespoon peeled and finely chopped onion

½ teaspoon ground turmeric

1–3 fresh hot green chilies, each slit in half lengthwise

1 teaspoon salt

½ teaspoon tamarind concentrate (sold in bottles)

½ teaspoon nice red chili powder

FOR THE TARKA

3 tablespoons olive or peanut oil

Generous pinch of ground asafetida

½ teaspoon whole brown mustard seeds

1–2 dried hot red chilies

3 cloves garlic, peeled and lightly crushed

8–10 fresh curry leaves, lightly crushed in your hand

Sour greens, both red-leafed and green-leafed, are used throughout India's south and west. If you cannot get sorrel, double the spinach and increase the amount of tamarind. The dish should taste slightly sour.

S. Sampoorna is a housewife who cooks with great efficiency and joy. She belongs to the business-orientated Chowdhary community, lives in Vijaywada (Andhra Pradesh), and specializes in Telengana foods. Her family eats meat, but she always includes a selection from her vast repertoire of local vegetarian dishes. For all her meals, she likes to include a savory and a sweet as well.

Serve this dal with a rice dish, a vegetable dish, and perhaps S. Sampoorna's Simple Seasoned Yogurt, Telengana-Style (see page 327). SERVES 4

꣑꣑꣑꣑꣑꣑꣑꣑꣑꣑꣑꣑꣑꣑꣑꣑꣑꣑꣑꣑꣑꣑꣑꣑꣑꣑꣑꣑꣑꣑꣑

From S. Sampoorna

1. Soak the toovar dal in a generous covering of water for about 1 hour. Drain.

2. Put the dal in a heavy-based pan, add 3½ cups water, and bring to a boil on medium-high heat. Skim the froth off the surface, then add the spinach, sorrel, tomatoes, onions, turmeric, and green chilies. Stir, then cover partially and cook gently for 40 minutes. Add the salt, tamarind concentrate, and chili powder. Stir and taste to check the balance of flavors. Keep cooking, partially covered on low heat, for another 15 minutes, stirring now and again.

3. Put the oil in a small frying pan and set over medium-high heat. When hot, add the asafetida, then the mustard seeds. As soon as the seeds start to pop, a matter of seconds, throw in the red chilies. They will darken quickly. Add the garlic and brown lightly on both sides. Quickly stir in the curry leaves (take care, as they will splutter), then tip the contents of the pan over the top of the dal. Cover to entrap the aromas. Stir before serving.

HYDERABADI "SOUR" DAL

KHATTI DAL

੶੶੶੶੶੶੶੶੶੶੶੶੶੶੶੶੶੶੶੶੶੶੶੶੶੶੶੶੶੶੶੶੶੶੶੶੶੶

1 cup plain toovar dal, picked over and washed in several changes of water

¼ teaspoon ground turmeric

1 teaspoon salt

1–2 fresh hot green chilies, cut crosswise into thin slices

10–12 fresh curry leaves, lightly crushed in your hand

2–3 tablespoons chopped fresh cilantro

¼ teaspoon nice red chili powder

1 teaspoon peeled and finely grated fresh ginger

7 cloves garlic, peeled, 1 crushed, 6 small ones left whole

2 good-sized tomatoes, peeled and finely chopped

¾–1 teaspoon tamarind concentrate (sold in bottles)

2 tablespoons olive or peanut oil

¼ teaspoon whole brown mustard seeds

½ teaspoon whole cumin seeds

3 dried hot red chilies

Southern Indian dals tend to be hot and sour. When Muslim Moghul governors were sent south from Delhi to conquer and eventually rule the Hyderabad area in the seventeenth and eighteenth centuries, they succumbed to the local flavors and seasonings they found there, and slowly incorporated them into their own foods. (One thing that Muslims never took to in all of India, from Kashmir in the north to Kerala in the south, was asafetida. They used garlic instead!) Sour foods stimulate the appetite in hot climates, as do very spicy ones. That may well be the explanation. Perhaps these northerners just liked the taste. At any rate, what is now called Hyderabadi cuisine includes many sour and fiery dishes like this dal, which is always served, southern-style, with rice. You can serve a yogurt relish and perhaps the Spinach with Dill (see page 111) on the side.

In the India of today, this entire dish is made in a pressure cooker and, when done, given a final tarka (see page xxii). I am assuming that most people in the West do not have a pressure cooker, so I have used an ordinary saucepan.   SERVES 4–5

੶੶੶੶੶੶੶੶੶੶੶੶੶੶੶੶੶੶੶੶੶੶੶੶੶੶੶੶੶੶੶੶੶੶੶੶੶੶

From Sanjeeda Shareef

1. Put the dal in a bowl with a generous covering of water and leave to soak for 30 minutes. Drain.

2. Tip the dal into a heavy-based pan, add 3 cups water, and bring to a boil. Skim off the froth that rises to the surface, then stir in the turmeric. Cover partially and cook for 30–40 minutes or until tender. Mash the dal coarsely with a potato masher. Add the salt, green chilies, curry leaves, fresh cilantro, chili powder, ginger, crushed garlic, tomatoes, tamarind concentrate, and

½ cup water. Stir and bring to a boil, then cover and simmer gently for 15–20 minutes.

3. Put the oil in a very small pan and set over medium-high heat. When hot, add the mustard seeds. As soon as they pop, a matter of seconds, add the cumin seeds and, 5 seconds later, the 6 whole garlic cloves and the red chilies. As soon as the garlic browns lightly, tip the contents of the pan over as much of the surface of the dal as you can. Cover to entrap the aromas. Stir before serving.

SOUTH INDIAN DAL WITH VEGETABLES

SAMBAR

¾ cup plain toovar dal, picked over and washed in several changes of water

¼ teaspoon ground turmeric

Scant 3 tablespoons olive or peanut oil

½ medium onion, peeled and chopped into ½ inch dice

Salt

1 medium tomato, peeled and finely chopped

1 teaspoon tamarind concentrate

½ small yellow squash, cut into ½ inch dice

15 green beans, cut crosswise into ½ inch pieces

1 teaspoon rice flour (also called rice powder) mixed with 1 tablespoon water

2 teaspoons sambar powder, or to taste

¼ teaspoon ground asafetida

¼ teaspoon whole brown mustard seeds

¼ teaspoon whole fenugreek seeds

1–2 dried hot red chilies, broken in half, or 1–2 fresh hot green chilies, slit in half lengthwise

10–15 fresh curry leaves, lightly crushed in your hand

2 tablespoons chopped fresh cilantro

A well-made sambar is one of the glories of South India. It is actually just a humble dal that is eaten daily with all manner of dosas (pancakes), idlis (steamed cakes), and plain rice. Generally, it has a fairly thin, soupy texture, though you can make it thicker if you prefer. Its daily variation comes from the addition of different vegetables, which changes its taste. Gourds and squashes are particularly popular, but whole small shallots, the New World chayote (sayote or chow chow), green beans, okra, peas, eggplant, and radishes can also be used. Many of these vegetables will need to be pre-boiled first in lightly salted water with the addition of a tiny bit of tamarind concentrate. Okra is better if it is lightly sautéed first and then pre-boiled.

A good sambar needs a good sambar spice mix or sambar masala. You do not need to make it yourself because many excellent brands are available in the market. Look for a good South Indian one, such as the MTR brand, in an Indian grocery.

Think of the sambar as a vegetable stew. I often serve it in soup plates and pass around plain rice, chutneys, and a yogurt relish (a South Indian pachadi would be ideal) to round off this main course. Sambar is always served with South Indian pancakes, such as plain dosas (see page 258). You can also serve it with the other pancakes in this book, or with plain rice or any of the upmas.

SERVES 4

1. Put the dal in a bowl with a generous covering of water and leave to soak for 30 minutes. Drain.

2. Tip the dal into a heavy-based pan, add 3 cups water, and bring to a boil. Skim off the froth that rises to the surface, then stir in the turmeric. Cover partially, lower the heat, and cook very gently for 50 minutes or until tender.

3. Meanwhile, put 1 teaspoon of oil in a smallish pan and set over medium heat. When hot, add the diced onions and cook for about 3 minutes or until almost translucent. Do not let them brown.

4. Add 1 cup water, ¼ teaspoon salt, the tomatoes, and the tamarind concentrate. Stir, cover, and cook over low heat for 20 minutes.

5. Add the squash and beans and bring to a simmer again. Cover and cook over low heat for 6–7 minutes or until the vegetables are tender.

6. Once the dal is cooked, mash it well, using a potato masher. Stir in ½ teaspoon salt, the rice flour mixture, and the sambar powder (start with 1 teaspoon, adding more as needed). Mix well. Add the vegetable mixture, stir, and check for salt. Thin out the sambar with about ½ cup hot water. You can add more if you wish.

7. Put 2 tablespoons of the oil in a small frying pan and set over medium-high heat. When hot, add the asafetida and, a second later, the mustard seeds. As soon as the seeds pop, a matter of seconds, add the fenugreek seeds and the red chilies. Stir once, then throw in the curry leaves (take care, as they will splutter). Pour the spices and oil over the sambar. Stir to mix, then scatter fresh cilantro over the top.

SOYA GRANULES WITH POTATOES

MOCK KEEMA ALOO

꧁꧂꧁꧂꧁꧂꧁꧂꧁꧂꧁꧂꧁꧂꧁꧂꧁꧂꧁꧂꧁꧂꧁꧂꧁꧂꧁꧂

1 cup soya granules

4 tablespoons olive or peanut
    oil

2 potatoes (12 oz in all), peeled
    and cut into 1 inch chunks

Salt and freshly ground black
    pepper

Generous pinch of ground
    asafetida

1 large onion (7 oz), peeled
    and chopped

2 medium tomatoes (about
    12 oz in all), peeled and
    finely chopped

A 1-inch piece of fresh ginger,
    peeled and very finely
    grated

3 cloves garlic, peeled and
    crushed

¼ teaspoon ground turmeric

¼–1 teaspoon nice red chili
    powder

1 teaspoon ground coriander

1 teaspoon garam masala

3 tablespoons chopped fresh
    cilantro

First of all, what kind of a name is Dell' Arte Inde? Well, it is a Frenchified and made-up name for a jewelry shop in my favorite hotel, the Taj Mahal Palace in Bombay. The Dell' stands for Delhi, where the family started its jewelry business many decades ago. When I embarked on this cookbook, I was very curious to know what various groups of people in India ate and to learn more about their eating habits. India is not a homogeneous country. The Taj Hotel's many shops were a good place to start.

There are three brothers who run the Dell' Arte jewelry business today: Rohit, Kapil, and Yogesh. They are Punjabi Hindus and all live together as a joint family. They are strict vegetarians.

The brothers arrive at the shop at different times for a long day of work: Kapil and Yogesh, the younger two, arrive at 8:30 and 9 a.m., while Rohit comes at 11 a.m. Lunch is anywhere between 1:30 and 4 p.m., depending on work. Lunch for thirty, the brothers and all the employees, comes from home. It is cooked by the wives, with the help of a Maharashtrian maid, who helps skew the seasonings in a westerly direction.

The lunch for the brothers is packed in dabbas, lunch boxes with compartments. The boxes are then put inside a checkered and very large insulated plastic carrying case. Lunchtime is usually declared at around 2 p.m. A display case, the one with a mirror for viewing how glittering jewels look on delicate ears and necks, is cleared, and a tablecloth is spread on top. There is already a bench near it; more chairs are added. The checkered plastic case is emptied. Plates, cutlery, and then all the food come dribbling out. Normally, there is one dal (chickpeas on the day I was there), one vegetable (okra), one paneer dish (scrambled paneer), and a big stack of chapatis. We also had an extra dish, keema (mock minced meat) made with soya granules. This recipe comes from Sarita, Rohit's wife.

All Indian grocers sell small soya granules. They are sometimes labeled "soy vadis." This dish may be served with rice or chapatis or naans, a vegetable such as okra or cauliflower, a yogurt dish, and a chutney or salad. You could also have it with just rice and a green salad.   SERVES 4

ಲಾ

From Dell' Arte Inde

1. Soak the soya granules in 1 cup hot water for 5 minutes. Drain, saving the soaking water.

2. Put the oil into a 10 inch, preferably nonstick frying pan and set over medium-high heat. When hot, add the potatoes and fry until golden brown on all sides. They do not have to cook through. Lift them out with a slotted spoon and spread them on a plate lined with a paper towel. Sprinkle lightly with salt and pepper.

3. Remove all but 2 tablespoons of the oil from the pan. Still over medium-high heat, add the asafetida and then the onions. Stir and fry the onions for 7–8 minutes or until they brown at the edges. Add the tomatoes and ½ teaspoon salt. Stir rapidly for 5–6 minutes or until the tomatoes are dark and soft.

4. Add the ginger and garlic, stirring for 2–3 minutes. Reduce the heat to medium low and stir in the turmeric, chili powder, and coriander. Now add the soaked soya granules, the soaking liquid plus enough water to make 1¼ cups, the potatoes, and another ½ teaspoon salt. Bring to a simmer. Cover and cook over low heat for about 15 minutes, stirring now and then.

5. Before serving, sprinkle the garam masala and fresh cilantro over the top and stir to mix.

GRAINS:

RICE, SEMOLINA, AND QUINOA

PLAIN BASMATI RICE

SAADAY BASMATI CHAWAL

ശശശശശശശശശശശശശശശശശശശശശശശശശശശ

2 cups of basmati rice

Here is the easiest way for you to cook basmati rice. Salt is generally not added, as the rice is meant to be eaten with well-seasoned food.

SERVES 4

ശശശശശശശശശശശശശശശശശശശശശശശശശശശ

1. Wash the rice in several changes of water. Drain and put in a bowl. Cover generously with water and leave to soak for 30 minutes. Drain thoroughly.

2. Preheat the oven to 325°F.

3. Bring 2¾ cups water to a boil in a heavy ovenproof pan with a tight-fitting lid. Add the rice, stir, and bring back to a boil. Cover tightly (using a layer of foil between the lid and the pan and crinkling the edges, if needed, to get a tight seal) and place in the oven for 30 minutes. Remove and let the rice sit, undisturbed, for 10 minutes. Fluff up the grains with a fork and serve.

PLAIN JASMINE RICE

SAADI JASMINE RICE

1½ cups jasmine rice

Put 2¼ cups water in a pan and bring to a boil. Add the rice, stir, and bring back to a boil. Cover tightly and cook over very low heat for 25 minutes. Leave covered until you are ready to eat.

RICE WITH DILL AND PEAS

SOOA AUR MATAR KI TAHIRI

꙰꙰꙰꙰꙰꙰꙰꙰꙰꙰꙰꙰꙰꙰꙰꙰꙰꙰꙰꙰꙰꙰꙰꙰꙰꙰꙰꙰꙰꙰꙰꙰꙰꙰

2 cups basmati rice

3 tablespoons olive or peanut
    oil

1 medium onion, peeled and
    cut into fine half rings

1 teaspoon garam masala

¾ cup well-packed fresh dill,
    feathery leaves and fine
    stems only, finely chopped

1 teaspoon salt

1 cup fresh or frozen peas,
    cooked and drained

I make this rice dish quite frequently when I have guests for dinner (and I so enjoy eating it the next day if any is left). It is aromatic and satisfyingly delicious. I like to serve it with Chana Dal with Spinach and Tomato and Carrot Raita (see pages 127 and 333). For a party, I add Green Beans with Potatoes (see page 63).

SERVES 4–6

꙰꙰꙰꙰꙰꙰꙰꙰꙰꙰꙰꙰꙰꙰꙰꙰꙰꙰꙰꙰꙰꙰꙰꙰꙰꙰꙰꙰꙰꙰꙰꙰꙰꙰

1. Wash the rice in several changes of water. Drain and put in a bowl. Cover generously with water and leave to soak for 30 minutes. Drain and leave in a strainer set over a bowl.

2. Preheat the oven to 325°F.

3. Put the oil in a heavy ovenproof pan and set over medium-high heat. When hot, add the onions and cook for 7–8 minutes or until reddish brown. Add the rice, garam masala, dill, and salt and reduce the heat to medium. Stir very gently to mix, lifting the rice from the bottom and turning it over as you would if mixing a soufflé. The tender rice grains break easily at this stage. When well mixed, pour in 2¾ cups water and bring to a boil.

4. Cover tightly with foil and a lid and put in the oven for 25 minutes. Quickly tip the drained peas on top of the rice, re-cover with the foil and the lid, and return the pan to the oven for another 5 minutes.

5. Set the pan of rice aside and leave undisturbed for 10 minutes. Fluff up the grains with a fork and serve. If you wish to hold the rice for an hour, cover the pan with heavy towels.

RICE WITH MOONG DAL AND POTATOES

KHILI KHICHRI

༄ఌఌఌఌఌఌఌఌఌఌఌఌఌఌఌఌఌఌఌఌఌఌఌఌఌఌఌఌఌఌఌ

¼ cup moong dal (skinned
    and split mung beans)

2 cups basmati rice

3 tablespoons olive or peanut
    oil or ghee (clarified
    butter)

½ teaspoon whole cumin
    seeds

1 medium waxy potato, peeled
    and cut into ½ inch dice
    (red potatoes work well)

1 teaspoon peeled and very
    finely diced fresh ginger

1 teaspoon garam masala

2 teaspoons ground coriander

1 teaspoon salt

¼ teaspoon nice red chili
    powder

½ teaspoon ground turmeric

This dish is both comforting and delicious. Sometimes I add tiny onions, browned slowly in a little oil, to the rice at about the same time as I add the water. This dish can be served with eggplant, greens, dals, and all manner of relishes. You could also have it by itself with a salad.

SERVES 4–6

༄ఌఌఌఌఌఌఌఌఌఌఌఌఌఌఌఌఌఌఌఌఌఌఌఌఌఌఌఌఌఌ

1. Wash the dal in several changes of water, then leave to soak for 3 hours. Drain.

2. Wash the rice in several changes of water and leave to soak for 30 minutes. Drain.

3. Put the oil or ghee in a heavy pan with a tight-fitting lid and set over medium-high heat. When hot, add the cumin seeds and, 10 seconds later, the potatoes. Stir and fry until the potatoes are lightly browned. Add the ginger and stir a few times, then reduce the heat to medium. Now add the rice, dal, garam masala, coriander, salt, chili powder, and turmeric. Sauté gently for 2–3 minutes, always lifting the rice from the bottom to avoid breaking the grains.

4. Add 2¾ cups water and bring to a boil. Cover tightly and cook over very low heat for 25 minutes.

SPICED HYDERABADI RICE

BAGHARE CHAVAL

∽∽∽∽∽∽∽∽∽∽∽∽∽∽∽∽∽∽∽∽∽∽∽∽∽∽∽∽∽∽∽

2 cups basmati rice

3 tablespoons olive or peanut
oil

4 tablespoons peeled and
finely sliced shallots

A 2-inch cinnamon stick

4 cloves

4 cardamom pods

¼ teaspoon black cumin seeds
(use ordinary cumin as a
substitute)

1 large clove garlic, peeled and
crushed

1 teaspoon peeled and finely
grated fresh ginger

1 teaspoon salt

1–2 fresh hot green chilies, slit
in half lengthwise

A lovely, well-flavored rice dish, this is what is served with Hyderabad's famous "dalcha," a dish of toovar dal, squash, and meat. The vegetarian version, Chana Dal with Yellow Squash, Chayote, or Doodhi, is on page 130. For more on Hyderabadi Muslim food, see the introduction to Tomato Kut on page 286.

This dish is usually made with basmati rice for special occasions, but with the more ordinary sona masoori, a smaller-grained rice, for everyday meals. Here I have made it with basmati rice. If you wish to use the sona masoori rice, follow this recipe but increase the cooking water to 3 cups.   SERVES 4–6

∽∽∽∽∽∽∽∽∽∽∽∽∽∽∽∽∽∽∽∽∽∽∽∽∽∽∽∽∽∽∽

From Sanjeeda Shareef

1. Wash the rice in several changes of water. Drain and put in a bowl. Cover generously with water and leave to soak for 30 minutes. Drain and leave in a strainer set over a bowl.

2. Preheat the oven to 325°F.

3. Put the oil in a heavy ovenproof pan and set over medium-high heat. When hot, add the shallots, cinnamon stick, cloves, cardamom pods, and cumin seeds. Stir as you let the shallots turn slightly brown. Add the garlic and ginger and stir for about a minute or until golden. Pour in 2¾ cups water and bring to a boil. Add the rice, salt, and green chilies. Stir and bring to a boil, then cover tightly with foil and a lid.

4. Put the pan in the oven for 30 minutes. Remove and let the rice sit undisturbed for 10 minutes. Fluff up the grains with a fork and serve.

LEMON RICE

NIMMAKAYA PULIHORA

cucucucucucucucucucucucucucucucucucucucucucucucucucucu

1½ tablespoons olive or peanut
oil
¼ teaspoon whole brown
mustard seeds
¼ teaspoon whole cumin
seeds
2 tablespoons raw skinless
peanuts
1 teaspoon chana dal
7–8 fresh curry leaves
(use basil leaves as an
alternative)
1 teaspoon peeled and very
finely chopped fresh
ginger
1–2 fresh hot green chilies,
finely chopped
½ teaspoon ground turmeric
1 teaspoon salt
1 recipe freshly made Plain
Jasmine Rice (see
page 173)
Finely grated rind from
1 lemon
1 tablespoon lemon juice

A light, summery rice dish that can be served with vegetables, dal, and relishes, and also by itself as a snack. This one most resembles Chinese stir-fried rice, except that all the ingredients are Indian.   SERVES 4

cucucucucucucucucucucucucucucucucucucucucucucucucucucu

Put the oil in a nonstick medium frying pan and set over medium heat. When hot, add the mustard seeds. As soon as they pop, a matter of seconds, add the cumin seeds and let them sizzle for a few seconds. Stir in the peanuts and chana dal, and as soon as the nuts begin to take on a golden color, add the curry leaves (take care, as these will splutter), ginger, and green chilies. Stir a few times and turn the heat to low. Add the turmeric and salt, stir once, then add all the cooked rice, lemon rind, and lemon juice. Break up all the rice lumps with the back of a wooden spoon and mix gently but thoroughly as you reheat the mixture. Serve hot.

TOMATO RICE

THAKKALI SADAM *OR* TOMATO ANNAM

ୡ୰

1½ tablespoons olive or peanut oil

8 raw cashews, split lengthwise into their natural halves

1 tablespoon raw peanuts

Generous pinch of ground asafetida

1 teaspoon urad dal

½ teaspoon whole brown mustard seeds

1 teaspoon peeled and very finely chopped fresh ginger

6–7 fresh curry leaves, lightly crushed in your hand

¾ cup tomato puree

2 or more fresh hot green chilies, finely chopped

¼ teaspoon ground turmeric

¾ teaspoon salt, or more as needed

1 recipe Plain Jasmine Rice (see page 173)

Rice with lime or lemon, rice with tamarind, rice with yogurt, and rice with tomatoes are all very popular throughout South India. These dishes have some things in common. Plain, unseasoned rice is cooked ahead of the meal. It is then spread out in a thali (metal platter) and seasoned, sauced, and well mixed. The sauce is generally sour and spicy. Because the temperature in the south is typically balmy, there is little danger of the rice getting icy cold, as there is in northern India. These mixed rices are always served at room temperature.

So what do we, who live in the West, do in our colder climes? I have worked out my own way of serving these dishes. I make my rice so it is ready just before we eat. I make my sauce ahead of time too, if possible. As we are getting ready to eat, I heat up the sauce, pour it over the rice in its pan, and mix it in. This way the rice may not be hot but it is still warm.

Serve at mealtimes with a dal, vegetables, and relishes. See the introduction to Cabbage Fritters (page 13) to get a sense of a meal it could be served with.   SERVES 4

ୡ୰ୡ୰ୡ୰ୡ୰ୡ୰ୡ୰ୡ୰ୡ୰ୡ୰ୡ୰ୡ୰ୡ୰ୡ୰ୡ୰ୡ୰ୡ୰ୡ୰ୡ୰ୡ୰ୡ

Based on a recipe from a mess in Rajahmundry, Andhra Pradesh

1. Put the oil in a small pan and set over medium heat. When hot, add the cashews and peanuts. Stir and fry them until they are golden. Remove with a slotted spoon and spread them out on a paper towel to drain.

2. Add the asafetida to the empty pan, and a second later add the dal. As soon as the dal starts to take on color, add the mustard seeds. As soon as the seeds pop, a matter of seconds, add the

ginger and then the curry leaves (take care, as they will splutter). Stir once, then pour in the tomato puree and 1½ cups water. Add the chilies, turmeric, salt, and nuts. Stir and bring to a simmer, then cover and simmer gently for 10 minutes.

3. Your rice should be ready around the same time as you are getting ready to eat. Heat up the sauce and pour it over the rice, which should still be in its pan. Mix gently but thoroughly, then serve.

BERRY PILAF

BERRY PULAV

୧୨୧୨୧୨୧୨୧୨୧୨୧୨୧୨୧୨୧୨୧୨୧୨୧୨୧୨୧୨୧୨୧୨

2 cups best-quality basmati
  rice from India

1 teaspoon saffron threads

3 tablespoons sugar

3 tablespoons very hot milk

About ½ cup dried barberries
  or dried cranberries

3 tablespoons olive or peanut
  oil

1 large onion, peeled and cut
  in half lengthwise, then
  into fine half rings

1½ tablespoons salt

5 cardamom pods

2½ inch cinnamon stick

1 bay leaf

3 cloves

3 tablespoons melted butter

The restaurant where this pilaf is served has been in existence since 1923. It is a Bombay landmark. The original owner, a Zoroastrian named Rashid Kohinoor, came from Iran and started out serving Iranian dishes. His son, Boman, married a Parsi, an Indian Zoroastrian, and she added many local Parsi dishes to the menu. A third generation heads the kitchen today.

It was Boman, ninety years old, who took us to our seats and offered us a fresh lime soda on a very hot day. "As they say, it will 'bit the hit' [beat the heat]"—one Indian with an accent mocking other Indians with worse accents. Indians do that all the time. He laughed boisterously. He joked around and was full of stories. When I asked him for the berry pilaf recipe, he laughed again and told us that the British ambassador (he probably meant the American ambassador) once asked him for the same recipe and he answered, "If you give me the recipe for Coca-Cola, I will hand over the recipe for berry pilaf." I never did get the Persian-Indian recipe from him, so I have created my own version, and without the chicken meatballs they add to it. At the restaurant this pilaf, called Chicken Berry Pulav, is served with meats, but I have left those out. I do not recommend this restaurant to vegetarians. Just use this recipe to make my aromatic yellow and white vegetarian version of their great signature dish.

The berry used here is the tiny Iranian barberry or zareshk, sold by Indian and Persian grocers. If you cannot find it, use dried cranberries. The final flavors are sweet and sour. As there is expensive saffron in it as well, I often make this pilaf for a dinner party. I find that it goes very well with eggplant, spinach, and paneer dishes.   SERVES 4–6

୧୨୧୨୧୨୧୨୧୨୧୨୧୨୧୨୧୨୧୨୧୨୧୨୧୨୧୨୧୨୧୨୧୨

1. Wash the rice in several changes of water. Put in a bowl, cover generously with water, and set aside to soak for 3 hours.

2. Combine the saffron and 1 tablespoon of the sugar in a mortar and pound together so you have a powder. Put in a small bowl. Add the hot milk, stir, then set aside for 3 hours.

3. Rinse the berries a few times and leave to soak for 20 minutes. Drain and pat dry.

4. Put the oil in a medium frying pan and set over medium-high heat. When hot, add the onions and cook for 5 minutes or until they start to brown. Reduce the heat to medium low and continue cooking until they are reddish brown. Add the drained berries and the remaining 2 tablespoons sugar. Stir once or twice, then remove from the heat.

5. Preheat the oven to 325°F.

6. Bring about 10 cups of water to a rolling boil. Add the salt, cardamom pods, cinnamon stick, bay leaf, and cloves. Stir once and add the rice. Let it cook in the boiling water for about 5½ minutes or until it is three-quarters cooked but still has a thin, hard core. Drain in a colander.

7. Working quickly now, spread 1 tablespoon of the melted butter in a medium ovenproof pan. Spread half the rice over it. Spread another tablespoon of the butter, plus half the saffron mixture and half the onion-berry mixture and some of its oil on top of the rice. Spread the remaining rice on top of the first layer. Pour the remaining tablespoon of butter over it, followed by the remaining saffron mixture and onion-berry mixture. Cover tightly with foil and a lid and bake in the oven for 30 minutes.

8. Remove and let the pan sit undisturbed for 10 minutes. Toss the rice gently to mix before serving.

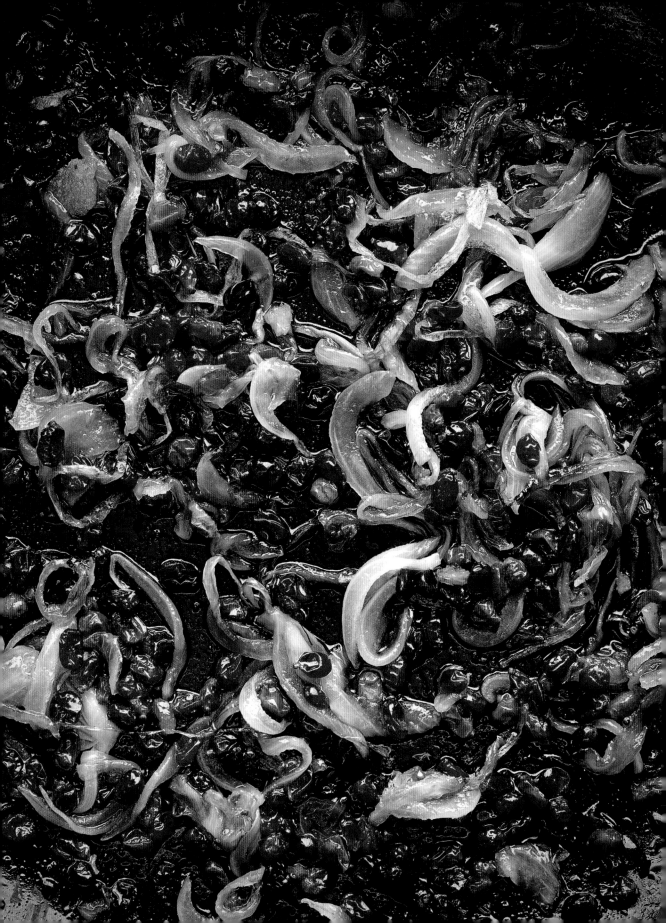

PLEASE DO NOT ARGUE
WITH MANAGEMENT

MANAGEMENT HAS GOT RIGHT
TO CHECK ANY ARTICLE OR
INDIVIDUAL ON SUSPICION

CUSTOMERS ARE REQUESTED TO
TAKE CARE OF THEIR BELONGINGS

RIGHT TO ADMISSION RESERVED

RESERVED

RICE WITH EGGPLANT

VANGI BHAAT

ଈଈଈଈଈଈଈଈଈଈଈଈଈଈଈଈଈଈଈଈଈଈଈଈଈଈଈଈଈଈଈ

1 recipe Plain Jasmine Rice
  (see page 173), but add
  1 teaspoon salt to the
  cooking water
1 medium eggplant (12 oz), cut
  into 1½ x 2 inch chunks
3 tablespoons olive or peanut
  oil
½ teaspoon urad dal
A 2-inch cinnamon stick
½ teaspoon whole brown
  mustard seeds
2 dried hot red chilies
6–8 fresh curry leaves, lightly
  crushed in your hand
1 medium onion (5½ oz), cut
  into ½ inch dice
¾–1 teaspoon salt (start with
  the smaller amount)
2 teaspoons ground coriander
1 teaspoon ground cumin
½ teaspoon ground turmeric
¼ teaspoon nice red chili
  powder, or to taste
1 tablespoon lemon juice
4 tablespoons tomato puree
2–3 tablespoons chopped
  fresh cilantro

This is a great dish for entertaining. The recipe can easily be doubled, if needed. Add a dal, a green vegetable, chutneys, and a yogurt relish. When this dish is made in western India, the eggplants tend to be quite spicy. They mellow a bit when mixed with the plain rice. You can make your own decision about the spiciness, adding as much chili powder as you like.

If you cannot find an eggplant of the weight you want, use two smaller or narrower ones, or use part of a large one. The usable pieces should weigh about 12 oz.   SERVES 4

ଈଈଈଈଈଈଈଈଈଈଈଈଈଈଈଈଈଈଈଈଈଈଈଈଈଈଈଈଈଈଈ

1. While the rice is cooking, soak the eggplant chunks in a large bowl of water.

2. Put the oil in a medium nonstick frying pan and set over medium heat. When hot, add the urad dal and cinnamon stick. Stir until the dal starts to take on color, a few seconds. Add the mustard seeds and red chilies. Stir until the seeds pop and the chilies darken, a few seconds. Quickly add the curry leaves (take care, as they will splutter), followed immediately by the onions. Stir and fry for 1 minute.

3. Drain the eggplant and add the chunks to the pan along with the salt. Stir and fry for about 10 minutes or until the pieces look slightly glazed. Turn the heat to low and sprinkle in the ground coriander, cumin, turmeric, and chili powder. Cook, stirring, for 2 minutes.

4. Add the lemon juice, tomato puree, and about ½ cup water. Stir and bring to a simmer, then cover and cook on very low heat

for 20 minutes, stirring gently from the bottom now and then. Check the salt, adding more if needed.

5. Just before serving, spread the hot rice on a large, warmed platter, breaking up any lumps with the back of a spoon. Empty the eggplant and its juices over the top and mix gently, being careful not to break the eggplant chunks. Sprinkle the fresh cilantro over the top.

VEGETABLE BIRYANI WITH CAULIFLOWER, CARROTS, AND PEAS

GOBI, GAJAR AUR MATAR KI BIRYANI

2 cups of basmati rice

2 tablespoons olive or peanut
    oil or ghee (clarified
    butter), or a combination
    of the two

A 2-inch cinnamon stick

1–2 bay leaves

4–5 cloves

4–5 cardamom pods

¼ teaspoon whole black
    cumin seeds (use ordinary
    cumin seeds if you do not
    have them)

12 cashews, split in half
    lengthwise

2 tablespoons golden raisins

½ medium onion, peeled and
    cut into fine half rings

1½ teaspoons salt

FOR THE VEGETABLES

2 tablespoons olive or peanut
    oil or ghee (clarified
    butter), or a combination
    of the two

¼ teaspoon whole cumin
    seeds

½ medium onion, peeled and
    cut into fine half rings

2 teaspoons peeled and finely
    grated fresh ginger

2 cups small cauliflower
    florets, about ½ inch wide

Biryanis are generally complicated affairs: you partially cook the rice, you partially cook the vegetables, you brown onions by themselves, and then you layer the three in a pan and let them bake together. In my effort to simplify the dish for this book, what I have done is to cook the rice by itself, then quickly stir-fry the vegetables with onions, and then put everything together in a large warmed platter or serving bowl. Biryanis are usually served with a yogurt relish and a salad, but you could add a dal, such as the Black-eyed Peas with Cilantro and Green Chilies (see page 122).

I like to remove the large spices, such as the bay leaf, cardamom pods, cloves, and cinnamon, from the rice before mixing it with the vegetables. (No one does this in India, as we know they are not meant for eating. We just gently push them aside on the plate.)

Here is my timetable for making the dish: I first wash the rice and set it to soak. While it is soaking, I chop up everything needed to make the vegetables. Then I cook the rice. While it is in the oven, I cook the vegetables. If I am eating immediately, I warm up a large serving bowl and empty the rice into it, gently breaking up any lumps. I empty the vegetables on top of it and mix gently but thoroughly. If I am eating much later, I wrap the pan of rice in a heavy towel and set it aside. It will stay hot for 2 hours. If it has cooled off too much, I reheat it in the oven for 20 minutes or so. The vegetables are left in the pan and they warm up easily over low heat. Then I mix the two together. SERVES 4–6

1. Wash the rice in several changes of water. Place the rice in a bowl, cover generously with water, and leave to soak for 30 minutes. Drain.

and 1 inch long, well
washed and drained
1 medium carrot, peeled and
diced to the size of peas
¼ teaspoon ground turmeric
¼–½ teaspoon nice red chili
powder
1 cup cooked fresh peas or
defrosted frozen peas
2–4 fresh hot green chilies,
finely chopped
¾ teaspoon salt
Freshly ground black pepper
½ teaspoon garam masala
1 tablespoon lime or lemon
juice

2. Preheat the oven to 325°F.

3. Put the oil or ghee for the rice in a heavy ovenproof pan with a well-fitting lid and set over medium heat. When hot, add the cinnamon stick, bay leaves, cloves, cardamom pods, and cumin seeds. Stir for a few seconds, then add the cashews. As soon as they are golden, add the raisins. They will plump up immediately. Quickly add the onions and fry until reddish. Add the drained rice, 2¾ cups water and the salt. Stir and bring to a boil, then cover tightly with foil and a lid. Place in the oven for 25 minutes.

4. Meanwhile, make the vegetables. Put the oil into a medium, preferably nonstick frying pan and set over medium-high heat. When hot, add the cumin seeds and let them sizzle for a few seconds. Add the onions, ginger, cauliflower, carrots, turmeric, and chili powder. Stir gently for about 3–4 minutes, still over medium-high heat, until the onions and cauliflower are lightly browned.

5. Reduce the heat to medium low and add the peas, green chilies, salt, black pepper, garam masala, and lime juice. Stir gently and cook for another 3–5 minutes or until the vegetables are just done.

6. Take the rice out of the oven when it is ready and let it sit for 10 minutes. After that, empty it into a warmed bowl and break up any lumps without breaking the grains. Add all the ingredients from the frying pan and mix gently but thoroughly. Serve immediately.

A NOTE ON UPMA, POHA, AND SOOJI

UPMA The Western world has no real equivalent for upma. It is somewhat like a risotto, except that it is not as dense and heavy, and not so wet and molten either. It is perhaps more like Chinese fried rice, except that it is a little wet and tends to collect in small clumps. Upma is, in the last analysis, deliciously itself. It is light and easy to prepare and often thrown together quickly as breakfast, a light lunch, or a snack. It tends to be spicy—very spicy if you like it that way. The basic ingredient is always a grain. Vegetables and spices are added to it for nutrition and flavoring.

The grains that are most commonly used to make upma are sooji and poha, discussed below. Both are ingredients worth having in your pantry on a continuous basis, as they can help you to turn out extraordinarily tasty, nutritious meals very quickly. Upmas can also be made with bread (I have one made with whole-grain bread in this book) and quinoa (you will find that here as well).

FLATTENED RICE (POHA) A friend of mine in Bombay, Vikram Doctor, who has a vast knowledge of Indian food, was wondering with me why it was that other countries with ancient histories of rice culture do not have any version of flattened rice. Some have puffed rice, another "instant" version suitable for a quick meal, but no one, to my knowledge, has the much-loved Indian poha.

Also called "phov," "cheewra," "chivra," "chuda," and "aval," it is used with great frequency in the rice-growing regions of eastern, western, and southern India as a breakfast and snack food. Travelers in ancient times carried a bag of it, reconstituting it with water whenever they were hungry, and perhaps accompanying it with a chutney or pickle, or soaking it in milk, like a cereal.

Today large quantities of poha are made in factories, but if you go to Indian villages with rice fields, you can still see poha being made the old-fashioned way. Actually, villages seem to have their own individual techniques. In one tribal village in Jharkhand (south of Bihar), the rice grains are put into vats with a little water for steaming/parboiling. This ancient process pushes the goodness of the hull and husk right into the heart of each grain. Then the grains are roasted rather casually, in a broken section of a rounded terracotta pot set on top of a small wood fire. The grains then go into a large mortar, and two women holding a long pole-like pestle pound rhythmically to flatten it. After the rice is flattened and the husk and hull are winnowed away, what you have is poha. Here it is not cooked any further, but eaten as it is with milk and sweetened with jaggery, a form of raw lump sugar. Further north it is eaten with sweetened yogurt, or crisped up and eaten at breakfast with Peas and Potatoes Cooked in a Bihari Style (see page 103).

The coastal Konkan region of western India produces a very nutritious red rice that is partially milled and also made into poha. It is put into hot milky tea in the mornings to give extra energy to workers going to the fields and to children going to school.

Poha is used in many religious ceremonies as well. One requirement in Baroda (Gujarat) is that it be made fresh just before it can be put into poha kheer, a pudding served as holy food at the Ram Temple after the Ram Navami prayers to celebrate Ram's birthday. In Baroda the rice grains are soaked for three days, drained thoroughly, roasted in a large cast-iron karhai (wok), pounded to the desired thickness in a mortar, then winnowed and dried.

But the poha dishes that I like best and crave constantly are the western and southern Indian ones that require the poha to be partly reconstituted and stir-fried quickly with spices and vegetables to make the wonderful risotto-like dish called upma. It cooks very easily and everyone loves it. Friendly ingredients for mixing with it include onions, potatoes, corn, tomatoes, cauliflower, peas, and mung bean sprouts. Poha may also be added to puddings and yogurt dishes. It is always added to that wonderful mélange of spicy nuts and seeds sold as Bombay Mix. Poha is light, nutritious, and very digestible, a good version of rice to know about and to have in your pantry.

In India, three thicknesses of poha are generally available, but I have used only what is sold as "thick" poha. It needs to be rinsed and soaked. (Each recipe in this book gives the necessary instructions.)

For reheating the poha upmas in this section, sprinkle generously with water and place over very low heat. Toss gently, using a flat spatula to fold the poha over from the bottom, rather like you might mix a soufflé, so the delicate grains do not get broken.

I had quite a revelatory experience recently. My husband and I were going to stay with a friend on an island off the coast of Maine. Since I seem to cook wherever I go and not much is available in the small island market, I was taking with me, among other things, all the ingredients to make a poha dish. It would be quick and easy. As I unpacked the mustard seeds, cumin seeds, chilies, potatoes, limes, and onions, I realized that I had left the poha behind. It had taken us nine hours to drive up there, plus a boat ride, so there was no going back. I thought of substitutes—semolina, bulgar, farina—nothing was available. My friends did have quinoa, though, and it worked so well that I have developed a recipe for it—cooked in the poha upma style!

SOOJI (INDIAN SEMOLINA) Sooji is not really a true semolina. Real semolina, the kind used for Italian pasta, is a granular flour made from hard durum wheat. Indian sooji is made from soft wheat, using the same method that is used for making true semolina. However, many Indian stores call it semolina, so do not let yourself get confused.

Buy from an Indian grocer and ask for "sooji/farina." Don't get the fine grind, if that is what the label says. Also, do not get roasted semolina, as you should roast it yourself (the process takes just a few minutes). A packet simply labeled "sooji" will be fine. You can tell your grocer that you want it to make upma (the *u* is pronounced like the "ou" in "could"). In South India, sooji is called "rava," which just means any granular flour. If you find yourself with a southern grocer, first try asking for sooji/farina. If he does not respond (though I am sure he will), try asking for wheat rava.

Indian semolina behaves rather like polenta, but cooks much faster and ends up with a much lighter, fluffier texture. A simple dish of it can be prepared in less than fifteen minutes, which makes it a very popular breakfast food and makes sooji a wonderful ingredient to have on hand. For breakfast, many Indians much prefer to eat their sooji/farina in a fluffy and savory form, not a sweet one. As one South Indian friend said to me, "We don't like our breakfasts to be sweet. We like them hot and spicy." Indeed, in India many Western breakfast companies have been selling instant cooking cereals filled with Indian spices and no sugar!

Sooji upmas can be served as breakfast, lunch, and dinner as well. In some North Indian cities, sooji is made into rich halvas, with lots of ghee and sugar (see Sooji Halva, page 376). These are eaten for breakfast on special occasions with Puffed Fried Breads (see page 235).

A little sooji is often added to Indian foods, such as the Savory Pastry Strips with Ajowan Seeds (see page 22), in order to make them extra crispy.

FLATTENED RICE WITH POTATOES

PHOVA USLI, AN UPMA

౿ఴ౿ఴ౿ఴ౿ఴ౿ఴ౿ఴ౿ఴ౿ఴ౿ఴ౿ఴ౿ఴ౿ఴ౿ఴ౿ఴ౿ఴ౿ఴ౿ఴ

2 medium waxy potatoes,
    boiled, cooled, and peeled
2 cups thick poha (flattened
    rice)
3 tablespoons olive or peanut
    oil
Generous pinch of ground
    asafetida
½ teaspoon urad dal
½ teaspoon whole brown
    mustard seeds
½ teaspoon whole cumin
    seeds
1 dried hot red chili (see
    introduction for other
    options)
10–15 fresh curry leaves,
    lightly crushed in your
    hand
½ medium onion, peeled and
    chopped
Salt
1 teaspoon sugar
2–3 tablespoons chopped
    fresh cilantro, to garnish
4 lime or lemon wedges, to
    serve

This is an absolutely delicious and simple breakfast or snack dish from the coastal Konkan region of western India. The texture is rice-like, but soft and much airier, and can collect in delicate lumps. I often make it for lunch and serve it with a large salad filled with lettuce, cucumbers, and tomatoes. You can use one whole dried red chili if you want the dish mild, and two (snapped in half) if you want the dish hotter. Many Indians prefer to add fiery fresh green chilies instead, one, two, or three, either split in half lengthwise or sliced into thin rings. Lime or lemon wedges should be served on the side.

To reheat, sprinkle with a tablespoon or two of water, cover, and put over very low heat. Toss gently now and then.

SERVES 3–4

౿ఴ౿ఴ౿ఴ౿ఴ౿ఴ౿ఴ౿ఴ౿ఴ౿ఴ౿ఴ౿ఴ౿ఴ౿ఴ౿ఴ౿ఴ౿ఴ౿ఴ

1. Cut the potatoes into ½ inch dice.

2. Put the poha into a sieve and wash gently but thoroughly under cold running water. Empty it into a bowl, cover generously with water, and leave to soak for 2 minutes. Drain and leave in the sieve set over a bowl.

3. Put the oil into a large nonstick frying pan and set it over medium-high heat. When hot, add the asafetida and the urad dal. As soon as the dal starts to pick up a little color, add the mustard seeds, cumin seeds, and the chili (whatever type you are using). As soon as the mustard seeds start to pop, a matter of seconds, add the curry leaves (take care, as they will splutter), then the onions and potatoes. Lower the heat to medium and fry, stirring now and again, until the onions and potatoes are slightly browned, 3–4 minutes. Sprinkle ¼ teaspoon salt over the top and stir.

FACING PAGE: Dried turmeric

4. Add the poha, gently breaking up any lumps, and sprinkle ½ teaspoon salt and the sugar over the top. Cook over low heat for 3–4 minutes, tossing frequently by lifting all the ingredients from the bottom with a flat spatula and folding them over, until the poha is heated through. Cover and set aside until you are ready to eat.

5. To reheat, sprinkle with a tablespoon or two of water and warm over very low heat. Toss gently now and then. Garnish with the fresh cilantro and serve with lime or lemon wedges.

FLATTENED RICE WITH CAULIFLOWER AND PEAS

PHOOL GOBI AUR MATAR WALA POHA

3 cups thick poha (flattened
rice)

3 tablespoons olive or peanut
oil

Generous pinch of ground
asafetida

¾ teaspoon urad dal

½ teaspoon whole brown
mustard seeds

½ teaspoon whole cumin
seeds

10–15 fresh curry leaves,
lightly crushed in your
hand

1 medium onion (about 4 oz),
peeled and chopped

2 teaspoons peeled and very
finely grated fresh ginger

2 cups very small cauliflower
florets, ½ inch wide and
1 inch long, well washed
and drained

¼ teaspoon ground turmeric

1 cup fresh cooked peas or
defrosted frozen peas

1–3 fresh hot green chilies,
finely chopped

Salt

1 tablespoon lime juice

A grand dish that looks splendid and tastes as good as it looks. Sometimes I eat this all by itself. Other dishes, such as Mixed Dal, Marwari-Style (see page 154), could be added to the meal, as well as a raita, popadams, and chutneys. It is also perfect for brunch.

In India most people like their poha upmas to be fairly spicy, but you can use as many or as few green chilies as you like.

SERVES 4

1. Put the poha into a sieve and wash gently but thoroughly in running water. Place in a bowl, cover generously with water, and soak for 2 minutes. Drain and leave in a sieve set over a bowl.

2. Put the oil into a large nonstick frying pan and set it over medium-high heat. When hot, add the asafetida and the urad dal. As soon as the dal starts to pick up a little color, add the mustard seeds and cumin seeds. When the mustard seeds start to pop, a matter of seconds, add the curry leaves (take care, as they will splutter), then the onions, ginger, cauliflower, and turmeric. Stir gently for about 3–4 minutes, still over medium-high heat, until the onions and cauliflower are lightly browned.

3. Reduce the heat to medium low and add the peas, green chilies, ½ teaspoon of salt, and the lime juice. Stir gently for 1–2 minutes, always lifting the ingredients from the bottom, so the peas heat/cook through.

4. Add all the poha, gently breaking up any lumps. Sprinkle another ½ teaspoon of salt over it and mix gently over a very low heat for 3–4 minutes, using a flat spatula and lifting the mixture from the bottom and folding it over the rest. When the ingredients are well blended and the poha has heated through, cover and set aside until you are ready to eat.

FLATTENED RICE WITH INDIAN-STYLE BEAN SPROUTS

PHUTI MOONG AUR POHA KA UPMA

꒰ꘛ꒰ꘛ꒰ꘛ꒰ꘛ꒰ꘛ꒰ꘛ꒰ꘛ꒰ꘛ꒰ꘛ꒰ꘛ꒰ꘛ꒰ꘛ꒰ꘛ꒰ꘛ꒰ꘛ꒰ꘛ

2 cups thick poha (flattened rice)

2 tablespoons olive or peanut oil

Generous pinch of ground asafetida

½ teaspoon urad dal

1 teaspoon whole brown mustard seeds

10–15 fresh curry leaves, lightly crushed in your hand

1 medium onion, peeled and chopped

¼ teaspoon ground turmeric

1 teaspoon peeled and finely grated fresh ginger

1–3 fresh hot green chilies, finely chopped

1 cup Indian-style mung bean sprouts (see page 142)

1 teaspoon salt, or to taste

Lime wedges, to serve

A very nutritious dish often eaten for breakfast in western India, it can also be eaten as a snack. Serve it with a yogurt lassi or a yogurt relish, or just plain old tea or coffee.

To reheat, sprinkle with a tablespoon or two of water, put over very low heat, and cover, tossing gently now and then.

SERVES 3–4

꒰ꘛ꒰ꘛ꒰ꘛ꒰ꘛ꒰ꘛ꒰ꘛ꒰ꘛ꒰ꘛ꒰ꘛ꒰ꘛ꒰ꘛ꒰ꘛ꒰ꘛ꒰ꘛ꒰ꘛ꒰ꘛ

1. Put the poha into a sieve and wash gently but thoroughly under running water. Empty it into a bowl, cover generously with water, and leave to soak for 2 minutes. Drain and leave in a sieve set over a bowl.

2. Put the oil into a large nonstick frying pan and set it over medium-high heat. When hot, add the asafetida and urad dal. As soon as the dal starts to pick up a little color, add the mustard seeds. When the seeds start to pop, a matter of seconds, add the curry leaves (take care, as they will splutter) and then the onions. Stir and fry for 6–7 minutes, until the onions just start to brown. Add the turmeric, ginger, and green chilies. Stir for a minute, then add the bean sprouts and ⅓ cup water. Bring to a simmer. Cover and simmer very gently for 10 minutes, adding a little water if the pan starts to dry out.

3. Add the poha and salt and cook over low heat for 3–4 minutes, tossing frequently by lifting all the ingredients from the bottom and folding them over, until the poha is heated through. Cover and set aside until you are ready to eat. Serve with the lime wedges.

FLATTENED RICE WITH TOMATOES

TIMATAR KA POHA UPMA

⌣⌣⌣⌣⌣⌣⌣⌣⌣⌣⌣⌣⌣⌣⌣⌣⌣⌣⌣⌣⌣⌣⌣⌣⌣⌣⌣⌣⌣⌣⌣⌣

2 cups thick poha (flattened rice)

2 tablespoons peanut or olive oil

½ teaspoon urad dal

Generous pinch of ground asafetida

1 teaspoon whole mustard seeds

½ teaspoon whole cumin seeds

10–15 fresh curry leaves, lightly crushed in your hand

1 medium onion, peeled and chopped

1–3 fresh hot green chilies, finely chopped

¼ teaspoon ground turmeric

1 teaspoon peeled and very finely grated fresh ginger

2 medium tomatoes (about 12 oz in all), peeled and chopped

About ¾ teaspoon salt, or to taste

½ teaspoon sugar

A lovely poha recipe sent to me by my friend and brilliant Indian food writer Vikram Doctor.

I have served this on summer days outdoors with a beet and hard-boiled-egg salad, for which I use the same dressing as Tomato Salad (see page 40), plus Green Beans with Potatoes (see page 63) and a green salad. It is a perfect lunch. In the winter it can be paired with an eggplant dish and a paneer dish, or just have it with a cup of hot tea.

To reheat, sprinkle with a tablespoon or two of water, put over very low heat, and cover, tossing gently now and then.   SERVES 4

⌣⌣⌣⌣⌣⌣⌣⌣⌣⌣⌣⌣⌣⌣⌣⌣⌣⌣⌣⌣⌣⌣⌣⌣⌣⌣⌣⌣⌣⌣⌣⌣

From Vikram Doctor

1. Wash the poha gently but thoroughly under running water. Empty it into a bowl, cover generously with water, and leave to soak for 2 minutes. Drain and leave in a sieve set over a bowl.

2. Pour the oil into a medium, preferably nonstick pan and set over medium-high heat. When hot, add the urad dal and the asafetida. As soon as the dal begins to change color, add the mustard seeds. When they start to pop, a matter of seconds, add the cumin seeds and, a second later, the curry leaves (take care, as they will splutter). Quickly add the onions, green chilies, and turmeric. Reduce the heat to medium and fry for 3–4 minutes or until the onions are translucent.

3. Add the ginger and stir for a minute. Now add all the tomatoes, ½ teaspoon of the salt, and the sugar. Increase the heat to medium high and fry for 3–4 minutes or until the tomatoes have softened.

4. Add all the poha and sprinkle another ¼ teaspoon of salt over the top. Cook over low heat for 3–4 minutes, gently breaking up any lumps and tossing the mixture with a flat spatula, lifting the ingredients from the bottom and turning them over. Add a sprinkling of water now and then. When heated through, cover and set aside until you are ready to eat.

FLATTENED RICE WITH GREEN BEANS AND GINGER

SEM KA POHA UPMA

೭೨೭೨೭೨೭೨೭೨೭೨೭೨೭೨೭೨೭೨೭೨೭೨೭೨೭೨೭೨೭೨೭೨೭೨೭೨೭

2 medium waxy potatoes, boiled, cooled, and peeled

Salt

1½ cups green beans (rounded or flat), cut crosswise into pieces ¼ inch thick

3 cups thick poha (flattened rice)

3 tablespoons olive or peanut oil

Generous pinch of ground asafetida

¾ teaspoon urad dal

¾ teaspoon whole brown mustard seeds

¾ teaspoon whole cumin seeds

2 dried hot red chilies, or 2 fresh hot green chilies, finely chopped

10–15 fresh curry leaves, lightly crushed in your hand

1 small onion (3 oz), peeled and chopped

1 teaspoon peeled and very finely grated fresh ginger

¼ teaspoon ground turmeric

1 teaspoon sugar

1 tablespoon lime juice

2–3 tablespoons chopped fresh cilantro, to serve

Here is yet another variation of poha upma, this time with ginger-flavored green beans. By now you will know how to put flattened rice together with almost any vegetable and any flavoring of your choice.　　　　　　　　　　　　　SERVES 4

೭೨೭೨೭೨೭೨೭೨೭೨೭೨೭೨೭೨೭೨೭೨೭೨೭೨೭೨೭೨೭೨೭೨೭೨೭೨೭

1. Cut the potatoes into ½ inch dice.

2. Bring 4 cups water to a boil in a medium pan. Stir in 2 teaspoons salt, then add the beans and boil for 4 minutes. Drain and refresh under cold water. Set aside.

3. Wash the poha gently but thoroughly under running water. Empty it into a bowl, cover generously with water, and leave to soak for 2 minutes. Drain and leave in a sieve set over a bowl.

4. Put the oil into a large nonstick frying pan and set it over medium-high heat. When hot, add the asafetida and urad dal. As soon as the dal starts to pick up a little color, add the mustard seeds, cumin seeds, and chilies. As soon as the mustard seeds start to pop, add the curry leaves (take care, as they will splutter), then the onions, ginger, and turmeric. Stir for a minute and add the potatoes. Stir and fry over medium heat for 3–4 minutes, until the onions and potatoes are slightly browned. Sprinkle ¼ teaspoon of salt over the top. Mix gently, then gently stir in the beans.

5. Over low heat, add all the poha, gently breaking up any lumps. Sprinkle in 1 teaspoon of salt, then the sugar and lime juice. Mix gently, using a flat spatula, lifting the ingredients from the bottom and folding them over. Keep tossing this way and cooking for about 3–4 minutes or until the poha is heated through. Cover and set aside until you are ready to eat. Garnish with the fresh cilantro and serve.

BREAD UPMA

DOUBLE ROTI KA UPMA

᭡᭡᭡᭡᭡᭡᭡᭡᭡᭡᭡᭡᭡᭡᭡᭡᭡᭡᭡᭡᭡᭡᭡᭡᭡᭡᭡᭡᭡᭡᭡᭡᭡᭡

3 tablespoons olive or peanut
    oil

½ teaspoon urad dal

½ teaspoon whole brown
    mustard seeds

Generous pinch of ground
    asafetida

7–8 fresh curry leaves, lightly
    crushed in your hand

1 medium onion (5 oz), peeled
    and finely sliced

½–2 fresh hot green chilies,
    finely chopped

A ½-inch piece of fresh ginger,
    peeled and very finely
    diced

Generous pinch of ground
    turmeric

1 good-sized tomato (6 oz),
    chopped

Salt

4 large slices of whole-grain
    bread, cut or broken into
    ½ inch cubes

2 tablespoons chopped fresh
    cilantro

If you come in from work and are tired and hungry, this upma can be prepared in no time. With it you could have a light salad, a bowl of soup, or just a cup of hot tea. You can also serve it with eggs. It is a good way to use up day-old bread. I like to make my upma with whole-grain bread, but white bread will do as well.

SERVES 2–3

᭡᭡᭡᭡᭡᭡᭡᭡᭡᭡᭡᭡᭡᭡᭡᭡᭡᭡᭡᭡᭡᭡᭡᭡᭡᭡᭡᭡᭡᭡᭡᭡᭡᭡

From Jayanti Rajagopalan

1. Put the oil in a medium nonstick pan and set over medium heat. When it is hot, add the urad dal. As soon as the dal begins to take on color, add the mustard seeds and asafetida. When the seeds start to pop, a matter of seconds, throw in the curry leaves (take care, as they will splutter). A second later, add the onions, green chilies, and ginger. Stir and sauté for about 3 minutes or until the onions start to soften. Add the turmeric and stir once. Now add the tomatoes and a generous pinch of salt. Reduce the heat to medium low and cook, stirring now and then, until the tomato softens.

2. Add the bread and increase the heat to medium high. Stir briskly until the spice mixture coats the bread and all the ingredients are well mixed. Cover, reduce the heat, and cook over low heat for another 2–3 minutes. Check the salt, adding more if needed. Sprinkle the fresh cilantro over the top and serve.

QUINOA "UPMA" WITH CORN AND MINT

BHUTTA, PUDINA AUR QUINOA KA UPMA

ᶜᵇ

1 cup quinoa

3 tablespoons olive or peanut oil

Generous pinch of ground asafetida

½ teaspoon urad dal

½ teaspoon whole brown mustard seeds

½ teaspoon whole cumin seeds

1 dried hot red chili

10–15 fresh curry leaves, lightly crushed in your hand

½ large onion, peeled and chopped

¼ teaspoon ground turmeric

1 cup corn kernels, fresh (from 1–2 cobs) or frozen and cooked through

1–2 fresh hot green chilies, finely chopped

2 tablespoons chopped fresh cilantro

1 tablespoon finely chopped fresh mint

Salt and freshly ground black pepper

1 teaspoon sugar

1 tablespoon lime or lemon juice

Lime or lemon wedges, to serve

In South India, upmas are pilaf-like, well-spiced, savory dishes that can be made with different grains, such as semolina (sooji) and flattened rice (poha). I have discovered, completely by accident, that they can also be made with Western grains, such as quinoa. This tiny, nutritious seed needs to be cooked first and then stir-fried with the chosen vegetables and seasonings. Here I have used corn and mint. I like to use fresh corn in the summer, but frozen cooked corn kernels may be used during the rest of the year.

This upma can be served as a snack at any time of day with a cup of tea or coffee. It makes a perfect breakfast food or brunch item. For a light lunch, serve it with a green salad, to which you can add grapefruit or tomatoes, cucumbers, and peppers.

SERVES 4

ᶜᵇ

1. Pour 2 cups water into a pan and bring to a boil. Add the quinoa, stir, and cover. Cook gently over very low heat for 15 minutes. Turn off the heat and let the pan rest, covered, for another 15 minutes.

2. Put the oil into a large nonstick frying pan and set it over medium-high heat. When hot, add the asafetida and the urad dal. As soon as the dal starts to pick up a little color, add the mustard seeds, cumin seeds, and the red chili. When the mustard seeds start to pop and the chili darkens, a matter of seconds, add the curry leaves (take care, as they will splutter), then the onions and turmeric. Stir and fry over medium heat until the onions are slightly browned, 3–4 minutes. Add the corn, green chilies, fresh cilantro, mint, and a generous pinch of salt. Stir and cook gently for about 2 minutes.

3. Add the cooked quinoa, gently breaking up any lumps, and sprinkle ¾ teaspoon of salt, a few grinds of pepper, the sugar,

and the lime or lemon juice over the top. Cook over very low heat for 3–4 minutes, tossing frequently by lifting all the ingredients from the bottom with a flat spatula and folding them over. When the quinoa is heated through, check the seasonings and make the necessary adjustments. Cover and set aside until you are ready to eat. Reheat with sprinklings of water. Serve with lime or lemon wedges.

SEMOLINA UPMA WITH GREEN BEANS, PEAS, AND CARROTS

SOOJI KA UPMA

ɕɔɕɔɕɔɕɔɕɔɕɔɕɔɕɔɕɔɕɔɕɔɕɔɕɔɕɔɕɔɕɔɕɔɕɔ

1 cup semolina (see note on
    page 197)

2 tablespoons olive or peanut
    oil

½ teaspoon whole brown
    mustard seeds

1–2 hot red dried chilies

6–7 fresh curry leaves, lightly
    crushed in your hand

½ medium onion, peeled and
    chopped

1 fresh hot green chili, finely
    sliced (optional)

½ cup green beans, cut into
    rounds ⅓ inch thick

½ cup fresh peas or defrosted
    frozen peas

1 medium carrot, peeled and
    cut into ¼ inch dice

Salt

This dish is from south Karnataka. It can be served as a snack or for breakfast with a sprinkling of lime juice and a yogurt relish, or at lunch or dinner with a sambar (see page 166), as well as chutneys and relishes. I have also been known to serve it as a first course with, quite heretically, a generous sprinkling of Parmigiano Reggiano cheese.

To reheat, add a generous sprinkling of water as you stir and mix, breaking up lumps with the back of a wooden spoon. You should do this on medium or medium-low heat for 4–5 minutes or until it is heated through and soft.   SERVES 3–4

ɕɔɕɔɕɔɕɔɕɔɕɔɕɔɕɔɕɔɕɔɕɔɕɔɕɔɕɔɕɔɕɔɕɔɕɔ

From Swaranlatha and her mother, Rajalaxmi, in Mysore

1. Put a wok or medium frying pan over medium-high heat. When hot, add the semolina and stir it around for 3–4 minutes or until you get a roasted aroma. The semolina should not change color much. Transfer to a large bowl and set aside.

2. Clean out the pan and set over medium heat. Add the oil and, when it is hot, add the mustard seeds and red chilies. Stir until the seeds pop and the chilies darken, a few seconds. Add the curry leaves (take care, as they will splutter) and, a second later, the onions and green chilies (if using). Stir for a minute.

3. Add the beans, peas, and carrots and sauté for 2–3 minutes. Add 4 tablespoons of water and ¼ teaspoon of salt. Cover and cook over a low heat for about 4 minutes or until the vegetables are just done. Remove the lid and add 2¼ cups water and ¾ teaspoon of salt. Bring to a simmer over medium-high heat.

4. Pick up a fistful of semolina and begin adding it to the pan in a slow drizzle, stirring as you go. Keep doing this until all the semolina is used up. Never stop stirring. This will take about 5 minutes. Reduce the heat to medium low and keep stirring and breaking up lumps for another 2 minutes. Continue to stir and break up lumps, now over low heat, for another 3–4 minutes or until the upma is soft and fluffy. Serve immediately, or cover and reheat as suggested above.

"RISOTTO" OF DAL, RICE, AND VEGETABLES

GEELI KHICHRI

꘎꘎꘎꘎꘎꘎꘎꘎꘎꘎꘎꘎꘎꘎꘎꘎꘎꘎꘎꘎꘎꘎꘎꘎꘎꘎꘎꘎꘎꘎

1 cup moong dal (skinned and split mung beans), already cooked for stock as on page 2 (with the 5 cups of liquid already removed)

½ cup basmati or jasmine rice, washed in several changes of water and drained

1 teaspoon ground cumin

1 teaspoon ground coriander

½ teaspoon ground turmeric

¼ teaspoon nice red chili powder

1 medium onion, peeled and finely chopped

1½ cups cauliflower, finely chopped

1 cup fresh peas or defrosted frozen peas

1½ teaspoons salt

FOR THE TARKA

2 teaspoons olive or peanut oil or ghee (clarified butter)

Generous pinch of ground asafetida

¼ teaspoon whole brown mustard seeds

¼ teaspoon whole cumin seeds

2 dried hot red chilies

6 tablespoons tomato puree

Khichri is an ancient Indian dish made with the nutritious combination of dal and rice. If you add vegetables, it becomes a complete meal. It comes in a dry form, rather like rice, and a wet form, rather like a risotto or porridge. This is the latter.

I like to serve it spread out on an old-fashioned soup plate with a pat of butter or ghee, some lemon juice, some crisply fried shallot slivers, chopped green chilies, finely chopped fresh ginger, and a few pinches of garam masala on the top. You can serve this as a first course in small portions, or as a main course.

I originally made this dish with the dal left over from making the stock for Red Pepper and Tomato Soup (see page 2). If you have not made the soup and still want to make the "risotto," just combine 1 cup dal, rice, cumin, coriander, turmeric, chili powder, onions, ginger, cauliflower, peas, and 12 cups water in a big pan. Bring to a boil, cover partially, and simmer gently for 1½ hours, adding boiling water as needed if the porridge gets too thick. Stir more frequently when the porridge thickens. Add the salt and mix it in. Do the tarka (see page xxii) at the end.

SERVES 6

꘎꘎꘎꘎꘎꘎꘎꘎꘎꘎꘎꘎꘎꘎꘎꘎꘎꘎꘎꘎꘎꘎꘎꘎꘎꘎꘎꘎꘎꘎

1. Put the remaining dal in a large pan (the stock should already have been removed) and add all the other ingredients, apart from those for the tarka. Pour in 6 cups water and bring to a boil. Cover partially, lower the heat, and simmer gently for 45 minutes, stirring frequently as the mixture thickens, and mashing the vegetables a bit.

2. To make the tarka, put the oil in a small frying pan over medium heat. When hot, add the asafetida and, a second later, the mustard seeds. As soon as they pop, add the cumin seeds and red chilies. Stir until the chilies darken, then add the tomato puree. Stir once or twice, then pour the contents of the pan over the khichri. Stir and serve as suggested above.

GRAINS:

BREADS, PANCAKES, SAVORIES, AND NOODLES

CHAPATIS

ೞೞೞೞೞೞೞೞೞೞೞೞೞೞೞೞೞೞೞೞೞೞೞೞೞೞೞ

1 cup chapati flour, plus extra
for dusting
1 teaspoon olive or peanut oil

Chapatis are the simplest of flatbreads. The name "chapati" probably comes from the same source as the word *chapat*, which means "to slap." There is much slapping done as chapatis are made, and it is probable that initially the chapatis were not rolled out at all but simply slapped into shape. This is still done in many Indian villages.

Chapatis are made with finely ground whole-grain flour and eaten over a great area of North India. They can be thick or thin, small or large, depending on who is making them. In villages they tend to be large and thick, and are often called "roti." Most people in little towns and big cities seem to like them small and very thin. This delicate version of the chapati is also known as "phulka."

I have been making my chapatis the same way for the last sixty years. It is the way they were made at our home in Delhi when I was growing up. But this year I happened to travel to Mysore, where a woman I met, Zubaida Vagh, told me that she had worked out a no-fail way to make chapatis. It did not involve any gadgets, such as chapati/tortilla presses—the chapatis were still rolled out by hand—but the dough did have a tiny bit of oil in it. The difference lay mainly in the timing after the chapati is slapped onto the tava or cast-iron griddle. I have used this new method here. My directions may be long but the process is in fact quite fast and simple. A chapati cooks in a little over a minute.

Chapati flour is very finely ground. It is best to buy it from an Indian grocery, where it is also called "ata" (pronounced *ah-ta*), with many variations in the spelling, including "atta." You can put butter or ghee on the top of each chapati as soon as it is made, if you like. MAKES 6

ೞೞೞೞೞೞೞೞೞೞೞೞೞೞೞೞೞೞೞೞೞೞೞೞೞೞೞ

1. Put the flour into a large bowl. Dribble in the oil and rub it into the flour until you have a breadcrumb-like texture. Slowly add water (you will need about ½ cup water or a little bit less), mixing it to form a soft dough. Shape it into a ball and knead for 10 minutes or until smooth. Form into a smooth ball, cover with a damp cloth, and set aside for 30–60 minutes.

2. Knead the dough again for a few minutes, then divide into 6 equal balls. Flatten them slightly between your palms and cover them with a damp cloth.

3. Set a medium cast-iron frying pan or tava, an Indian griddle, over medium heat. Have a small wad of cloth handy, as well as a plate lined with a dish towel to put the chapatis in as they get made.

4. Dust your work surface with flour. Take one of the flattened balls, keeping the rest covered, and roll it out, flipping it over a few times and dusting it with flour whenever needed, until you have an even circle about 6 inches in diameter. Lay it on one palm and then slap it onto the other palm to get rid of the excess flour. Now slap the chapati onto the hot pan for just 5 seconds. Using a fine-edged spatula, turn it over and leave for about 30 seconds or until the bottom has a few nice brown spots. Flip the chapati again, this time pressing down on it with the wadded cloth, and turning it slightly with each press. These will be quick motions—press and turn slightly, press and turn, and so on—lasting only about another 30 seconds. The chapati should puff up, but even if it does not, it will be delicious. Put each chapati on one half of the towel and cover with the other half.

5. Make all chapatis this way, turning the heat down to medium low when you are doing the rolling, and turning it up again when you are almost ready to slap it onto the pan.

PLAIN DELHI PARATHAS

DILLI KAY TIKAUNAY PARATHAY

1 cup chapati flour, plus extra
for dusting

⅓ teaspoon salt

3–4 tablespoons olive or
peanut oil, melted butter,
or ghee (clarified butter)

Parathas are much richer than chapatis, so they tend not to be eaten on a daily basis. Not only are they layered with butter, oil, or ghee, but they are also cooked in it, like pancakes. However, like pancakes, they are utterly delicious, and one does need to succumb to them every now and then. They can be eaten at breakfast with pickles, chutneys, and relishes, or served at any meal with dals and vegetable dishes.

Parathas can be made plain, as in this recipe, or they can be stuffed with spiced potatoes, cauliflower, radishes, and even eggs. Some recipes for these follow. In the Delhi tradition, these parathas are triangular and made with whole-grain chapati flour, also sold by Indian grocers as "ata" (see page 219 for more about this flour).

MAKES 6

1. Put the flour and salt into a large bowl. Dribble in 2 teaspoons of the oil, butter, or ghee and rub it into the flour until it has a breadcrumb-like texture. Slowly add about ½ cup water, working it into the flour. You are aiming for a ball of soft dough, so you might not need all the water. Once the ball is formed, knead it for 10 minutes or until smooth. Shape it into a ball, oil or otherwise grease it, and slip it into a plastic bag. Set aside for 30–60 minutes.

2. Knead the dough again for a few minutes, then divide into 6 equal balls. Flatten them slightly between your palms and cover them with a damp cloth.

3. Set a medium cast-iron frying pan or tava over medium-low heat.

4. Meanwhile, dust your work surface with flour. Take one of the flattened balls, keeping the rest covered, and roll it out, flipping

it over a few times and dusting it with flour whenever needed, until you have an even circle about 6 inches in diameter. Brush it with about ½ teaspoon of the oil, butter, or ghee and fold it in half. Brush again with ¼ teaspoon of oil, butter, or ghee and fold in half again. Dusting with flour as needed, roll the triangle into a larger triangle, about 6 inches on each side. Lay it on one palm with your fingers spread out, then slap it onto the other palm to get rid of the excess flour.

5. Put 1 teaspoon of oil in the hot pan and slap the paratha right in the center. Dribble ½ teaspoon oil over it and cook for 45–60 seconds, until the paratha has golden-brown spots on the underside. Using a fine-edged spatula, turn it over and cook for another 45–60 seconds, until the second side has a few nice brown spots too. Flip the paratha again, leave for 10 seconds, then flip again and leave for another 10 seconds. It should now be done—crisp on the outside and soft and layered inside. Transfer to a large plate and cover with an upside-down plate.

6. Make all the parathas in the same way, taking the pan off the heat if it gets too hot as you do your rolling out, and then putting it back a little before you slap the next bread in.

EGG PARATHAS

UNDAY KAY PARATHAY

⌐⌐⌐⌐⌐⌐⌐⌐⌐⌐⌐⌐⌐⌐⌐⌐⌐⌐⌐⌐⌐⌐⌐⌐⌐⌐⌐⌐⌐⌐⌐⌐⌐⌐⌐⌐

1 cup chapati flour, plus extra for dusting

Salt

3–4 tablespoons olive or peanut oil, melted butter, or ghee (clarified butter)

4 eggs

2–4 fresh hot green chilies, finely chopped

3 tablespoons peeled and finely chopped shallots

4 cherry tomatoes, chopped

2 tablespoons chopped fresh cilantro

Freshly ground black pepper

4 generous pinches of garam masala

This is very similar to the previous recipe, except that this paratha is a bit larger and stuffed with spiced eggs. I love it for breakfast with Simple Yogurt Dipping Sauce (see page 328) and a cup of hot tea.   MAKES 4

⌐⌐⌐⌐⌐⌐⌐⌐⌐⌐⌐⌐⌐⌐⌐⌐⌐⌐⌐⌐⌐⌐⌐⌐⌐⌐⌐⌐⌐⌐⌐⌐⌐⌐⌐⌐

From Jayanti Rajagopalan

1. Put the flour and ⅓ teaspoon of salt into a large bowl. Dribble in 2 teaspoons of the oil, butter, or ghee and rub it into the flour until it has a breadcrumb-like texture. Slowly add about ½ cup water, working it into the flour. You are aiming for a ball of soft dough, so you might not need all the water. Once the ball is formed, knead it for 10 minutes or until smooth. Shape it into a ball, oil or otherwise grease it, and slip it into a plastic bag. Set aside for 30–60 minutes.

2. Knead the dough again for a few minutes and divide into 4 equal balls. Flatten them slightly between your palms and cover them with a damp cloth.

3. Break the eggs into 4 separate bowls and beat each one lightly. Put a quarter of the chilies, shallots, tomatoes, and cilantro into each bowl. Add some salt, pepper, and garam masala and mix well.

4. Set a medium cast-iron frying pan or tava, an Indian griddle, over medium-low heat.

5. Meanwhile, dust your work surface with flour. Take one of the flattened balls, keeping the rest covered, and roll it out, flipping it over a few times and dusting it with flour whenever needed, until you have an even circle about 7 inches in diameter. Brush it with about ½ teaspoon of the oil, butter, or ghee and fold it in

half. Brush again with ¼ teaspoon of oil, butter, or ghee and fold in half again. Dusting with flour as needed, roll the triangle into a larger triangle, about 7 inches on each side. Lay it on one palm with your fingers spread out, then slap it onto the other palm to get rid of the excess flour.

6. Put 1 teaspoon of oil in the hot pan and slap the paratha right in the center. Dribble ½ teaspoon of oil over it and cook for 45–60 seconds, until the paratha has golden-brown spots on the underside. Using a fine-edged spatula, turn it over and cook for another 30 seconds. Now lift the top flap of the paratha and pour 1 bowlful of egg mixture inside. It may not all fit, so keep the flap open and fold or scrape in the rest of the egg. Flip the paratha and leave for 20 seconds, then flip again and leave for 10 seconds. It should now be done. Transfer to a large plate and cover with an upside-down plate.

7. Make all the parathas in the same way, taking the pan off the heat if it gets too hot as you do your rolling out, and then putting it back a little before you slap the next bread in.

PARATHAS WITH AJOWAN SEEDS AND RED CHILI FLAKES

AJWAIN KAY PARATHAY

ტღტღტღტღტღტღტღტღტღტღტღტღტღტღტღტღტღტღტ

Pinch of ajowan seeds

Dash of red chili flakes

Follow the recipe for Plain Delhi Parathas (see page 221), but with the following difference.   MAKES 6

ტღტღტღტღტღტღტღტღტღტღტღტღტღტღტღტღტღტღტ

When you have rolled a paratha into a 6 inch circle and brushed it with ½ teaspoon of oil, butter, or ghee, sprinkle with the ajowan seeds and chili flakes before folding the circle in half. Ajowan (or ajwain) seeds have a thyme-like taste and smell, so you can use fresh thyme leaves—about ½ teaspoon for each paratha—if you prefer.

PARATHAS STUFFED WITH SPICED CAULIFLOWER

GOBI PARATHA

ოოოოოოოოოოოოოოოოოოოოოოოოოოოოოოოოოოოო

1 cup chapati flour, plus extra
　　for dusting

Salt

8 tablespoons olive or peanut
　　oil, melted butter, or ghee
　　(clarified butter)

1 tablespoon peeled and finely
　　chopped shallot or onion

1½ cups grated cauliflower
　　(see introduction)

1–2 fresh hot green chilies,
　　finely chopped

A 1-inch piece of fresh ginger,
　　peeled and very finely
　　chopped

About 1 teaspoon garam
　　masala

About ¼ teaspoon nice red
　　chili powder

Great in the school lunch box or as travel food, these parathas are also among my favorite Sunday breakfast dishes. All I need with them is Simple Yogurt Dipping Sauce (see page 328) and some hot tea.

When grating the cauliflower, use the largest hole in the grater and grate just the florets, not the stems. Any bigger pieces that break and fall in can be finely chopped by hand. MAKES 6

ოოოოოოოოოოოოოოოოოოოოოოოოოოოოოოოოოოოო

1. Put the flour and ½ teaspoon salt into a large bowl. Dribble in 2 teaspoons of the oil, melted butter, or ghee and rub it into the flour until it has a breadcrumb-like texture. Slowly add about ½ cup water, working it into the flour. You are aiming for a ball of soft dough, so you might not need all the water. Once the ball is formed, knead it for 10 minutes or until smooth. Shape it into a ball, oil or otherwise grease it, and slip it into a plastic bag. Set aside for 30–60 minutes.

2. Meanwhile, make the stuffing: combine the shallots or onions, cauliflower, green chilies, and ginger in a bowl and mix them together.

3. Knead the dough again for a few minutes and divide into 6 equal balls. Flatten them slightly between your palms and cover them with a damp cloth.

4. Set a cast-iron frying pan or tava, an Indian griddle, over medium heat.

5. Meanwhile, dust your work surface with flour. Take one of the flattened balls, keeping the rest covered, and roll it out, flipping it over a few times and dusting it with flour whenever needed, until you have an even circle about 5½ inches in diameter. Brush

it with about 1 teaspoon of the oil, butter, or ghee. Put 2 heaping tablespoons of the cauliflower mixture in the center and sprinkle with a little salt, garam masala, and chili powder. Make folds all around the edges to form a pouch. Pinch the folds together and give the top a twist for good measure. Dusting with flour as needed, and with the twisted side down, roll out the pouch until it is 5½ inches in diameter. Lay the paratha on one palm and then slap it onto the other palm to get rid of the excess flour.

6. Put 1 teaspoon of oil in the hot pan and slap the paratha, folds side down, right in the center. Dribble ½ teaspoon of oil over it, then press down with your spatula and cook for about 1 minute, until the paratha has golden-brown spots on the underside. Turn it over, pressing down on it again, and leave for another minute or more or until the second side has a few nice brown spots too. Some of the cauliflower might get exposed, but that's fine. Flip the paratha again, this time for 5 seconds, and then again for another 5 seconds. It should now be done. Transfer to a large plate and cover with an upside-down plate.

7. Make all the parathas in the same way, taking the pan off the heat if it gets too hot as you do your rolling out, and then putting it back a little before you slap the next bread in.

PARATHAS WITH RINGS

LACHCHHEYDAR PARATHA

୧୧୧୧୧୧୧୧୧୧୧୧୧୧୧୧୧୧୧୧୧୧୧୧୧୧୧୧୧୧

This paratha is layered in rings.   MAKES 6

୧୧୧୧୧୧୧୧୧୧୧୧୧୧୧୧୧୧୧୧୧୧୧୧୧୧୧୧୧୧

1 cup chapati flour, plus extra for dusting

⅓ teaspoon salt

½ teaspoon sugar

About 6 tablespoons ghee (clarified butter) or olive or peanut oil

About ½ cup warm milk (use only as much as is needed to make a soft dough)

1. Put the flour, salt, and sugar into a large bowl. Dribble in 1 teaspoon of the ghee or oil and rub it into the flour until it resembles breadcrumbs. Slowly add the milk, mixing it in and gathering the flour into a ball. You are aiming for soft dough, so you might not need all the milk. Once the dough is formed, knead it for 10 minutes or until smooth. Shape it into a ball, oil or otherwise grease it, and slip it into a plastic bag. Set aside for 30–60 minutes.

2. Knead the dough again for a few minutes and divide into 6 equal balls. Flatten them slightly between your palms and cover them with a damp cloth.

3. Set a medium cast-iron frying pan or tava, an Indian griddle, over medium-low heat.

4. Meanwhile, dust your work surface with flour. Take one of the flattened balls, keeping the rest covered, and roll it out, flipping it over a few times and dusting it with flour whenever needed, until you have an even circle about 6½ inches in diameter. Brush it with about ½ teaspoon of the ghee or oil, then dust it lightly with flour. Now pleat it tightly toward you, making ½ inch folds, as if making a fan. Stand the pleated paratha on its long edge and roll into a tight pinwheel, tucking the end in firmly. Flatten the pinwheel, dust with flour as needed, and roll into a circle about 6½ inches in diameter. Lay it on one palm with your fingers spread out, then slap it onto the other palm to get rid of the excess flour.

5. Put 1 teaspoon of the ghee or oil in the hot pan and slap the paratha right in the center. Dribble ½ teaspoon of oil over it and

cook for 35–45 seconds or until the paratha has golden-brown spots on the underside. Using a fine-edged spatula, turn it over and cook for another 35–45 seconds or until the second side has a few nice brown spots too. Flip the paratha again, this time for 10 seconds, and then again for another 10 seconds. It should now be done, crisp on the outside and soft and layered inside. Transfer to a large plate and cover with an upside-down plate.

6. Make all the parathas in the same way, taking the pan off the heat if it gets too hot as you do your rolling out, and then putting it back a little before you slap the next bread in.

MARWARI LAYERED GRIDDLE BREADS

MARWARI TAVEY KI ROTI OR BATIA

ᏮᏮᏮᏮᏮᏮᏮᏮᏮᏮᏮᏮᏮᏮᏮᏮᏮᏮᏮᏮᏮᏮᏮᏮᏮᏮᏮᏮᏮᏮᏮᏮ

1 cup chapati flour, plus extra
 for dusting

⅓ teaspoon salt

¾ teaspoon ground cumin

1 or 2 generous pinches of
 nice red chili powder

Pinch of nigella seeds (kalonji,
 optional)

Pinch of ajowan seeds
 (optional)

About 6 tablespoons olive
 or peanut oil or ghee
 (clarified butter)

Very easy to make, this is really a layered paratha, only the layers are circular. I like to serve it with Potatoes Cooked in a Banarasi Style or Marwari Style (see pages 107 and 108), Cauliflower with Peas (see page 75), any simple dal, and a yogurt relish. It is also a wonderful bread to take out on picnics, carry on train journeys, and put into lunch boxes, as Indians often do. All you need to add is a vegetable dish and an Indian relish.

Marwaris (see page 108 for more about this community) tend to make this bread with ghee, but you can use oil if you prefer. I do.   MAKES 6

ᏮᏮᏮᏮᏮᏮᏮᏮᏮᏮᏮᏮᏮᏮᏮᏮᏮᏮᏮᏮᏮᏮᏮᏮᏮᏮᏮᏮᏮᏮᏮᏮ

From Vinita Pittie's home

1. Put the flour into a large bowl. Add the salt, cumin, chili powder, and nigella and ajowan seeds (if using). Dribble in 1 teaspoon of the oil or ghee and rub it into the flour until it has a breadcrumb-like texture. Slowly add about ½ cup water, working it into the flour. You are aiming for a ball of soft dough, so you might not need all the water. Once the ball is formed, knead it for 10 minutes or until smooth. Shape it into a ball, oil or otherwise grease it, and slip it into a plastic bag. Set aside for 30–60 minutes.

2. Knead the dough again for a few minutes and divide into 6 equal balls. Flatten them slightly between your palms and cover them with a damp cloth.

3. Set a medium cast-iron frying pan or tava, an Indian griddle, over medium-low heat.

4. Meanwhile, dust your work surface with flour. Take one of the flattened balls, keeping the rest covered, and roll it out, flipping it over a few times and dusting it with flour whenever

needed, until you have an even circle about 6½ inches in diameter. Brush it with about ½ teaspoon of the oil or ghee, then roll it tightly inward, forming a snake. Now roll the snake into a tight pinwheel, tucking in the end firmly. Dusting with flour as needed, roll out the pinwheel into a circle about 6½ inches in diameter. Lay it on one palm with your fingers spread out, then slap it onto the other palm to get rid of the excess flour.

5. Put 1 teaspoon of oil in the hot pan and slap the bread right in the center. Dribble ½ teaspoon of oil over it and cook for 35–45 seconds or until the bread has golden-brown spots on the underside. Using a fine-edged spatula, turn it over and cook for another 35–45 seconds or until the second side has a few nice brown spots too. Flip the bread again, this time for 10 seconds, then again for another 10 seconds. It should now be done, crisp on the outside and soft and layered inside. Transfer to a large plate and cover with an upside-down plate.

6. Make all the parathas in the same way, taking the pan off the heat if it gets too hot as you do your rolling out, and then putting it back a little before you slap the next bread in.

A Banjara woman in Andhra grinds millet for bread.

PUFFED FRIED BREADS

POORI

᪑᪑᪑᪑᪑᪑᪑᪑᪑᪑᪑᪑᪑᪑᪑᪑᪑᪑᪑᪑᪑᪑᪑᪑᪑᪑᪑᪑

2 cups chapati flour, plus extra
    for dusting
½ teaspoon salt
1 tablespoon olive or peanut
    oil, plus more for deep-
    frying

These very popular breads are reserved for special occasions—festivals, weddings, picnics, train journeys, and even Sunday breakfasts! They are generally eaten with potatoes and other vegetables, just as chapatis might be. As they are rich (traditionalists cook them in pure ghee), they are not eaten every day. Using whole milk rather than water to make the dough keeps them nice and pliable, especially if you are taking them to work or school, or are traveling with them.

These breads are always deep-fried in an Indian karhai, which most resembles a wok but is a bit deeper. It uses oil in the most economical manner, but you can use a wok or a deep frying pan instead.

MAKES 12

᪑᪑᪑᪑᪑᪑᪑᪑᪑᪑᪑᪑᪑᪑᪑᪑᪑᪑᪑᪑᪑᪑᪑᪑᪑᪑᪑᪑

1. Put the flour and salt into a bowl and mix lightly. Dribble in the oil and rub it into the flour evenly. Slowly add about ½ to 1 cup water or whole milk, working it into the flour. You are aiming for a soft dough, so you might not need all the liquid. Once the dough is formed, knead it for 10 minutes or until smooth. Shape it into a ball, oil or otherwise grease it, and slip it into a plastic bag. Set aside for 30–60 minutes. You could even refrigerate it and hold it longer.

2. Shortly before you are ready to eat, pour a 1½ inch depth of oil into a karhai, wok, or frying pan and set it over medium heat.

3. Meanwhile, knead the dough again and divide into 12 equal balls. Flatten them slightly between your palms and cover them with a damp cloth.

4. Dust the work surface very lightly with the flour. Take one of the flattened balls, keeping the rest covered, and roll it out,

CHILI MARKET: chilies being sold in sacks

flipping it over a few times and dusting it with flour whenever needed, until you have a 5½ inch circle. When the oil is very hot, carefully lay the poori on the surface. It may sink to the bottom, but will rise to the top again immediately and start to sizzle. Using the back of a slotted spoon, push the poori gently into the oil with tiny, swift strokes. In just seconds it should puff up. Turn it over and cook the second side for a few seconds. Remove with a slotted spoon and transfer to a platter lined with a paper towel.

5. Make all the pooris in the same way and serve them hot. If you wish to serve them later, stack them and keep them covered. When cool, place in an airtight tin or ziplock bag.

PUFFED FRIED LEAVENED BREADS

BHATURA

2 cups flour, plus extra for
dusting
½ teaspoon baking powder
¼ teaspoon baking soda
½ teaspoon sugar
¼ teaspoon salt
1 teaspoon olive or peanut oil,
plus extra for deep-frying
6 tablespoons plain yogurt

If you have ever eaten the fried dough served by Native Americans, you will find this very similar. Bhaturas are a lot like pooris (see previous recipe), except that the leavening makes their texture a bit spongier. They are a speciality of the Punjab, where they are often served with chickpea dishes. Add the Tomato, Onion, and Cucumber Koshambari (see page 341) and a yogurt relish, and you have a fine lunch in front of you. I also love bhaturas with cauliflower and potato dishes.

Ideally, they should be eaten hot, as soon as they are made. If you cannot do that, line a plate with a paper towel, stack the bhaturas one on top of the other as they are made, and keep covered all the time with an upside-down plate.

If you have children waiting impatiently as you are preparing dinner, give them a small piece of a bhatura dusted with a little confectioner's sugar. It will bring smiles. MAKES 8

1. Put the flour, baking powder, baking soda, sugar, and salt into a large wide bowl and mix lightly with your fingers. Add the teaspoon of oil and all the yogurt. Mix until the dough is crumbly but still loose. Add about 2½ tablespoons of water and gather the dough together to make a smooth ball. Knead for a few minutes. Wash your hands, then put a little oil on them and rub it on the ball. Knead for another 8–10 minutes, until smooth. Rub a little more oil on the ball and slip it into a plastic bag. Set aside 40–60 minutes or longer if you wish.

2. Shortly before you are ready to eat, pour a 1½ inch depth of oil into a karhai, wok, or frying pan and set it over medium heat.

3. Meanwhile, knead the dough again and divide into 8 equal balls. Flatten them slightly between your palms and cover with a damp cloth.

4. Dust the work surface very lightly with the flour. Take one of the flattened balls, keeping the rest covered, and roll it out, flipping it over a few times and dusting it with flour whenever needed, until you have a 5 inch circle. When the oil is very hot, carefully lay it on the surface of the oil. It may sink to the bottom, but it will rise back to the top immediately and start to sizzle. Using the back of a slotted spoon, push the bhatura gently into the oil with tiny, swift strokes. In just seconds it should puff up. Turn it over and cook the second side for a few seconds. Remove with a slotted spoon and transfer to a platter lined with a paper towel.

5. Make all the bhaturas in the same way, taking the pan off the heat if it gets too hot as you do your rolling out, then putting it back a little before you slap the next bread in. Serve the bhaturas hot. If you wish to serve them later, stack them and keep them covered. When cool, place in an airtight tin or ziplock bag.

SOOJI PANCAKES

RAVA DOSA

ᏈᏈᏈᏈᏈᏈᏈᏈᏈᏈᏈᏈᏈᏈᏈᏈᏈᏈᏈᏈᏈᏈᏈᏈᏈᏈᏈᏈᏈᏈᏈᏈ

½ cup plain yogurt

1 cup sooji (see page 197)

½ cup rice flour (also called
  rice powder)

2 tablespoons flour

1 teaspoon salt

About 4 tablespoons olive or
  peanut oil

2–3 tablespoons chopped
  fresh cilantro (optional)

1 fresh hot green chili, finely
  chopped (optional)

½ teaspoon whole cumin
  seeds (optional)

These pancakes are soft, satiny, and filled with tiny depressions. They are very similar to crêpes, but spongier and much easier to prepare. Excellent in their savory form with Potato and Onion Mélange (see page 99) stuffed inside them, they are just as good served as a dessert in their sweet form (see page 379). They may also be served plain for breakfast, with chutneys and a yogurt relish. If you are going to stuff them, you do not need to add any seasoning other than the salt.   MAKES 12

ᏈᏈᏈᏈᏈᏈᏈᏈᏈᏈᏈᏈᏈᏈᏈᏈᏈᏈᏈᏈᏈᏈᏈᏈᏈᏈᏈᏈᏈᏈᏈᏈ

1. Empty the yogurt into a bowl. Using a fork or whisk, beat it lightly until smooth and creamy. Slowly add 2½ cups water, mixing it well as you go.

2. Put the sooji, rice flour, flour, and salt in a separate and larger bowl. Slowly add the yogurt-water combination, mixing it in until everything is thoroughly blended and there are no lumps. Set aside for at least 1 hour. A little longer is fine too.

3. When you're ready to cook, put the oil in a small bowl and stick a teaspoon in it. Set a nonstick frying pan over medium heat and add 1 teaspoon of oil. Meanwhile, add the cilantro, green chilies, and cumin seeds (if using) to the batter and stir well. Measure ⅓ cup water into a ladle and mentally note the level to get an idea of how much batter you will need each time. Take a ladleful of the batter and pour it slowly into the pan, letting it expand into a circle about 6 inches in diameter. This batter is very forgiving, so you can fill up any holes and round off the pancake to get the shape you want. Let it cook for a minute or so, until golden red on the underside. Flip the pancake over and cook for another minute or so, until the second side is golden red as well.

4. If you are serving the pancake plain and unstuffed, lift it with a spatula and slide it onto a plate. It is best eaten fresh.

5. If you are stuffing the pancake, flip it onto a plate, place the stuffing on it slightly to one side, and roll it up like a wrap.

6. Make only as many pancakes as you need, remembering to stir the batter thoroughly each time. The batter can be stored in the refrigerator for several days.

RICE FLOUR AND FLATTENED RICE PANCAKES

CHAWAL KAY ATA AUR POHA KAY DOSAY

იო

1 cup rice flour (also called
　　rice powder)

½ cup plain yogurt

2 tablespoons flattened rice/
　　thick poha (see page 195)

½ teaspoon salt

Pinch of ground asafetida

1 teaspoon peeled and finely
　　grated fresh ginger

Coarsely ground black pepper

1–2 fresh green chilies (such
　　as bird's-eye), very finely
　　chopped

2–3 tablespoons chopped
　　fresh cilantro

About 1 tablespoon olive or
　　peanut oil

I love all Indian savory pancakes that can be included in the general category known as "dosas." And I am always looking for dosas that do not need fermentation, as they are far easier to make. Here is just such a dosa. It is made mainly with rice flour and can be eaten as a snack with chutneys, pickles, and swigs of hot tea, of course, or like a chapati as part of a meal.

These dosas are made rather like crêpes. It is best to eat them as soon as they are made. Each takes less than 2 minutes to cook, so make a stack and then sit down to eat.

MAKES 7–8 SMALL DOSAS

იო

From Rita D'Souza

1. Put the rice flour in a bowl and add the yogurt, poha, salt, asafetida, and ¾ cup water. Mix well, then set aside for 15 minutes. Pour the mixture into a blender and whiz until smooth. Pour it back into a clean, dry bowl and add the ginger, black pepper, chilies, and cilantro. Mix, cover, and set aside for 2 hours.

2. When you're ready to cook, check your batter. It should be a flowing, creamy mixture, rather like the one for crêpes. I usually need to add another tablespoon of water to it at this stage to thin it out a bit. Mix well.

3. Line two large plates with a paper towel and place them near you. Pour the oil into a small bowl, stick a teaspoon in it, and set that nearby too. Place a 6 inch nonstick frying pan over medium heat and brush it with a little oil. Measure ⅓ cup water into a ladle and mentally note the level to get an idea of how much batter you will need each time. When the pan is hot, dip your ladle into the batter, stir it around, and pick up the measured amount.

Pour the batter into the center of the frying pan, quickly tilting it to make the batter flow to the edges. Let the dosa sit there for 45–60 seconds, until the top is set. Little bubbles may appear and the underside should get nice reddish spots. Pour a few drops of oil over it and around the edges, then turn and cook the second side for another 45 seconds. Using a spatula, transfer it to a prepared plate and cover with the other prepared plate.

4. Make all the dosas in the same way, stacking them on top of each other between the paper-lined plates. Serve immediately.

RICE FLOUR PANCAKES
CHAWAL KAY ATA KAY DOSAY

༄ཉ༄ཉ༄ཉ༄ཉ༄ཉ༄ཉ༄ཉ༄ཉ༄ཉ༄ཉ༄ཉ༄ཉ༄ཉ༄ཉ༄ཉ༄ཉ

½ cup plain yogurt

1 cup rice flour (also called
rice powder)

½ teaspoon salt

About 3 tablespoons olive or
peanut oil

2 tablespoons finely chopped
fresh cilantro

1–2 fresh hot green chilies,
finely chopped

1 tablespoon peeled and finely
chopped shallot

Eaten for breakfast or as a snack food, these are served with chutneys and pickles. You can also wrap them around any vegetable dish of your choice and serve them at lunch with a salad.

MAKES 8

༄ཉ༄ཉ༄ཉ༄ཉ༄ཉ༄ཉ༄ཉ༄ཉ༄ཉ༄ཉ༄ཉ༄ཉ༄ཉ༄ཉ༄ཉ༄ཉ

From Rita D'Souza

1. Empty the yogurt into a bowl. Using a fork or whisk, beat it lightly until smooth and creamy. Slowly add 1½ cups water, mixing it well as you go.

2. Put the rice flour and salt in a separate and larger bowl. Slowly add the yogurt-water combination, mixing it in until everything is thoroughly blended and there are no lumps. Set aside for 1–2 hours. A little longer is fine too.

3. When you're ready to cook, put the oil in a small bowl and stick a teaspoon in it. Set a nonstick frying pan over medium heat and add 1 teaspoon oil. Meanwhile, add the cilantro, green chilies, and shallots to the batter and stir well. Measure ⅓ cup water into a ladle and mentally note the level to get an idea of how much batter you will need each time. Take a ladleful of the batter and pour it slowly into the pan, letting it expand into a circle about 6 inches in diameter. This batter is very forgiving so you can fill up any holes and round off the pancake to get the shape you want. Let it cook for about 2 minutes or until the underside is golden red. Flip it over and cook the other side for another 2 minutes or so, until it is golden red as well. Pick up the pancake with a spatula and slide it onto a plate. You can fold

it in half and then into quarters if you wish. Keep covered as you make the other pancakes in the same way, remembering to stir the batter thoroughly each time.

4. Make only as many pancakes as you need. The batter can be stored in the refrigerator for several days.

SAVORY WHOLE-WHEAT PANCAKES

ATA KAY DOSAY

꽃꽃꽃꽃꽃꽃꽃꽃꽃꽃꽃꽃꽃꽃꽃꽃꽃꽃꽃꽃꽃꽃꽃꽃꽃꽃

1 cup chapati flour or ordinary whole-wheat flour

¼ teaspoon salt

¼ teaspoon nice red chili powder

½ teaspoon ground coriander

¼ teaspoon whole cumin seeds

½ medium tomato, finely diced

4 tablespoons peeled and finely chopped onion

1 fresh hot green chili, finely chopped

3 tablespoons chopped fresh cilantro

About 3 tablespoons olive or peanut oil or ghee (clarified butter)

These pancakes are similar to crêpes except that they are made with whole-wheat flour, well spiced, and eggless. Very popular in Maharashtra and along India's west coast, they are generally eaten for breakfast with chutneys, yogurt relishes, and pickles. They can also be served at lunch or dinner as flatbreads.

The pancakes are best served fresh, as soon as they are made, when they are both crisp and flexible. If you cannot manage that, stack them one on top of the other on a plate as you make them and keep them well covered with an upside-down plate. To freeze them, slip a layer of parchment paper or waxed paper between each pancake, allowing more of the paper for the top and the bottom, and let them cool completely. Slide the whole bundle into a ziplock bag and freeze flat. Defrost before reheating, then slap the pancakes, one at a time, onto a hot cast-iron griddle or frying pan, giving each a few seconds on both sides until nice and hot.

MAKES 7

꽃꽃꽃꽃꽃꽃꽃꽃꽃꽃꽃꽃꽃꽃꽃꽃꽃꽃꽃꽃꽃꽃꽃꽃꽃꽃

1. Put the flour, salt, chili powder, and ground coriander into a bowl. Slowly add about 1 cup water, mixing with a wooden spoon and breaking up lumps as you go, until you have a thinnish, smooth batter. Alternatively, whiz the ingredients in a blender, putting the water in first, then the flour and ground seasonings. Transfer to a bowl. Set the batter aside for 2 hours. Add all the other ingredients except the oil and stir to mix.

2. When you're ready to cook, put the oil in a small bowl and stick a teaspoon in it. Place a 6 inch nonstick frying pan over medium heat and add ½ teaspoon of oil. (The pan I use is 7 inches at the widest part of the diameter, but narrows at the bottom.) Measure ⅓ cup water into a ladle and mentally note the level to get an idea of how much batter you will need each

time. When the frying pan is hot, stir the batter from the bottom and pour a ladleful of it into the center of the pan. Tilt the pan quickly in all directions until the mixture reaches the edges. Any holes may be quickly filled in with a little bit of extra batter. Cook for about 2 minutes, dribbling another ½ teaspoon oil over the top of the pancake. Peek underneath to see if the pancake has turned golden red. Slide a fine-edged spatula all the way under the pancake to loosen it and flip it over. Cook the second side for another 1½–2 minutes, pressing down in the center with the back of a spatula. This side should have many brownish-red spots. Turn the pancake over twice more, leaving it for just a few seconds each time. Put the pancake on a large plate and cover with an upside-down plate.

3. Make all the pancakes in the same way and serve immediately, if possible.

CHICKPEA FLOUR AND TOMATO PANCAKES

BESAN TAMATAR OMLATE

cacacacacacacacacacacacacacacacacacacacacacacacacaca

1 cup chickpea flour (besan or
   gram flour)

¾ teaspoon salt

¼ teaspoon ground turmeric

¼ teaspoon nice red chili
   powder

Generous pinch of ground
   asafetida

¼ teaspoon garam masala

1 cup tomato, finely diced

1 medium onion, peeled and
   finely diced

1 fresh hot green chili, finely
   chopped (use more if you
   wish)

About 3 tablespoons olive or
   peanut oil

In western India, many vegetarians refer to this dish as an omelet, and eat it with toast and tea or coffee. It can be eaten for breakfast, or even as a snack. Chutneys are always offered on the side.

Follow the introduction to the preceding recipe for instructions on making these pancakes ahead of time.   MAKES ABOUT 7

cacacacacacacacacacacacacacacacacacacacacacacacacaca

1. Sift the flour, salt, turmeric, chili powder, asafetida, and garam masala into a bowl. Slowly add about 1¼ cups water, mixing with a wooden spoon and breaking up any lumps as you go, until you have a thin, smooth batter. Alternatively, whiz the ingredients in a blender, putting the water in first, then the flour and ground seasonings. Transfer to a bowl. Set the batter aside for 2 hours. Add all the other ingredients, except the oil, and stir to mix.

2. When you're ready to cook, put the oil in a small bowl and stick a teaspoon in it. Place a 6 inch nonstick frying pan over medium heat and add ½ teaspoon of oil. (The pan I use is 7 inches at the widest part of the diameter, but narrows at the bottom.) Measure ⅓ cup water into a ladle and mentally note the level to get an idea of how much batter you will need each time. When the oil is hot, stir the batter from the bottom and pour a ladleful of it into the center of the pan. Tilt the pan quickly in all directions until the mixture reaches the edges. Any holes and empty spaces can be quickly filled with a little bit of extra batter. Cook for about 2 minutes, dribbling another ½ teaspoon of oil over the top of the pancake. Peek underneath to see if the pancake has turned golden red. Slide a fine-edged plastic spatula all the way under the pancake to loosen it and flip it over. Cook the second side for another 1½–2 minutes, pressing down in the

center with the back of a spatula. This side should have many brownish-red spots. Turn the pancake over twice more, leaving it for just a few seconds each time. Put the pancake on a large plate and cover with an upside-down plate.

3. Make all the pancakes in the same way and serve immediately, if possible.

WHOLE MUNG BEAN PANCAKES

PESARATTU

∽∾∽∾∽∾∽∾∽∾∽∾∽∾∽∾∽∾∽∾∽∾∽∾∽∾∽∾∽∾∽∾∽∾∽∾

1 cup whole mung beans

15 or so whole fenugreek seeds

1–3 fresh hot green chilies, chopped

A ¾-inch piece of fresh ginger, peeled and finely chopped

Generous pinch of ground asafetida

½ teaspoon ground cumin

Handful of fresh cilantro leaves

1 teaspoon salt

¼ teaspoon ground turmeric

1 tablespoon rice flour (also called rice powder)

About 6 tablespoons olive or peanut oil

One of the glories of Andhra Pradesh, these highly nutritious pancakes are made for breakfast with great flourish at the grand Falaknuma Palace Hotel in Hyderabad, right in front of the guests who order them. A ladleful of mung batter is dropped onto a massive oiled griddle. It is spread out quickly using the back of the ladle with a spiral motion, so it thins out like a crêpe into a very large oval. Finely sliced onions and peppers may be strewn over the top, and the crisp pancake served at once with a chutney such as Fresh Cilantro, Ginger, and Coconut Chutney (see page 310). Guests just gobble them up.

Pesarattus are equally popular with less affluent locals traveling on the highways of Andhra. A family of three riding on one motorbike may decide to jump off it as they get tempted by a pesarattu stand on the roadside. I never can resist one. Here several griddles are set up to take many different types of orders. You can have it plain, with chutneys and podis (dry chutneys) or slathered with a thin layer of semolina upma (a savory, spicy porridge; see page 212) and folded over. One order came in for an egg pesarattu. For this, an egg was broken over the pancake and spread around, some podi was sprinkled over the top, and the pesarattu was turned over to let the egg cook. I decided to try one too. It was delicious.

The batter for this plain pesarattu, as all others, can be made a day ahead, covered, and refrigerated. It can also be frozen.

MAKES ABOUT 9

∽∾∽∾∽∾∽∾∽∾∽∾∽∾∽∾∽∾∽∾∽∾∽∾∽∾∽∾∽∾∽∾∽∾∽∾

From the Taj Falaknuma Palace hotel

1. Put the beans and fenugreek seeds into a bowl and wash them in several changes of water. Drain, then cover generously in fresh water and soak for 5–6 hours. Drain and put into a

blender. Add the chilies, ginger, asafetida, cumin, cilantro, salt, ¾ cup water, and the turmeric. Blend for several minutes, pushing down with a spatula when necessary, until you have a pancake-like batter. It will not be smooth, but the beans should be well ground. Add the rice flour, blend again, and empty into a bowl.

2. Put the oil in a small bowl and stick a teaspoon in it. Have two plates nearby to hold the pancakes as they are made. Measure ⅓ cup water into a ladle and mentally note the level to get an idea of how much batter you will need each time.

3. Add about 3 tablespoons of water to the batter and mix well. It should now be like flowing cream but with a lot of texture.

4. Set a medium nonstick frying pan over medium-low heat and add a teaspoon of the oil. When hot, stir the batter from the bottom and pour a ladleful into the center of the pan. Let it sit for a second or so, then lightly use the ladle or the back of a spoon to spread it outward in a continuous spiral motion. When it is about 5 inches in diameter, use a plastic spatula to spread the batter outward from the center as if scraping it to the edges. Spread evenly, using a light touch so you do not disturb the bottom layer. Aim for a diameter of 7–8 inches. Dribble a teaspoon of oil on the top and just outside the rim of the pancake, cover with a lid, and cook for about 2 minutes or until the underside has turned golden red. Flip the pancake over and cook the other side, uncovered, for 1 minute. Either serve right away or put the cooked pancake on a plate and cover with the second plate.

5. Make all the pancakes in the same way, stirring the batter from the bottom each time you make a new one.

WHOLE MUNG BEAN PANCAKES WITH EGG

GUDDU PESARATTU

ↄↄ

1 recipe Whole Mung Bean
    Pancake batter (see page
    250)
About 6 tablespoons olive or
    peanut oil, for frying

TOPPING PER PANCAKE

1 egg
¼ teaspoon Dry Chutney
    Made with Three Dals (see
    page 313), or a little salt,
    black pepper, and nice red
    chili powder

These pancakes are made exactly like those in the previous recipe except that they are topped with an egg. Serve with a fresh chutney. MAKES ABOUT 9

ↄↄ

Follow the previous recipe until you have spread out the batter to the required 7–8 inches. Now crack an egg and drop it onto the center of the pancake. Break the yolk with one edge of your spatula and quickly spread the egg out over the whole pancake. Dribble 1 teaspoon oil over the top and along the outside of the rim. Sprinkle the dry chutney over the egg, then cover with a lid and cook for 2 minutes. Uncover, turn the pancake over, and cook with the lid off for 1 minute. Serve immediately.

WHOLE MUNG BEAN PANCAKES WITH SHALLOTS AND PEPPERS

ULIPAYA PESARATTU

~~~~~~

1 recipe Whole Mung Bean
Pancake batter (see
page 250)
About 6 tablespoons olive or
peanut oil, for frying

TOPPING PER PANCAKE
1 tablespoon finely sliced
shallots
About 1 tablespoon finely
julienned red peppers
¼ teaspoon Dry Chutney
Made with Three Dals (see
page 313), or Spicy Peanut
Crumble (see page 311), or
a little salt, black pepper,
and nice red chili powder

Again, these pancakes are made exactly like the basic recipe for whole Mung Bean Pancakes, but are topped with finely sliced shallots and peppers. Those who like their food really spicy can add a few slivers of hot green chilies as well. Serve with a fresh chutney.   MAKES ABOUT 9

~~~~~~

From the Taj Falaknuma Palace hotel in Hyderabad

Follow the Whole Mung Bean Pancake recipe until you have spread out the batter to the required 7–8 inches. Now spread the shallots and peppers evenly over the top and press them in with the back of a spatula. Dribble 1 teaspoon of oil over the top and along the outside of the rim. Sprinkle the dry chutney over the shallots and peppers, then cover with a lid and cook for 2 minutes. Uncover, turn the pancake over, and cook with the lid off for 1 minute, pressing down on the pancake again. Serve immediately.

MOONG DAL PANCAKES

CHEELA, POORA

৩১

1 cup moong dal (skinned and
    split mung beans), washed
    and soaked in water for
    5–6 hours

1–3 fresh hot green chilies,
    chopped

A 1-inch piece of fresh ginger,
    peeled and finely chopped

2 cloves garlic, peeled and
    chopped

¼ teaspoon ground turmeric

Handful of fresh cilantro,
    chopped

1 teaspoon salt

1 large shallot, peeled and
    finely chopped

About 6 tablespoons olive or
    peanut oil

Made all over India, this savory pancake is exceedingly popular in the north as a breakfast dish. My mother often made it for us on Sundays. It is eaten with chutneys, pickles, and yogurt relishes (see page 303). You could also have it instead of a chapati at lunch or dinner, with a cauliflower or potato dish and a raita.

The batter can be made a day in advance, covered, and refrigerated. It can also be frozen.   MAKES ABOUT 9

৩১

1. Drain the dal and place in a blender. Add the chilies, ginger, garlic, turmeric, cilantro, salt, and ¾ cup water. Blend thoroughly, then empty into a bowl. Add the shallots, then stir in 3 tablespoons of water.

2. Put the oil in a small bowl and stick a teaspoon in it. Have two plates nearby to hold the pancakes as they are made. Measure ⅓ cup water into a ladle and mentally note the level to get an idea of how much batter you will need each time.

3. Set a medium nonstick frying pan over medium-low heat and add a teaspoon of the oil. When hot, stir the batter from the bottom and pour a ladleful into the center of the pan. Let it sit for a second or so, then lightly use the ladle or the back of a spoon to spread it outward in a continuous spiral motion. When it is about 5 inches in diameter, use a spatula to spread the batter outward from the center. Use a light touch so you do not disturb the bottom layer and spread evenly. Aim for a diameter of 7–8 inches. Dribble a teaspoon of oil on the top and just outside the rim of the pancake, cover, and cook for about 2 minutes or until the underside has turned golden red. Flip the pancake over and cook the second side, uncovered, for 1 minute, transfer it to a plate and cover with an upside-down plate.

4. Stir the batter from the bottom each time you make a new one.

FOUR-DAL PANCAKES

FOUR-DAL DOSAS

࿐࿐࿐࿐࿐࿐࿐࿐࿐࿐࿐࿐࿐࿐࿐࿐࿐࿐࿐࿐࿐࿐࿐࿐࿐

½ cup moong dal (skinned
   and split mung beans)

4 tablespoons plain toovar dal

4 tablespoons urad dal

4 tablespoons chana dal

4 tablespoons basmati rice

20–30 fresh curry leaves,
   finely chopped

Large handful of fresh
   cilantro, finely chopped

1½ teaspoons finely chopped
   fresh hot green chilies

1 teaspoon salt

About ½ cup olive or
   peanut oil

A very nutritious savory pancake made with four different types of split peas and a little rice, all combined together. Each dal adds its own distinct texture and taste. As with most Indian savory pancakes, these may be served at any meal, but are very commonly eaten for breakfast, accompanied by yogurt relishes and chutneys. I also like to roll them around a dryish vegetable dish, such as Goan Potatoes or Cauliflower with Potatoes (see pages 110 and 74), and serve them as wraps with a fresh green salad for lunch.

MAKES ABOUT 11

࿐࿐࿐࿐࿐࿐࿐࿐࿐࿐࿐࿐࿐࿐࿐࿐࿐࿐࿐࿐࿐࿐࿐࿐࿐

From Nina Chandavarkar

1. Put the 4 dals and the rice in a large bowl and wash them in several changes of water, rubbing them between your palms. Drain, cover generously with fresh water, and soak overnight.

2. Drain the dals and rice. Put 1 cup water in a blender, then add the dal mixture. Blend until you have a thick, grainy batter. Empty into a bowl and add the curry leaves, cilantro, chilies, and salt. Mix well. Add another ½ cup water and mix again. The batter should be like flowing cream but with a lot of texture. If you later find it hard to spread out, you may need to add another 3–4 tablespoons of water.

3. Put the oil in a small bowl and stick a teaspoon in it. Have two plates nearby to hold the pancakes as they are made. Measure ⅓ cup water into a ladle and mentally note the level to get an idea of how much batter you will need each time.

4. Set a nonstick frying pan over medium-low heat and add a teaspoon of the oil. When hot, stir the batter from the bottom and pour a ladleful into the center of the pan. Let it sit for a

second or so, then lightly use the ladle or the back of a spoon to spread it outward in a continuous spiral motion. When it is about 5 inches in diameter, use a spatula to spread the batter outward from the center as if scraping it to the edges. Again, use a light touch so you do not disturb the bottom layer, and spread evenly. Aim for a diameter of 7–8 inches.

5. Dribble a teaspoon of oil on the top and just outside the rim of the pancake, then cover with a lid and cook for about 2 minutes or until the bottom has turned golden red. Flip the pancake over and cook the second side, uncovered, for 1½–2 minutes. Either serve right away or put the cooked pancake on a plate and cover with a second plate.

6. Make all the pancakes in the same way, stirring the batter from the bottom each time you make a new one.

RICE AND URAD DAL PANCAKES

DOSA

ᘈᘈᘈᘈᘈᘈᘈᘈᘈᘈᘈᘈᘈᘈᘈᘈᘈᘈᘈᘈᘈᘈᘈᘈᘈᘈᘈᘈᘈᘈᘈᘈᘈᘈᘈ

1 cup boiled rice (Indian parboiled rice)

15 or so fenugreek seeds

4 tablespoons urad dal

½ teaspoon salt

6 tablespoons olive or peanut oil

Times have changed since I first started writing cookbooks in 1967. Many more of the ingredients for regional Indian cooking are now widely available, and with the Internet, everyone has access to everything. I struggled with the wrong rice for making dosas for decades. In India they are made with "boiled rice," a parboiled medium-grain rice that is now available in nearly all Indian shops.

Dosas are very nutritious as they contain a grain (rice) and a legume (urad dal) and are generally eaten with a yogurt-based chutney to make a perfect meal. They can be eaten for breakfast, lunch, or dinner. Tomato, cilantro, and coconut chutneys are served on the side. Quick Yogurt and Pickle Chutney (see page 316) is another good choice. Dosas can also be folded over a stuffing of Potato and Onion Mélange (see page 99), or served with a bowl of sambar, South Indian Dal with Vegetables (see page 166).

MAKES ABOUT 9

ᘈᘈᘈᘈᘈᘈᘈᘈᘈᘈᘈᘈᘈᘈᘈᘈᘈᘈᘈᘈᘈᘈᘈᘈᘈᘈᘈᘈᘈᘈᘈᘈᘈᘈᘈ

1. Wash the rice and fenugreek seeds, then cover generously in water and leave to soak overnight.

2. Wash the dal in several changes of water, then cover generously in water and leave to soak overnight.

3. Drain both the rice and the dal and put in a blender along with 1 cup water. Blend thoroughly for at least 5 minutes, pushing down with a spatula when necessary, until you have a smooth paste. It will feel very slightly gritty because of the tiny, sand-like granules of rice. Just remember that you have to keep going until the granules are, indeed, sand-like and not bigger.

4. Empty the batter into a bowl. Cover and leave to ferment in a warm place for at least 8 hours. I find that my batter takes about

24 hours. You will recognize when fermentation has occurred, as the batter will rise.

5. Stir the batter and add the salt and about 5 tablespoons of water to it. Mix well. It should be just a little thicker than crêpe batter.

6. Put the oil in a small bowl and stick a teaspoon in it. Have two plates nearby to hold the pancakes as they are made. Measure ⅓ cup water into a ladle and mentally note the level to get an idea of how much batter you will need each time.

7. Set a medium nonstick frying pan over medium-low heat and add a teaspoon of the oil. When hot, stir the batter from the bottom and pour a ladleful into the center of the pan. Let it sit for a second or so, then lightly use the ladle or the back of a spoon to spread it outward in a continuous spiral motion. When it is about 5 inches in diameter, use a spatula to spread the batter outward from the center as if scraping it to the edges. Again, use a light touch so you do not disturb the bottom layer. Spread evenly, aiming for a diameter of 7–8 inches. Dribble a teaspoon of oil on the top and just outside the rim of the pancake, then cover with a lid and cook for about 1 minute or until the bottom has turned golden red. Turn the pancake over and cook the second side, uncovered, for 1 minute. Transfer the cooked pancake to a plate and cover with the second plate.

8. Make all the pancakes in the same way, stirring the batter from the bottom each time you make a new one.

CABBAGE AND ONION PATTIES

BANDH GOBI KI ANGLO-INDIAN PATTY

1 medium green cabbage
    (about 2 lbs)

3 tablespoons olive or peanut
    oil

½ teaspoon whole brown
    mustard seeds

½ teaspoon whole cumin
    seeds

½ teaspoon whole fennel
    seeds

2 onions (about 10 oz in all),
    peeled and cut into fine
    half rings

2 teaspoons peeled and finely
    grated fresh ginger

1 fresh hot green chili, finely
    chopped

1 tablespoon hot curry powder

2 tablespoons tomato purée

2 teaspoons salt

Flour, for dusting

1¾ lbs frozen puff pastry
    (I buy the pastry in two
    14-oz blocks), defrosted

The patty man was such a welcome sight when I was growing up in India. I could spot his bicycle just as he turned into our gate and would watch him as he slowly came down our long, curving drive. There was a tin trunk attached to the back of his bike, and that is where my interest lay. This trunk contained a British-Indian speciality—patties. These were a little like British pasties, except that they were made with puff pastry, they were spicy, and they came in both vegetarian and non-vegetarian forms. The vegetarian ones were always triangular, with a little yellow from the turmeric in the curry powder temptingly oozing out at the corners. They were usually made with potatoes, but I have changed the stuffing a bit in these recipes; this set of patties is stuffed with spicy cabbage and onions, and the next one is stuffed with a lovely potato mixture. Serve with chutneys at teatime, or for lunch with a green salad using My Yogurt Dressing (see page 329).

You can make your own puff pastry, but I suggest that you buy it frozen from a supermarket. I get one sheet in each 14 oz packet, so I need two of them.

The recipe makes eight large patties. If you want just four, use only one pastry sheet and half the cabbage mixture. The cabbage can hold for several days in the refrigerator.

MAKES 8 LARGE PATTIES

1. Discard the outer leaves of the cabbage, quarter what remains, and remove the hard inner core. Now shred the cabbage as you would for coleslaw, chopping by hand or using a mandoline or a food processor.

2. Put 1 tablespoon of the oil in a large saucepan set over medium-high heat. When hot, throw in the mustard seeds. As soon as they start to pop, a matter of seconds, add the cumin and

fennel seeds. Two seconds later add the cabbage and onions. Stir and fry for 1–2 minutes, then cover and cook on low heat for 5 minutes. The cabbage should wilt.

3. Add the ginger, green chilies, curry powder, tomato purée, and salt. Stir and cook for a minute.

4. Pour the remaining 2 tablespoons oil into a large nonstick frying pan or wok and set over medium heat. When hot, empty all the contents of the cabbage pan into the frying pan. Stir and fry for 15–20 minutes or until the cabbage has browned a bit and is dry. Set aside to cool.

5. Preheat the oven to 425°F. Line two baking sheets with parchment paper.

6. Flour your work surface and the pastry. If you have bought the pastry in one block, cut it in half. Roll out each piece so that you have a sheet that is 12 inches square. Trim off any excess pastry. Cut each sheet into 4 squares so that you have 8 squares in total and prick each with the tines of a fork, going all the way down to your work surface. Divide the cabbage into 8 equal parts.

7. Take a square of pastry and, with one point facing you, fold it toward you into a triangle just to see where the fold will be. Open it up again and put one part of the cabbage mixture right at the fold line, spreading it evenly toward the two edges nearest you but staying ¼ inch away from the edges. Dip a finger in water and dab it generously on the two edges nearest you. Now fold the pastry into a triangle and seal the edges well by pressing down firmly with the balls of your fingers. Make all the patties in the same way.

8. Put the patties on the prepared baking sheets and place in the oven for 15 minutes. Turn the heat down to 375°F and cook for another 20 minutes or until golden brown and cooked through. Serve hot, warm, or at room temperature.

POTATO PATTIES

ALOO KI ANGLO-INDIAN PATTY

ഇഭ്യഭ്യഭ്യഭ്യഭ്യഭ്യഭ്യഭ്യഭ്യഭ്യഭ്യഭ്യഭ്യഭ്യഭ്യഭ്യ

Flour, for dusting

1¾ lbs frozen puff pastry
(I buy the pastry in two
14-oz blocks), defrosted

1 recipe Potatoes Cooked
in a Banarasi Style (see
page 107), made with
4 tablespoons of water
rather than ½ cup, and
cooled

Before making these patties, please read the introduction to the previous recipe (see page 260). The quantities below can easily be halved. Any leftover potatoes will keep for several days in the refrigerator, so they can be used to make another batch of patties or eaten at a meal with Indian flatbreads.

MAKES 8 LARGE PATTIES

ഇഭ്യഭ്യഭ്യഭ്യഭ്യഭ്യഭ്യഭ്യഭ്യഭ്യഭ്യഭ്യഭ്യഭ്യഭ്യഭ്യ

1. Preheat the oven to 425°F. Line two baking sheets with parchment paper.

2. Flour your work surface and the pastry. If you have bought the pastry in one block, cut the pastry in half. Roll out each piece so that you have a sheet that is 12 inches square. Trim off any excess pastry. Cut each sheet into 4 squares so that you have 8 squares in total and prick each with the tines of a fork, going all the way down to your work surface. Divide the potatoes into 8 equal parts.

3. Take one square of pastry and, with one point facing you, fold it toward you into a triangle just to see where the fold will be. Open it up again and put one part of the potato mixture right at the fold line, spreading it evenly toward the two edges nearest you but staying ¾ inch away from the edges. Dip a finger in water and dab it generously on the two edges nearest you. Now fold the pastry into a triangle and seal the edges well by pressing down firmly with the balls of your fingers. Make all the patties in the same way.

4. Put the patties on the prepared trays and place in the oven for 15 minutes. Turn the heat down to 375°F and cook for another 20 minutes or until golden brown and cooked through. Serve hot, warm, or at room temperature.

BOMBAY SANDWICHES

TOASTIES

꙰꙰꙰꙰꙰꙰꙰꙰꙰꙰꙰꙰꙰꙰꙰꙰꙰꙰꙰꙰꙰꙰꙰꙰

2 waxy potatoes (about 8 oz
    in all), freshly boiled,
    cooled, and peeled (do not
    refrigerate)
2 medium tomatoes
½ large green or red pepper
1 medium onion
Butter
4 large slices of your favorite
    bread
Salt and freshly ground black
    pepper
About 2 tablespoons Green
    Chutney (see page 304)
2 slices of cheese, such as
    cheddar

These sandwiches are a newish addition to Bombay street food. They were certainly not around when I was a child. The sandwich-wallah today sits with other snack vendors, with his handheld grilling cage held over an open fire. He is making India's version of a grilled cheese sandwich, only it has many more ingredients than you would get in the United States: sweet peppers, potatoes, tomatoes, onions, and the all-important green chutney, which is what makes the sandwich Indian. It is now so popular that the Taj hotel's elegant Sea Lounge, where I went in the 1940s and 1950s for its delicate ham and cucumber tea sandwiches, now also offers spicy toasties. I love them with a cup of hot tea. You could also have them for lunch with a soup or salad. Make the toasties using a panini/sandwich maker or a cast-iron frying pan.

SERVES 2

꙰꙰꙰꙰꙰꙰꙰꙰꙰꙰꙰꙰꙰꙰꙰꙰꙰꙰꙰꙰꙰꙰꙰꙰

From the Taj Mahal Palace hotel

1. Cut each of the potatoes lengthwise into 5 ovals. Discard the rounded outer pieces. Slice the tomatoes, discarding the top and bottom slices. Cut off the top and bottom of the pepper and remove all the seeds. Cut the remaining flesh into thin, long slices. Peel the onion and cut into fine rings.

2. Butter the slices of bread. Working with just two, arrange as many potato slices on them as will fit easily. Dust lightly with salt and pepper. Put as many of the tomato slices as will fit easily on top of the potatoes and dust lightly with salt and pepper. Top with the pepper slices and onions. Dribble the chutney over the top, using only what fits easily. Put the cheese over the chutney. Top with the reserved bread slices and press down.

3. If using a sandwich maker, follow the manufacturer's instructions. Otherwise, set a heavy, preferably cast-iron frying pan over medium heat. When hot, melt about 1 tablespoon of butter in the center, then lay the two sandwiches on top of it. Keep pressing down hard on them with a spatula until the underside is reddish gold and the cheese has melted. Turn carefully, add a little more butter, and toast the second side in the same way.

4. Remove the sandwiches, cut into triangles, and serve immediately.

A NOTE ON SEVAI

South Indians make their own sevai (thin fresh rice noodles) using all manner of wooden, brass, and stainless steel presses to extrude rice dough, allowing the noodles to fall onto a lightly oiled plate set just below. They are then steamed and eaten with curries as a main meal, or just stir-fried with seasonings for a quick snack. They can also be doused with cardamom-flavored fresh coconut milk and eaten for breakfast.

These noodles are known variously as "idiappam" in Kerala, "nuputtu" in Coorg, and "sevai" in most other places. Taking the easy way out, I use the East Asian dried rice noodles known as rice sticks. Unfortunately, packets of rice sticks come in many different sizes and with a variety of cooking instructions, or incorrect instructions—or no instructions at all. My recipes call for about 5 oz noodles and serve 3–4.

A packet that declares its weight to be 5¼ oz is fine. For a packet marked 7 oz, you just have to break off a portion of the noodles while still dry and save them for another use. (They are wonderful in soups.)

HOW TO PREPARE RICE STICKS Bring a pan of water to a rolling boil. Drop in the folded rice sticks and boil rapidly for 3–7 minutes. Each brand is slightly different, and some cook in just a minute, so keep tasting until the noodles are soft, pliable, and fully cooked. Empty them into a colander and run cold water over them. The noodles are now ready to be stir-fried or reheated with a sauce or a little water whenever you are ready for them. This second heating will help them relax and expand much more. Remember that they are not salted, so add the salt as you reheat. Plain noodles may be served with curries.

THIN RICE NOODLES WITH MUSHROOMS AND TOMATOES

SEVAI WITH MUSHROOMS AND TOMATOES

ↄↄ

5 oz thin dried rice noodles, generally sold as rice sticks

3 tablespoons olive or peanut oil

1 teaspoon urad dal

1 teaspoon whole brown mustard seeds

2 dried hot red chilies

8–10 fresh curry leaves, lightly crushed in your hand

About 6 large, thick-capped fresh shiitake mushrooms (5 oz in all), stems removed and caps cut into 1 inch chunks (see introduction for alternatives)

1¼ teaspoons salt

2 good-sized tomatoes (11 oz in all), peeled and chopped

Freshly ground black pepper

In Kerala, plain rice noodles are called "idiappam" and often served with fiery fish curries. Here I have put them together with tomatoes and mushrooms to make a simple vegetarian dish.

I have used fresh shiitake mushrooms, now easily available. They are sold in different sizes, some being thin and small, and others quite large with thick, juicy tops. It is the large thick ones that I prefer here. I remove their stalks and quarter the caps. If you cannot find them, use whatever is available. You need chunky 1 inch pieces. White or cremini mushrooms can be used as a substitute, and in this case you do not have to remove the stems. Depending on their size, you can use them whole or cut into chunks.

SERVES 3–4

ↄↄ

1. Bring a medium pan of water to a rolling boil. Drop in the noodles and let them cook until they are just tender. They should turn soft, pliable, and slippery. This could take anywhere from 3 to 7 minutes, depending on the brand. Bite into a noodle to check that it is cooked through. Drain and run under cold water, then set aside in the strainer.

2. Put the oil in a medium nonstick frying pan and set over medium heat. When hot, add the urad dal. As soon as it begins to pick up a little color, stir in the mustard seeds and red chilies. When the mustard seeds start to pop, a matter of seconds, add the curry leaves (take care, as these will splutter) and, a few seconds later, the mushrooms and ¼ teaspoon salt. Stir and fry for about 4 minutes or until the mushrooms appear wet and glossy.

3. Add the tomatoes, some generous grinds of black pepper, ½ teaspoon of salt, and ½ cup water. Stir and bring to a simmer,

then cover and simmer over medium-low heat for about 10 minutes or until the tomatoes are soft and there are just a few tablespoons of sauce left. Reduce the heat if necessary.

4. Add the drained noodles and sprinkle another ½ teaspoon of salt over the top. Stir over low heat until the noodles have heated through and thoroughly combined with the sauce, about 2–3 minutes. The noodles should expand a bit more during this process.

THIN RICE NOODLES WITH LEMON AND PEAS

MATAR SEVAI

ဃဃဃဃဃဃဃဃဃဃဃဃဃဃဃဃဃဃဃဃဃဃဃဃဃဃ

5½ oz thin dried rice noodles, generally sold as rice sticks

2 tablespoons olive or peanut oil

1 teaspoon urad dal

1 teaspoon whole brown mustard seeds

8–10 fresh curry leaves, lightly crushed in your hand

2 tablespoons peeled and finely chopped shallots

1–3 fresh hot green chilies, finely chopped

1 cup peas, parboiled and drained if fresh, defrosted if frozen

1 teaspoon salt, or to taste

¼ teaspoon ground turmeric

2 teaspoons lemon juice

Finely grated zest of 1 lemon

3 tablespoons chopped fresh cilantro

This noodle dish may be eaten as a snack, or as part of a meal, or as the whole meal itself if you follow it with a salad with My Yogurt Dressing (see page 329). SERVES 3–4

ဃဃဃဃဃဃဃဃဃဃဃဃဃဃဃဃဃဃဃဃဃဃဃဃဃဃ

1. Bring a medium pan of water to a rolling boil. Drop in the noodles and let them cook until they are just tender. They should turn soft, pliable, and slippery. This could take anywhere from 3 to 7 minutes, depending on the brand. Bite into a noodle to check that it is cooked through. Drain and run under cold water, then set aside in the strainer.

2. Put the oil in a medium nonstick frying pan and set over medium heat. When hot, add the urad dal. As soon as it begins to pick up a little color, add the mustard seeds. When the seeds start to pop, a matter of seconds, add the curry leaves (take care, as these will splutter), then the shallots and chilies. Stir and cook over medium-low heat until the shallots have softened. Add the peas and stir for a minute.

3. Reduce the heat to low, then add the noodles, salt, turmeric, lemon juice, and lemon zest. Stir gently and heat the noodles through, taking about 2–3 minutes to do so. The noodles should expand a bit more during this process. Taste for balance of seasonings and adjust as necessary. Add the fresh cilantro and toss.

EGGS AND DAIRY

CHILI-FRIED EGGS FROM SRI LANKA

CHILI EGGS

ೞೞೞೞೞೞೞೞೞೞೞೞೞೞೞೞೞೞೞೞೞೞೞೞೞೞ

4 teaspoons olive or peanut oil

4 tablespoons peeled and
finely diced shallots

1 fresh hot green chili, finely
chopped

¼ cup finely diced tomato

Salt

2 eggs

This is a simple and delicious version of fried eggs from Sri Lanka, inspired by those served at Sun House in Galle. Here I am using a new technique for frying eggs that I have recently learned. It requires the eggs to be broken into a cold pan and uses much less oil.

The recipe can easily be doubled; just use a medium frying pan instead of a small one. Serve the eggs with toast. MAKES 2

ೞೞೞೞೞೞೞೞೞೞೞೞೞೞೞೞೞೞೞೞೞೞೞೞೞೞ

From Jeffrey Dobbs, the Sun House in Galle, Sri Lanka

1. Put 2 teaspoons of the oil in a small nonstick frying pan and set over medium heat. When hot, add the shallots and green chilies and cook, stirring now and then, until the shallots start to soften, about 2 minutes. Add the tomatoes and a generous pinch of salt. Stir and cook for another 1½ minutes or until the tomatoes are soft, turning the heat down a bit if necessary. Set the spicy mixture aside on a plate, taste for salt, and add more if required.

2. Wash and dry the frying pan. Add the remaining 2 teaspoons of oil and break the eggs into the pan while it is still cold, letting them lie side by side. Cover the pan and place over medium-low heat. Keep lifting the cover now and then to see if the eggs are done to your liking. I like my yolks soft and the whites completely set, which takes about 3 minutes to achieve. The yolks turn hard very quickly, so be vigilant.

3. Once ready, transfer the eggs to a serving dish and salt very lightly. Top with the spicy tomato mixture and serve immediately.

SIMPLE SCRAMBLED EGGS

KHICHRI UNDA

℣℥℣℥℣℥℣℥℣℥℣℥℣℥℣℥℣℥℣℥℣℥℣℥℣℥℣℥℣℥℣℥℣℥

4 eggs, broken into a bowl

Salt

2 teaspoons olive or peanut oil

2 scallions, cut into fine rings
halfway up their green
sections

2 tablespoons finely chopped
tomatoes

1 hot fresh green chili (or
more if you wish), very
finely chopped

2 tablespoons finely chopped
fresh cilantro

Freshly ground black pepper

These are the simplest scrambled eggs, soothing and satisfying, but also spicy or they would not be Indian. I make them without thinking, just the way I have been doing for the last sixty years. As I break the first egg, I go on autopilot.

In Indian towns and villages scrambled eggs are served either with flatbreads, such as Plain Delhi Parathas (see page 221), or with toasted or untoasted slices of bread. Pickles and chutneys may be offered on the side.   SERVES 2

℣℥℣℥℣℥℣℥℣℥℣℥℣℥℣℥℣℥℣℥℣℥℣℥℣℥℣℥℣℥℣℥℣℥

1. Beat the eggs until light and frothy, then sprinkle a generous pinch of salt over them.

2. Put the oil into a medium nonstick frying pan and set over medium heat. When hot, add the scallions. Stir a few times, then add the tomatoes, green chilies, and cilantro. Stir for a minute, then sprinkle a little salt and pepper over the top.

3. Pour in the beaten eggs and let the mixture flow to the edges. Begin to fold all the ingredients together, mixing them gently. When the eggs have set to the consistency you like, remove them quickly and serve.

PARSI SCRAMBLED EGGS

AKOORI

～～～～～～～～～～～～～～～～～～～～～～～～～～～～～～

4 eggs

2 tablespoons milk

Salt and freshly ground black
    pepper

1 tablespoon butter, ghee
    (clarified butter), or olive
    oil

4 tablespoons peeled and
    finely chopped onions

⅛ teaspoon ground cumin

⅛ teaspoon ground turmeric

1–3 fresh hot green chilies,
    finely chopped

1 teaspoon peeled and finely
    grated fresh ginger

2–3 tablespoons chopped
    fresh cilantro

4 medium cherry tomatoes,
    each cut into 8 pieces

Parsis are Zoroastrians whose ancestors, fleeing religious perse-cution, originally came to India from Iran during the eighth cen-tury. They have kept their culture and cuisine alive all these years. Eggs feature prominently in their everyday foods, and akoori, or scrambled eggs, is a speciality that rises to the level of a main dish. It can be served at breakfast, lunch, or dinner, with slices of bread, toast, or Indian flatbreads. For lunch or a light dinner, a salad to follow is all you would need.   SERVES 2

～～～～～～～～～～～～～～～～～～～～～～～～～～～～～～

1. Break the eggs into a bowl. Add the milk, ⅛ teaspoon of salt, and some pepper. Beat until light and frothy, then set aside.

2. Put the butter, ghee, or oil into a medium nonstick frying pan and set over medium heat. When hot, add the onions and fry for a minute. Add the cumin, turmeric, chilies, ginger, and cilantro. Mix well and cook for another 2–3 minutes. Add the tomatoes and ¼ teaspoon of salt. Stir for a minute.

3. Pour in the egg mixture, stirring gently inward from the out-side, forming large curds and cooking the eggs to a consistency that is just a little runnier than you like. Remove from the heat and continue to stir gently. The eggs will keep cooking. You are looking for soft, large curds. Serve immediately.

OMELET WITH PEAS AND GREEN PEPPERS

MATAR AUR SHIMLA MIRCH KA OMLATE

ଙଙଙଙଙଙଙଙଙଙଙଙଙଙଙଙଙଙଙଙଙଙଙଙଙଙଙଙଙ

4 tablespoons olive or peanut
  oil

Scant ¼ teaspoon whole
  cumin seeds

2 tablespoons peeled and
  finely chopped shallots

1 teaspoon peeled and finely
  grated fresh ginger

1 fresh hot green chili, finely
  chopped

¾ cup peas, parboiled and
  drained if fresh, defrosted
  if frozen

4 tablespoons diced green
  pepper, seeds removed (the
  dice should be the same
  size as the peas)

Salt and freshly ground black
  pepper

2 tablespoons finely chopped
  fresh cilantro

4 eggs

Here the omelet has a deliciously gingery stuffing of spicy peas and peppers. You can use just red peppers, or a mixture of green and red if you wish.

For serving suggestions, see previous recipe.   SERVES 2

ଙଙଙଙଙଙଙଙଙଙଙଙଙଙଙଙଙଙଙଙଙଙଙଙଙଙଙଙଙ

1. Put 2 tablespoons of the oil in a medium nonstick frying pan and set over medium heat. When hot, add the cumin seeds. Let them sizzle for 10–15 seconds, then add the shallots and fry for a minute. Add the ginger and chili and fry for 30 seconds. Stir in the peas and green peppers and cook for about 4 minutes, adding a light sprinkling of water if the pan gets too dry. Add ¼ teaspoon of salt and some black pepper. Taste for balance of seasonings and adjust as necessary. Stir in the cilantro and take off the heat.

2. Break the eggs into two separate bowls and beat until frothy. Salt and pepper them lightly.

3. Put 1 tablespoon of oil in a medium nonstick frying pan and set over medium heat. Pour in one lot of beaten eggs and stir gently to scramble lightly, while tilting the pan to let the wet mixture to flow to the edges. When slightly set, spread half the pea mixture over half the omelet. Fold the plain half over it. Using a wide spatula, turn the omelet over and press down on it lightly. If no liquid egg oozes out, it is done; otherwise, keep over low heat and turn a few more times. Make the second omelet in the same way and serve hot.

SPICY CAULIFLOWER OMELETS
GOBI KA OMLATE

꿍꿍꿍꿍꿍꿍꿍꿍꿍꿍꿍꿍꿍꿍꿍꿍꿍꿍꿍꿍꿍꿍꿍꿍꿍꿍

Served with toast or crusty bread and a salad, these omelets make a lovely, light lunch or supper. You can also serve them the Indian way, with Plain Delhi Parathas (see page 221) and chutneys.

When grating the cauliflower, use the largest holes on the grater and grate just the flower part, not the stems. Any bigger pieces that break and fall in can be finely chopped by hand.

SERVES 2

꿍꿍꿍꿍꿍꿍꿍꿍꿍꿍꿍꿍꿍꿍꿍꿍꿍꿍꿍꿍꿍꿍꿍꿍꿍꿍

About 4 tablespoons olive or peanut oil

¼ teaspoon whole brown mustard seeds

¼ teaspoon whole cumin seeds

5–6 fresh curry leaves, finely chopped (optional)

3 tablespoons peeled and finely chopped shallots

A 1-inch piece of fresh ginger, peeled and finely chopped

1 cup finely grated cauliflower (see introduction)

1–2 fresh hot green chilies, finely chopped

½ teaspoon garam masala

¼ cup finely diced tomato

3 tablespoons chopped fresh cilantro

Salt and freshly ground black pepper

4 eggs

1. Put 2 tablespoons of the oil in a medium frying pan and set over medium-high heat. When hot, add the mustard seeds. As soon as they pop, a matter of seconds, add the cumin seeds. Let them sizzle for a second or two, then add the curry leaves, if using (take care, as these will splutter), the shallots, ginger, cauliflower, chilies, and garam masala. Stir and fry for 3–4 minutes, until the mixture is lightly browned. Add the tomatoes, cilantro, and black pepper. Stir and cook for a minute, then take off the heat.

2. Break the eggs into two separate bowls and beat until frothy. Salt and pepper them lightly.

3. Just before you wish to eat, add ¼ teaspoon of salt to the cauliflower mixture. Stir and taste. If you want more salt, add it now.

4. Put 1 tablespoon of oil in a medium nonstick frying pan and set over medium heat. Pour in one lot of beaten eggs and stir gently to scramble lightly, while tilting the pan to let the wet mixture flow to the edges. When slightly set, spread half the cauliflower mixture over half the omelet. Fold the plain half over it. Using a wide spatula, turn the omelet over and press down on it lightly. If no liquid egg oozes out, it is done. If not, keep over low heat and turn a few more times. Make the second omelet in the same way and serve hot.

SIMPLE HARD-BOILED EGG CURRY

KODIGUDDU MASALA VEPADU

ʊʊʊʊʊʊʊʊʊʊʊʊʊʊʊʊʊʊʊʊʊʊʊʊʊʊʊʊʊ

4 hard-boiled eggs

1 tablespoon ghee (clarified butter) or unsalted butter

⅛ teaspoon ground turmeric

⅛–¼ teaspoon salt, or to taste

Freshly ground black pepper

⅛ teaspoon chili powder, or to taste

This is the simplest of egg curries and is beloved in the Telengana region of Andhra Pradesh, where it is served with a khichri (see Rice with Moong Dal and Potatoes, page 175), tamarind rasam, and crisp popadams.

You can increase the number of eggs and the amount of seasoning. No real measurements are required here. You can easily improvise. SERVES 2–4

ʊʊʊʊʊʊʊʊʊʊʊʊʊʊʊʊʊʊʊʊʊʊʊʊʊʊʊʊʊ

From Shobhana and Padma Reddy

1. Peel the eggs, then cut 4–5 long slits in the whites going from somewhere near the top to somewhere near the bottom but not meeting.

2. Put the ghee or butter in a small frying pan and set over medium heat. When hot, add the turmeric, salt, pepper, and chili powder. Stir together, then add the eggs and roll them around for about a minute, or until they are golden. Remove the pan from the heat and serve.

EGGS IN A MUSTARD SAUCE

ANGREZI MUSTARD WALAY UNDAY

∽∽∽∽∽∽∽∽∽∽∽∽∽∽∽∽∽∽∽∽∽∽∽∽∽∽∽∽∽

3 tablespoons English mustard
    powder

½ teaspoon ground turmeric

¼ teaspoon nice red chili
    powder

1 fresh hot green chili, finely
    chopped

1 teaspoon peeled and finely
    grated fresh ginger

Salt

3 tablespoons tomato purée

2 teaspoons olive or peanut oil

Generous pinch of whole
    mustard seeds

Generous pinch of whole
    cumin seeds

Generous pinch of whole
    nigella seeds (kalonji)

Generous pinch of whole
    fennel seeds

4 hard-boiled eggs, peeled and
    cut in half lengthwise

This recipe has been inspired by all the wonderful Bengali mustard sauces that I have enjoyed over the decades. For a meal, serve it with rice and other vegetables, such as spinach or peas. For breakfast, have it with slices of fresh Italian or French bread to soak up the good juices. Remember, as the sauce cooks, it loses most of its pungency.   SERVES 2

∽∽∽∽∽∽∽∽∽∽∽∽∽∽∽∽∽∽∽∽∽∽∽∽∽∽∽∽∽

1. Combine the mustard powder, turmeric, chili powder, green chilies, ginger, ½ teaspoon of salt, and the tomato purée in a bowl. Slowly add 1½ cups water, mixing well and breaking up any lumps as you do so. Set aside.

2. Put the oil in a medium nonstick frying pan and set over medium heat. Meanwhile, put all the seeds in a small bowl. When the oil is hot, add the seeds. When the mustard seeds start to pop, a matter of seconds, pour in the mustard sauce and bring to a simmer. Reduce the heat and simmer gently for 2–3 minutes.

3. Arrange all the egg halves in the sauce, yolk side up, and spoon the sauce over them until they heat up. Transfer carefully to a serving dish, again with yolks facing up. Pour the sauce over them and serve immediately.

COORG-STYLE EGG CURRY WITH POTATOES

MUTTA CURRY

4 small red potatoes (about
6 oz in all), boiled and left
to cool

2 tablespoons olive or peanut
oil

½ teaspoon whole brown
mustard seeds

½ teaspoon whole cumin
seeds

5–6 fresh curry leaves, lightly
crushed in your hand

1 onion (5 oz), peeled and
chopped

4 cloves garlic, peeled and
finely chopped

1 fresh hot green chili or
more, finely chopped

1 teaspoon ground coriander

1 teaspoon ground cumin

¼ teaspoon nice red chili
powder

2 tomatoes (about 1 cup in all),
peeled and chopped

1 teaspoon salt, or to taste

1 cup coconut milk, from a
well-shaken can

4–8 eggs, as desired, hard-
boiled and peeled

This is an excellent curry to serve at brunch or lunch with some plain rice. Some little relishes and chutneys would complete the meal. SERVES 4

From Mynah Pemmaiah

1. When the potatoes are cool, peel and quarter them. You need ¾ inch pieces. Set aside.

2. Put the oil in a medium wide pan and set over medium heat. When hot, add the mustard seeds. As soon as they pop, a matter of seconds, add the cumin seeds and let them sizzle for 10 seconds. Add the curry leaves (take care, as these will splutter) and, a few seconds later, the onions. Stir and fry for 5–6 minutes or until the onions are lightly browned. Add the garlic and green chilies and stir for 2 minutes. Stir in the coriander, ground cumin, and chili powder. Now add the tomatoes, salt, and 1½ cups water. Bring to a simmer, then cover and simmer very gently for 20 minutes.

3. Add the coconut milk, potatoes, and eggs to the sauce. Bring to a simmer, then cook, uncovered, on very low heat, for 3–4 minutes, stirring now and then. If the sauce seems too thick, add a few tablespoons of water.

EGGS IN A HYDERABADI TOMATO SAUCE

TOMATO KUT

ᥫ᭡

6 eggs

3 tablespoons chickpea flour
(besan or gram flour)

1½ cups tomato puree

½ teaspoon tamarind concentrate
(sold in bottles)

Salt

2 tablespoons olive or peanut oil

6–7 fresh curry leaves, lightly
crushed in your hand

2 teaspoons peeled and finely
grated fresh ginger

4 cloves garlic, peeled and
crushed

½ teaspoon ground cumin seeds

¼–½ teaspoon nice red chili
powder

¼ teaspoon ground turmeric

FOR THE TARKA (SEE PAGE xxii)

2 tablespoons olive or peanut oil

¼ teaspoon whole brown
mustard seeds

¼ teaspoon whole cumin seeds

3–6 dried hot red chilies

2 cloves garlic, peeled and halved
lengthwise, then cut into
lengthwise slivers

6–7 fresh curry leaves, lightly
crushed in your hand

PICTURED ON PAGES 288–289

Hyderabadi cuisine developed in the courts of the rulers of Hyderabad and in the homes of the mostly Muslim aristocratic families who followed Moghul generals sent from the Delhi imperial Moghul court to capture and then rule the southern Hyderabad area.

In the heat of a new climate zone, the northern Moghul cuisine began taking on southern accents. Wheat eaters became rice eaters without quite giving up their naans and kulchas and other baked goodies. The biggest changes were in the seasonings. Mustard seeds and curry leaves, popular in the south but unheard of in northern Muslim cuisine, became constants, as did tamarind. In fact, the love affair with sour foods, which aid digestion in hot climates, began early and has never ended. Tamarind, tomatoes, green mangoes, and limes are used with the same frequency as they are by the original inhabitants. The famous Hyderabadi "Sour" Dal (see page 164) is really not all that different from the local sambar (South Indian Dal with Vegetables, see page 166), and it too is eaten with rice.

This tomato kut is another sour dish served with rice. It is normally eaten at lunch or dinner, but I frequently serve it for brunch. It is quickly devoured!

I have allowed 1½ eggs per person, but there is enough sauce to increase the total to 8 eggs if you wish.   SERVES 4

ᥫ᭡

From Sanjeeda Shareef

1. Hard-boil the eggs. Peel them under cold running water and set them aside.

2. Put a small cast-iron frying pan over medium-high heat. When hot, add the chickpea flour and stir a few times until it

turns a shade darker. Transfer it to a medium bowl and leave to cool.

3. When the flour is cold, slowly add 6 tablespoons of water, stirring until you have a thick paste with no lumps. Now add the tomato puree, the tamarind concentrate, 1½ teaspoons salt, and 2½ cups water. Mix and set aside.

4. Put the 2 tablespoons of oil into a medium, preferably non-stick frying pan and set over medium heat. When hot, add the crushed curry leaves (take care, as these will splutter), followed by the ginger and garlic. Stir a few times, turn the heat to low, and add the ground cumin, chili powder, and turmeric. Stir a few times, then add the tomato puree mixture. Place over medium-high heat and bring to a boil, stirring constantly. Lower the heat and simmer gently for 10 minutes, stirring now and then. Check the salt. You might need to add another ¼ teaspoon or so.

5. To make the final tarka, put a small frying pan on medium-high heat and add 2 tablespoons of oil. When it is very hot, put in the mustard seeds. As soon as they pop, a matter of seconds, add the cumin seeds and red chilies. When the red chilies darken, put in the garlic pieces. Let the garlic brown lightly. Throw in the curry leaves (take care, as these will splutter) and quickly empty the contents of the pan evenly over the sauce. Stir well.

6. To serve, cut the eggs into halves lengthwise. Find a shallow serving dish that can fit the halves in a single layer. Arrange the eggs, yolk up, in the dish. Pour the sauce over them.

YOGURT RICE

CURD RICE

꿀꿀꿀꿀꿀꿀꿀꿀꿀꿀꿀꿀꿀꿀꿀꿀꿀꿀꿀꿀꿀꿀꿀꿀꿀

1 cup jasmine rice

2 cups plain yogurt

½ cup milk

2 teaspoons olive or peanut oil

2 tablespoons raw cashews,
    split in half lengthwise

2 teaspoons chana dal

1 teaspoon urad dal or yellow
    split peas

1 teaspoon whole brown
    mustard seeds

½ teaspoon whole cumin
    seeds

2–3 dried hot red chilies,
    broken in half

6–8 fresh curry leaves,
    chopped

1 teaspoon salt, or to taste

A 1-inch piece of fresh ginger,
    peeled and cut into minute
    dice

1–3 fresh hot green chilies,
    finely chopped (optional)

2–3 tablespoons chopped
    fresh cilantro

This is perhaps the simplest version of one of South India's most beloved dishes, usually offered at the end of the meal to soothe the fieriness of the foods eaten just preceding it. It is also offered in southern temples as holy, blessed food. Known variously as "daddojanam" (Andhra Pradesh), "thayyir saadam" (Tamil Nadu), "mosaranna" (Karnataka), and "curd rice" (by English speakers), it is typically eaten at the end of the meal with just pickles and chutneys, but it may be served with the meal as well, in individual bowls, like a salad. In fact, diced or grated cucumbers, grated carrots, diced grapes, and pomegranate seeds are often added to it.

You will find that the texture is perfect when the curd rice is initially made. If it sits for a few hours, it will thicken, so add more cold milk to thin it out. Grated cucumbers also help to keep it thinned out.

You can use 1–3 fresh hot green chilies, finely chopped, instead of the dry red chilies, adding them at the same time as the ginger. Or you can add both!   SERVES 4–8

꿀꿀꿀꿀꿀꿀꿀꿀꿀꿀꿀꿀꿀꿀꿀꿀꿀꿀꿀꿀꿀꿀꿀꿀꿀

From Malathi Srinivasan

1. Combine the rice and 2½ cups water in a small, heavy-based pan. Bring to a boil, then cover tightly and cook over very low heat for 25 minutes.

2. Empty all the rice into a large, wide bowl and stir gently to cool it. Stir in the yogurt, then mix in ½ cup of the milk.

3. Put the oil in a small pan and set over medium heat. When hot, add the cashews. Stir them around until they become golden, then remove them with a slotted spoon. Add the chana dal. As soon as it starts to color, add the urad dal and, a few seconds later, the mustard seeds, cumin seeds, and red chilies.

As soon as the mustard seeds pop, a matter of seconds, add the curry leaves, then empty the contents of this pan over the rice mixture. Add the salt, ginger, green chilies (if using), and cilantro. Stir well and taste for balance of seasonings. Garnish with the cashews just before serving. (If not serving straight away, see introduction.)

Spice box

A NOTE ON FRESH INDIAN CHEESE (PANEER)

Paneer means "cheese," and in India there is basically just one kind—a very fresh variety that is generally made and consumed the same day. With refrigeration, it can be made to last a few more days.

The process of making the cheese is very simple. Milk is brought to a boil, then a curdling agent—lime juice or vinegar or day-old whey—is added. The curds are drained off and pressed into a wheel in a piece of muslin. That's it.

In India most people just buy paneer fresh from the market. In the West all good Indian grocers sell it. Is is usually frozen into blocks, and it is very good quality. All you have to do is defrost it and cut it into pieces of the size you want, and you are ready to cook. If you are in a hurry, the defrosting can be done by immersing the plastic packet in warm water. If you have time, take the block out of the freezer a day before and refrigerate it. You could also leave it out at room temperature for a few hours.

Some paneer recipes appear in the following pages. There is also a recipe for Spicy Paneer Slices on page 9.

Note that paneer gets hard as it sits. When it is heated, it becomes soft again.

FRESH INDIAN CHEESE COOKED LIKE SCRAMBLED EGGS

PANEER KI BHURJI

ᑫᑐᑫᑐᑫᑐᑫᑐᑫᑐᑫᑐᑫᑐᑫᑐᑫᑐᑫᑐᑫᑐᑫᑐᑫᑐᑫᑐᑫᑐᑫᑐᑫᑐᑫᑐ

1 tablespoon olive or peanut oil

5 tablespoons peeled and finely chopped onion (about half a medium onion)

Generous pinch of ground turmeric

1 fresh hot green chili, finely chopped

1 teaspoon peeled and finely grated fresh ginger

4 medium cherry tomatoes, each cut into 8 pieces

7 oz fresh Indian cheese (paneer), crumbled into tiny pieces

3 tablespoons fresh cooked peas or defrosted frozen peas

½ teaspoon salt, or to taste

Freshly ground black pepper

2 tablespoons chopped fresh cilantro

It is best if this dish is cooked just before it is served, and it helps to prepare all the ingredients in advance. If you wish to cook it fully ahead of time, cover the finished dish until needed. Then, just before you eat, add a little water, cover again, and set the pan on low heat. Stir now and then until it is hot.

The original recipe was made without peas, and you can omit them if you wish.

In India, this bhurji is eaten all over the Punjab, from village homes to roadside truck stops. It is generally served with slices of bread or toast, or any plain flatbread. Pickles, chutneys, and relishes are often served on the side. SERVES 2

ᑫᑐᑫᑐᑫᑐᑫᑐᑫᑐᑫᑐᑫᑐᑫᑐᑫᑐᑫᑐᑫᑐᑫᑐᑫᑐᑫᑐᑫᑐᑫᑐᑫᑐᑫᑐ

From Dell' Art Inde and Sarita Malhotra

1. Put the oil in a medium nonstick frying pan and set over medium heat. When hot, add the onions and fry for a minute. Add the turmeric and green chilies. Stir and fry for another 2–3 minutes or until the onions have softened a bit. Add the ginger and stir a few times. Now add the tomatoes and stir for another minute.

2. Add the paneer, peas, and salt and cook over medium-low heat, stirring for 2–3 minutes. Everything should be heated through and the seasonings well mixed. Add the black pepper and fresh cilantro and stir again. Taste for balance of flavors.

STIR-FRIED FRESH INDIAN CHEESE WITH GREEN PEPPERS

CHILI PANEER

༺༺༺༺༺༺༺༺༺༺༺༺༺༺༺༺༺༺༺༺༺༺༺༺༺༺༺༺༺༺

14 oz fresh Indian cheese
(paneer), cut into ¾ inch
squares

1 tablespoon flour

Salt and freshly ground black
pepper

3 tablespoons olive or peanut
oil

1 large green pepper, seeded
and cut into ¾ inch
squares

¼ teaspoon whole cumin
seeds

1 onion (5 oz), peeled and
chopped

2 teaspoons peeled and finely
grated fresh ginger

3–4 cloves garlic, peeled and
crushed

1 fresh hot green chili, finely
chopped

1 teaspoon ground coriander

1 teaspoon ground cumin

¼ teaspoon nice red chili
powder

½ cup tomato puree

1½ tablespoons soy sauce

½ teaspoon sugar

2–3 tablespoons chopped
fresh cilantro

Chili paneer is a Chinese-inspired Indian dish that has gained much favor over the past twenty years. It is generally made very hot and can be eaten as a snack or with a meal. Serve it with rice or Indian flatbreads.

You might need to add a little water when reheating.

SERVES 4–5

༺༺༺༺༺༺༺༺༺༺༺༺༺༺༺༺༺༺༺༺༺༺༺༺༺༺༺༺༺༺

1. Put all the paneer pieces in a bowl. Sprinkle with the flour, ¼ teaspoon of salt, and some black pepper and toss to mix.

2. Put the oil in a nonstick wok, karhai, or frying pan and set over medium heat. Add all the paneer in a single layer and fry until golden on all sides. Using a slotted spoon, transfer to a bowl.

3. Add the green pepper pieces to the oil left in the pan and stir-fry for about a minute. Sprinkle very lightly with salt, then use a slotted spoon to transfer to the same bowl as the cheese.

4. Keep the oil left in the pan over medium heat and add the cumin seeds. Let them sizzle for 10 seconds, then add the onions. Stir-fry for 3–4 minutes or until they look glazed. Add the ginger, garlic, and green chilies. Stir-fry for a minute, then add the coriander, ground cumin, and chili powder. Stir for a minute. Add the tomato puree, soy sauce, sugar, ¼ teaspoon of salt, and ½ cup water. Stir and bring to a simmer.

5. Fold in the paneer and green peppers and cook gently, stirring now and then, until the paneer is heated through. Sprinkle the fresh cilantro over the top when serving. (You will need to add 4–5 tablespoons of water if the dish needs reheating.)

Sri Narasimha sign in Andhra Pradesh

FRESH INDIAN CHEESE WITH PEAS AND MUSHROOMS

PANEER, MATAR AUR KHUMBI

ಲಾಲಾಲಾಲಾಲಾಲಾಲಾಲಾಲಾಲಾಲಾಲಾಲಾಲಾಲಾಲಾಲಾ

This rich and satisfying dish is best eaten with Indian flatbreads, but you can serve it with rice if you prefer. A dal and some relishes may be served on the side. SERVES 4

ಲಾಲಾಲಾಲಾಲಾಲಾಲಾಲಾಲಾಲಾಲಾಲಾಲಾಲಾಲಾಲಾಲಾ

8 whole raw cashews

4 tablespoons tomato puree

1 teaspoon ground cumin

1 teaspoon ground coriander

¼ teaspoon ground turmeric

Generous pinch of ground cloves

Generous pinch of ground cinnamon

Generous pinch of ground cardamom

2 tablespoons olive or peanut oil

Generous pinch of ground asafetida

½ teaspoon whole cumin seeds

7 medium mushrooms (about 4 oz in all), quartered lengthwise

1 cup fresh cooked peas or defrosted frozen peas

1 teaspoon peeled and finely grated fresh ginger

7 oz fresh Indian cheese (paneer), cut into ¾ inch cubes

1 teaspoon salt

2 tablespoons heavy cream

1. Put the cashews, tomato puree, and 4 tablespoons of water into a blender and add the first six ground herbs and spices in the order listed. Blend until smooth, then pour into a bowl. Rinse the blender with ½ cup water and pour that into the bowl as well.

2. Put the oil into a medium nonstick frying pan and set over medium heat. When hot, add the asafetida and cumin seeds. Let the seeds sizzle for 10 seconds, then add the mushrooms. Stir-fry them for a minute or until they appear glossy. Add the peas and ginger and stir for a minute. Add the cheese cubes and the salt, stir for 2 minutes, then add the tomato mixture. Stir and bring to a simmer, then heat gently for about 3 minutes, until everything is warmed through and well mixed. Gently stir in the cream and serve.

FRESH INDIAN CHEESE IN A BUTTER-TOMATO SAUCE

PANEER MAKHANI

ᏨᏨᏨᏨᏨᏨᏨᏨᏨᏨᏨᏨᏨᏨᏨᏨᏨᏨᏨᏨᏨᏨᏨᏨᏨᏨᏨᏨᏨᏨ

1 cup tomato puree

1 cup heavy cream

2 teaspoons peeled and finely
   grated fresh ginger

1 teaspoon garam masala

2 teaspoons lemon juice

½ teaspoon sugar

1 fresh hot green chili, finely
   chopped

1¼ teaspoons salt

¼ teaspoon nice red chili
   powder

1 teaspoon ground roasted
   cumin seeds (see page xx)

1 tablespoon dried fenugreek
   leaves (kasuri methi),
   crumbled (optional)

14 oz fresh Indian cheese
   (paneer), cut into ¾ inch
   squares

Freshly ground black pepper

2 tablespoons unsalted butter

1 tablespoon olive or peanut
   oil

¼ teaspoon whole cumin
   seeds

2–3 tablespoons chopped
   fresh cilantro

This is the vegetarian version of chicken in a butter-tomato sauce, for which a tandoor-roasted bird is cut up and enfolded in a rich, creamy sauce. This vegetarian incarnation is much loved and generally eaten with Indian flatbreads, especially naans. There is no recipe for naans in this book, but you can buy them from grocers or Indian restaurants. Serve a chickpea dish or the Mixed Dal, Marwari-Style (see page 154) on the side, along with a chutney or relish. SERVES 4–6

ᏨᏨᏨᏨᏨᏨᏨᏨᏨᏨᏨᏨᏨᏨᏨᏨᏨᏨᏨᏨᏨᏨᏨᏨᏨᏨᏨᏨᏨᏨ

1. Combine the tomato puree, cream, ginger, garam masala, lemon juice, sugar, green chilies, 1 teaspoon of the salt, chili powder, ground roasted cumin, and dried fenugreek leaves (if using) in a bowl. Stir thoroughly and set aside.

2. Put the cubed cheese into another bowl. Add ¼ teaspoon of salt and some black pepper. Toss well to mix.

3. Put the butter, oil, and cumin seeds in a medium nonstick pan and set over medium heat. Put all the cheese cubes in the pan in a single layer and brown them very lightly on at least two sides. Pour the tomato sauce over the top and stir to mix. Bring to a simmer, then heat very gently for 4–5 minutes, stirring with a light hand as you do so. Sprinkle the fresh cilantro over the top before serving.

SPINACH WITH FRESH INDIAN CHEESE

SAAG PANEER

⌘⌘⌘⌘⌘⌘⌘⌘⌘⌘⌘⌘⌘⌘⌘⌘⌘⌘⌘⌘⌘⌘⌘⌘⌘⌘⌘⌘⌘⌘⌘

10 oz fresh spinach, well
   washed and lightly drained
1 good-sized tomato (about
   6 oz), chopped
2 generous handfuls of fresh
   cilantro leaves
1–2 fresh hot green chilies,
   chopped
2 tablespoons dried fenugreek
   leaves (kasuri methi),
   crushed between your
   palms or fingers into a
   powder
3 tablespoons olive or peanut
   oil
1 medium onion (5 oz), peeled
   and finely chopped
1 tablespoon peeled and very
   finely grated fresh ginger
2 cloves garlic, peeled and
   crushed
¼–¾ teaspoon chili powder
2 teaspoons ground coriander
1 teaspoon ground cumin
¼ teaspoon ground turmeric
1 teaspoon salt, or to taste
14 oz fresh Indian cheese
   (paneer), cut into ¾ inch
   cubes

There are dozens of recipes for saag paneer in the Punjab, where dairy products are a mainstay of the diet and where this dish originated. Here is one of the simplest. It is generally served with Indian flatbreads and a dal.

The size of the paneer cubes you cut will depend partly on the size of the block you buy.   SERVES 4–5

⌘⌘⌘⌘⌘⌘⌘⌘⌘⌘⌘⌘⌘⌘⌘⌘⌘⌘⌘⌘⌘⌘⌘⌘⌘⌘⌘⌘⌘⌘⌘

1. Bring a large pan of water to a rolling boil and drop all the spinach into it. As soon as it wilts, drain in a colander and run cold water over it. Set aside to drain for another 5 minutes. Do not try to squeeze any more water out of it.

2. Put the tomatoes, spinach, fresh cilantro, green chilies, and dried fenugreek leaves into a blender in the order listed and blend until smooth. Set aside.

3. Pour the oil into a medium nonstick frying pan and set over medium heat. When hot, add the onions and fry for 7–8 minutes or until soft and golden. Add the ginger and garlic and continue to stir-fry for another 2–3 minutes. The onions should pick up a little color. Stir in the chili powder, ground coriander, cumin, and turmeric. Now pour in the mixture from the blender, adding the salt, cheese, and ½ cup water. Stir and bring to a simmer, then cook over low heat for about 10 minutes, stirring gently now and then.

CHUTNEYS, RELISHES, AND SALADS

GREEN CHUTNEY

HARI CHUTNEY

ભ્

1 good-sized bunch fresh
  cilantro, the greenest you
  can find
1 tablespoon lime juice
2–3 fresh hot green chilies,
  sliced into fine rings
A 1-inch piece of ginger,
  peeled and finely chopped
1 tablespoon plain yogurt
Scant ½ teaspoon salt

This is the simplest version of the green chutney that all northern Indians eat in their homes. It is dribbled over snack foods, used as a dip for fritters, and many a child, including me, has been known to take a green chutney and cheese sandwich to school in his or her lunch box. You can also spread it on a Chapati (see page 219), along with leftovers of a cauliflower or potato dish, and roll it up for lunch or a snack.

Being a fresh chutney, this keeps for only a few days, though it can be frozen. Its bright green color seems to bear witness to its health-giving properties—basically, lots of vitamins—as it includes fresh cilantro, lime juice, green chilies, and ginger. It is hot and sour and totally unlike any preserved chutney.

MAKES ABOUT 1 CUP

ભ્

1. Cut off the leaf-free stalks of the cilantro. Wash and drain the remaining stalks and leaves. You should have 1½ well-packed cups. Chop well, as this will help in the blending.

2. Put the lime juice in your blender first, followed by the chilies, then the ginger, yogurt, and 4 tablespoons of water. Blend, then add the chopped cilantro. Whiz to a smooth paste, pushing down the mixture as needed. Pour the chutney into a small bowl, add the salt, and mix it in. Taste, and make necessary adjustments to the seasonings.

SIMPLE COCONUT CHUTNEY

NARIYAL CHUTNEY

½ cup fine coconut powder

1–2 fresh hot green chilies, chopped

1 teaspoon sugar

½ teaspoon salt

4 teaspoons lime or lemon juice

Made in less than five minutes, this chutney can be served with most meals. A coconut chutney is nearly always served with Indian dosas, the savory pancakes for which you will find many recipes in this book. The coconut powder used here is dry, unsweetened, and easy to store.　　SERVES 4–6

From Rita D'Souza

Combine all the ingredients in a blender along with ½ cup water. Blend until smooth. Refrigerate until needed. Coconut powder tends to thicken as it sits, so add a little more water before serving if you need to.

FRESH CILANTRO AND YOGURT CHUTNEY

DAHI AUR HARAY DHANIYAY KI CHUTNEY

ᎧᎧᎧᎧᎧᎧᎧᎧᎧᎧᎧᎧᎧᎧᎧᎧᎧᎧᎧᎧᎧᎧᎧᎧᎧᎧᎧᎧ

1 cup plain yogurt

1 tablespoon lime or lemon juice

1 well-packed cup cilantro, chopped

2–3 fresh hot green chilies, chopped

¼ teaspoon salt, or to taste

A simple, everyday chutney that could be served with most meals. It is also good drizzled over soups.　　SERVES 6

ᎧᎧᎧᎧᎧᎧᎧᎧᎧᎧᎧᎧᎧᎧᎧᎧᎧᎧᎧᎧᎧᎧᎧᎧᎧᎧᎧᎧ

1. Put 4 tablespoons of the yogurt plus all the remaining ingredients into a blender and whiz until smooth, pushing down with a rubber spatula if necessary. If your blender seems to stick, add a little more of the yogurt.

2. Empty the remaining yogurt into a bowl. Beat lightly with a fork or a whisk until smooth and creamy. Add the mixture from the blender and stir until well mixed.

SIMPLE TAMARIND CHUTNEY

AASAAN IMLI KI CHUTNEY

2 tablespoons tamarind
  concentrate (sold in
  bottles)
4 tablespoons sugar
¾ teaspoon salt
½ teaspoon ground roasted
  cumin seeds (see page xx)
¼ teaspoon nice red chili
  powder
¼ teaspoon ground ginger
  (optional)
¼ teaspoon finely crushed
  dried mint or ½ teaspoon
  very finely chopped fresh
  mint (optional)

Tamarind chutney is an essential component of many Indian snack foods. It is used as a dip for fritters and samosas, and it can be dribbled over such disparate things as sliced bananas, seasoned potato patties, and yogurt relishes. It is sour, sweet, hot, and quite delicious. It can be made by soaking tamarind, squeezing out its pulp, and then seasoning it. Today the quicker option is to use a ready-made tamarind paste or concentrate, which seem to be the same thing, though there is a dizzying variety available. I use the concentrate, sold under the name Tamicon, because of its uniformity.

MAKES ABOUT ½ CUP

1. Put the tamarind concentrate in a smallish bowl, removing as much of it as possible from the measuring spoon with the help of another spoon or your finger. Add 3 tablespoons of boiling water and mix thoroughly. Add the sugar, salt, roasted cumin seeds, and chili powder and mix again. Add either or both of the optional ingredients if you want them, and mix thoroughly.

2. You will now have a very thick chutney, good for dribbling on bananas but too thick to use as a dip for fritters, samosas, and other snacks such as the Salad of Puffed Rice, Cucumbers, Onions, and Tomatoes (see page 46). In any recipe that requires it, I indicate how much to thin it out.

FRESH CILANTRO, GINGER, AND COCONUT CHUTNEY

GUJARATI HARI CHUTNEY

∽∽∽∽∽∽∽∽∽∽∽∽∽∽∽∽∽∽∽∽∽∽∽∽∽∽∽∽∽∽∽

1 cup small leafy stems of
   fresh cilantro
A ½-inch piece of fresh ginger,
   peeled and finely chopped
½–3 fresh hot green chilies,
   chopped
7–8 fresh curry leaves,
   chopped
¼ teaspoon salt, or to taste
½ cup fine coconut powder
1 teaspoon olive or peanut oil
¼ teaspoon urad dal
Generous pinch of ground
   asafetida
¼ teaspoon whole brown
   mustard seeds

Similar fresh chutneys exist throughout western and southern India. This particular one comes from the Jains of Palanpur. For more information about them, see page 75.

You can serve this chutney with any Indian meal. It is particularly good with stuffed flatbreads and the dosa family of savory pancakes.

For this recipe it is best to buy a large bunch of cilantro and pick off the required weight of leaves with the small stems attached to them.   SERVES 6–8

∽∽∽∽∽∽∽∽∽∽∽∽∽∽∽∽∽∽∽∽∽∽∽∽∽∽∽∽∽∽∽

From Rajul Gandhi

1. Wash the fresh cilantro and drain, then chop well. Place in a blender along with the ginger, green chilies, curry leaves (if using), salt, and ½ cup water. Blend together, then add the coconut powder and blend again. Transfer to a small bowl. Check the salt, adding more if you wish.

2. Put the oil in a small frying pan set over medium-high heat. When hot, add the urad dal and asafetida. As soon as the dal begins to change color, put in the mustard seeds. When the mustard seeds start to pop, a matter of seconds, pour the contents of the frying pan into the bowl of chutney and stir to mix.

3. This chutney will keep for several days in the refrigerator.

SPICY PEANUT CRUMBLE

SHENGA HINDI

꒝꒞꒝꒞꒝꒞꒝꒞꒝꒞꒝꒞꒝꒞꒝꒞꒝꒞꒝꒞꒝꒞꒝꒞꒝꒞꒝꒞꒝꒞꒝꒞

½ cup roasted, unsalted peanuts

⅓ teaspoon salt

1 teaspoon nice red chili powder (or more if you like)

Not all chutneys are wet and flowing. There are many, particularly in the southern half of India, that take the form of a powder or coarse crumble. This chutney, from northern Karnataka, resembles breadcrumbs, some quite fine and some a little bit coarser. Northern Karnataka and Maharashtra grow a lot of peanuts (and sesame seeds), and all the local people, more so vegetarians, commonly use them to add protein to their meals. This particular chutney may be strewn over rice or sprinkled over bread and savory pancakes. **MAKES ABOUT 1 CUP**

꒝꒞꒝꒞꒝꒞꒝꒞꒝꒞꒝꒞꒝꒞꒝꒞꒝꒞꒝꒞꒝꒞꒝꒞꒝꒞꒝꒞꒝꒞꒝꒞

From Smita Kulkarni

Put all the ingredients in a grinder and grind until you have a mixture of coarse and fine "crumbs." Empty into a screw-top jar and store in a cool place.

SPICY PEANUT AND GARLIC CRUMBLE

SHENGA HINDI

૭ઙ૭ઙ૭ઙ૭ઙ૭ઙ૭ઙ૭ઙ૭ઙ૭ઙ૭ઙ૭ઙ૭ઙ૭ઙ૭ઙ૭ઙ૭ઙ૭ઙ૭ઙ૭ઙ

1 tablespoon olive or peanut
  oil
4 cloves garlic, peeled and
  chopped
½ cup roasted, unsalted
  peanuts
⅓ teaspoon salt
1 teaspoon nice red chili
  powder (or more if you
  like)

This chutney is very much like the previous one, except that it includes garlic. I find it very delicious. It too may be strewn over rice or sprinkled over bread and savory pancakes.

MAKES ABOUT 1 CUP

૭ઙ૭ઙ૭ઙ૭ઙ૭ઙ૭ઙ૭ઙ૭ઙ૭ઙ૭ઙ૭ઙ૭ઙ૭ઙ૭ઙ૭ઙ૭ઙ૭ઙ૭ઙ૭ઙ

From Smita Kulkarni

1. Put the oil and garlic in a small frying pan and set over low heat. Let the garlic slowly turn golden and crisp, stirring now and then. Lift the garlic out with a mesh spatula or slotted spoon and spread on a paper towel to cool and become even crisper. (The leftover oil can be used for salad dressings or to cook vegetables.)

2. Put the garlic and all the remaining ingredients in a grinder and grind until you have a mixture of coarse and fine "crumbs." Empty into a screw-top jar and store in a cool place.

DRY CHUTNEY MADE WITH THREE DALS

KANDI PODI

ଓଓଓଓଓଓଓଓଓଓଓଓଓଓଓଓଓଓଓଓଓଓଓଓଓଓଓଓଓଓ

4 tablespoons chana dal

4 tablespoons plain toovar dal

2 tablespoons urad dal

½ teaspoon whole cumin
seeds

4–6 dried hot red chilies

3 cloves garlic, peeled and
sliced

Generous pinch of asafetida

8–10 fresh curry leaves, lightly
crushed in your hand

Salt

Here is another dry chutney, this time made with three dals, all of which need to be slightly roasted first. It is very typical of Andhra Pradesh in South India, where such dry chutneys are known as "podis" (or gunpowder!), and eaten with savory pancakes and rice dishes.

This chutney can also be used as a seasoning for quick-cooked vegetables such as eggplant, okra, and bitter gourds. Generally speaking, the method is as follows: You put some oil in a pan and make a tarka (see page xxii) with urad dal, mustard seeds, cumin seeds, and curry leaves (take care, as these will splutter). Then you add a cut vegetable and sauté it until cooked through. Finally, you sprinkle some dry chutney over the top.

MAKES 1 CUP

ଓଓଓଓଓଓଓଓଓଓଓଓଓଓଓଓଓଓଓଓଓଓଓଓଓଓଓଓଓଓ

From Sayi Rani in Vishakhapatnam, Ardhra Pradesh

1. Set a small cast-iron frying pan over medium-low heat. When hot, add the chana dal and roast it, stirring, for about a minute. Add the toovar dal and keep roasting for another minute. Now add the urad dal, reduce the heat to low, and roast until the dals are all a golden-red color, about 5–6 minutes in all. Empty the dals into a bowl.

2. Put the cumin seeds, chilies, garlic, asafetida, and curry leaves into the empty frying pan, still over low heat. (Take care, as the curry leaves will splutter.) Stir and roast until the chilies

darken and the curry leaves dry up, about 5–6 minutes. Add these seasonings to the bowl of dals and set aside to cool.

3. Pour the contents of the bowl into a grinder, add ½ teaspoon of salt, and grind as finely as you can. The chutney will look like powder but be slightly granular. Taste for salt. It should be a little saltier than your normal food, so adjust as necessary. Store in a screw-top jar in a cool place.

QUICK YOGURT AND PICKLE CHUTNEY

DAHI AUR ACHAAR KI CHUTNEY

꒰꒱꒰꒱꒰꒱꒰꒱꒰꒱꒰꒱꒰꒱꒰꒱꒰꒱꒰꒱꒰꒱꒰꒱꒰꒱꒰꒱꒰꒱꒰꒱꒰꒱꒰꒱꒰꒱

½ cup plain yogurt

1 teaspoon (or more, if desired) any ready-made paste-like Indian pickle

I just made up this recipe one day when I was searching around for something simple and spicy to eat with my Moong Dal Pancakes (see page 255). I used what I had lying around in the kitchen, including something labeled Mango Thokku, which I had bought from the pickle section of my local Indian store. Any paste-like pickle will do. As long as it has no big chunks, it will work fine. Eggplant pickle is generally paste-like, as are many others. Some that are not, like most lime pickles, can be chopped finely to become paste-like. I just add a little of this pickle to yogurt and I am ready to eat. You could serve it with any of the pancakes in this book.

The day I made this chutney for the first time, my lunch was a big green salad from the produce in my garden, a moong dal pancake (two, if truth be told), and this chutney, which acted as a kind of dip. It was delicious. (This is also very good as a dip for potato chips.)   SERVES 1

꒰꒱꒰꒱꒰꒱꒰꒱꒰꒱꒰꒱꒰꒱꒰꒱꒰꒱꒰꒱꒰꒱꒰꒱꒰꒱꒰꒱꒰꒱꒰꒱꒰꒱꒰꒱꒰꒱

Put the yogurt in a small bowl and beat lightly with a fork until smooth and creamy. Add the pickle and mix it in thoroughly.

TOMATO AND GINGER CHUTNEY

TAMATAR-ADRAK KI CHUTNEY

2 tomatoes (12 oz in all),
    peeled, cored, and very
    finely chopped

2 teaspoons peeled and finely
    grated fresh ginger

2 cloves garlic, peeled and
    crushed

¼ teaspoon salt

¼ teaspoon nice red chili
    powder

2 tablespoons olive or peanut
    oil

¼ teaspoon urad dal

¼ teaspoon whole mustard
    seeds

5–6 fresh curry leaves, lightly
    crushed in your hand

Here is a hot, savory chutney, which can be eaten with almost any Indian meal. It comes from a South Indian Muslim cook in Albany, New York! He served it to me in the back of a small grocery store and I just guessed at what might be in it. A dollop of it in a soup, rather like a French rouille, perks it right up.   SERVES 4

1. Combine the tomatoes, ginger, garlic, salt, and chili powder in a small bowl.

2. Put the oil in a small nonstick frying pan and set over medium-high heat. When hot, add the urad dal. As soon as it starts to color, add the mustard seeds. When they pop, a matter of seconds, add the curry leaves (take care, as these will splutter), immediately followed by the contents of the small bowl. Stir continuously and fry for about 7–8 minutes or until you have a dark, thick paste. When cool, remove the curry leaves.

RED CHUTNEY FROM THE KONKAN COAST

KONKANI LAL CHUTNEY

೧೧೧೧೧೧೧೧೧೧೧೧೧೧೧೧೧೧೧೧೧೧೧೧೧೧೧೧೧೧೧೧

4 dried hot red chilies or
6–7 genuine Kashmiri or
byadgi chilies, if you can
get them

⅓ teaspoon salt

½ teaspoon dark brown sugar
or jaggery

8 tablespoons fresh grated
coconut, or defrosted if
frozen

¼ teaspoon ground roasted
cumin seeds (see page xx)

2 teaspoons sweet red paprika
(not needed if using
genuine byadgi chilies)

1 tablespoon olive or peanut
oil

Generous pinch of ground
asafetida

¼ teaspoon whole brown
mustard seeds

5–6 fresh curry leaves, lightly
crushed in your hand

The pretty, fertile Konkan Coast slithers down the western side of India from just north of Bombay all the way south to Mangalore, partially covering the narrow coastal plains of two states, Maharashtra and Karnataka. That is where this lovely chutney comes from. It has dozens of variations and may be eaten at all meals, including breakfast, when savory pancakes and steamed savory cakes are served in villages along the coast with hot coffee sweetened with liquid jaggery (raw brown sugar) stored in round-bottomed terracotta pots.

SERVES 6

೧೧೧೧೧೧೧೧೧೧೧೧೧೧೧೧೧೧೧೧೧೧೧೧೧೧೧೧೧೧೧೧

1. Put the chilies in a small bowl and pour ½ cup boiling water over them. Let them soak for 2–4 hours, until very soft. Lift them out of the water, remove the seeds, and chop the flesh. Save the water.

2. Put the chilies, salt, sugar, and reserved water into a blender. Add another 4 tablespoons of water and blend until smooth. Add the coconut, cumin, and paprika (if using) and blend again until the mixture is as fine as you can get it. Scrape the chutney into a bowl.

3. Put the oil into a small frying pan and set over medium-high heat. When hot, add the asafetida, quickly followed by the mustard seeds. As soon as the seeds start to pop, a matter of seconds, throw in the curry leaves (take care, as these will splutter). Quickly pour the contents of the pan into the chutney and mix well.

4. This chutney will keep for about 3 days in the refrigerator, but can also be frozen. It tends to get thicker as it sits, so feel free to add a little water to thin it out.

SWEET GREEN MANGO CHUTNEY

AAM KI MEETHI CHUTNEY

1½ lbs green, unripe sour
  mangoes
Salt
2 teaspoons olive or peanut oil
¼ teaspoon whole brown
  mustard seeds
2 hot dried red chilies
3 tablespoons sugar, or to taste

Green, unripe mangoes, sour and rich in pectin, are used throughout India to make all manner of sour pickles and sweet chutneys. Many of the latter are like preserves and can be kept for a long time. But mangoes can also be made into fresh chutneys, such as this one, which needs to be eaten within a day or two. However, it is so delicious, it will hardly last you a few hours! The recipe comes from a Bengali village, where my friend the documentary filmmaker Kavery Kaul was served it as a penultimate course, just before the sweets, by farmers returning home from a morning of tilling. In Bengal such chutneys are often eaten all by themselves in meals that start with fried foods, such as fritters (see pages 13, 15, and 18), go on to the rice, dal, and vegetable course, then to the chutney and finally to the sweetmeats, which Bengalis love and specialize in.

My mangoes were large, so I needed just two. You will find sour green mangoes in Indian groceries, especially from April to August. You might need to adjust the salt and sugar, as the amount of flesh and the sourness of mangoes can vary according to the variety and the time of picking.　　SERVES 6–8

1. Peel the mangoes, then cut the flesh off the stone and chop into rough dice. Put the dice into a medium saucepan, adding 1 cup water and ¼ teaspoon of salt. Bring to a boil, then cover and simmer gently for 7–8 minutes or until the mango pieces are very soft. Drain in a sieve.

2. Wash and dry the pan and set it over medium-high heat. Add the oil and, when hot, the mustard seeds and chilies. As soon as the seeds pop and the chilies darken, add the cooked mango. Stir in ¼ teaspoon of salt and the sugar, then mash up the mangoes as they cook for another 5–6 minutes. Taste for the balance of sugar and salt, adding more of whatever is needed. Serve at room temperature.

GINGERY CRANBERRY CHUTNEY WITH MUSTARD SEEDS

CRANBERRY KI CHUTNEY

〜〜〜〜〜〜〜〜〜〜〜〜〜〜〜〜〜〜〜〜〜〜〜〜〜〜〜〜〜〜〜

Two 1-lb cans of jellied
　　cranberry sauce
2 teaspoons olive or peanut oil
1 teaspoon whole yellow or
　　brown mustard seeds
1 cup cider vinegar
1 tablespoon peeled and very
　　finely grated fresh ginger
8 tablespoons sugar
½ teaspoon salt
¼ teaspoon nice red chili
　　powder (or more if you
　　wish)

This chutney is very easy to prepare. I make it with two cans of jellied cranberry sauce so no chopping or cutting is required. During the holiday season, I make enough to fill several jars that I take as gifts for friends. You may serve it at meals or on oatcakes or other savory biscuits with tea. Indians love the combination of hot tea with something a bit sweet, sour, and spicy.

MAKES ABOUT 3½ CUPS

〜〜〜〜〜〜〜〜〜〜〜〜〜〜〜〜〜〜〜〜〜〜〜〜〜〜〜〜〜〜〜

1. Place the cranberry sauce in a large bowl. Mash it as best as you can with a potato masher, or push it through a sieve or potato ricer. It will still be a little lumpy, but that is fine.

2. Put the oil in a medium saucepan and set over medium heat. When hot, add the mustard seeds. They should pop within seconds. Quickly pour in the vinegar and add the ginger, sugar, salt, and chili powder. Stir, then simmer vigorously on medium heat for 12–15 minutes, stirring every now and then, until the liquid has reduced by about half. Stir in the cranberry sauce and bring to a simmer, then simmer gently for 10 minutes, stirring frequently.

3. Let the sauce cool a little bit, then spoon it into sterilized jars. When the sauce has cooled completely, seal with lids and refrigerate. The sauce should be good for 2 weeks or more.

GREEN MANGO RELISH WITH MUSTARD SAUCE

AAM MAKHA

ಬ� (decorative border)

2 large hard, sour green
  mangoes (about 1½ lbs
  in all)
1 teaspoon salt
1 tablespoon sugar
1–2 fresh hot green chilies,
  finely chopped, or ¼–¾
  teaspoon nice red chili
  powder
1–2 tablespoons Homemade
  Mustard Sauce (see
  page 323)

Many Indian villages have mango trees that, as they grow larger, provide ample shade for whole families to spread cots (rope beds) under them and rest in the afternoons. Throughout the early summer, they also provide hard, sour (unripe) green mangoes that can be made into quick, refreshing salads. Here is one such relish/salad from Bangladesh, given to me by my physical therapist. Similar relishes can be found in the Indian state of West Bengal. They are eaten as part of the meal or as a snack. Kasundi, the spicy mustard sauce used to dress the relish, comes in a bottle and can be bought in some Indian and Bangladeshi shops. In case you can't find it, I have provided a quick version of my own.

Approximate seasonings are given for the relish because the sourness of mangoes can vary hugely. The amount of sugar used is really a matter of taste as well.   SERVES 4–6

(decorative border)

From Rifat Rahman

Peel the mangoes and grate them on the coarsest part of your grater. Place in a bowl, add all the other ingredients, and mix well.

HOMEMADE MUSTARD SAUCE

KASUNDI

ოთოოთოოთოოთოოთოოთოოთოოთოოთოოთოოთოოთოოთოოთოო

1 teaspoon white wine vinegar

½ teaspoon ground cumin

¼ teaspoon ground turmeric

1 teaspoon sugar

3 tablespoons ready-made
whole-grain mustard

In the West it is very hard to find a bottle of kasundi, the Bengali mustard sauce used in West Bengal, India, and Bangladesh as a dressing and a dip for all manner of sour fruit and vegetables (see my recipe for Green Mango Relish with Mustard Sauce on page 322). Use it anywhere a grainy mustard is required.

I do not exactly make the mustard sauce from scratch. I buy a bottle of whole-grain mustard and then add seasonings so it tastes and looks almost exactly like the real thing.

MAKES ABOUT ½ CUP

ოთოოთოოთოოთოოთოოთოოთოოთოოთოოთოოთოოთოოთოოთოო

1. Put 5 tablespoons of water in a small pan. Add the vinegar, cumin, turmeric, and sugar and bring to a gentle simmer over low heat. Stir and simmer gently for a minute, then set aside to cool.

2. Spoon the mustard into a small bowl. Slowly add the cooled contents of the pan, stirring to mix. Store in a screw-top jar in the refrigerator.

SIMPLE SEASONED YOGURT, SOUTH INDIAN—STYLE

MOSARU PACCHADI/PERUGU TALIMPU

〜〜〜〜〜〜〜〜〜〜〜〜〜〜〜〜〜〜〜〜〜〜〜〜〜〜〜〜〜〜

1 cup plain yogurt

¼ teaspoon salt

1 teaspoon olive or peanut oil

½ teaspoon urad dal or yellow split peas

¼ teaspoon whole brown mustard seeds

2 hot dried red chilies

5–6 fresh curry leaves

This is the simplest of generic South Indian yogurt relishes. At the Windflower Resort in Mysore it appears on the table with all orders of Indian food. SERVES 4

〜〜〜〜〜〜〜〜〜〜〜〜〜〜〜〜〜〜〜〜〜〜〜〜〜〜〜〜〜〜

From the Windflower Resort and Spa in Mysore

1. Put the yogurt and salt in a serving bowl. Beat lightly with a whisk or fork until smooth and creamy.

2. Put the oil in a small pan and set over medium-high heat. When hot, add the dal. As soon as it changes color, add the mustard seeds. When they pop, a matter of seconds, add the chilies, rolling them until they darken all over. Quickly add the curry leaves (take care, as these will splutter), then pour the contents of the pan over the yogurt. Do not stir—leave the seasonings on top as decoration.

SIMPLE SEASONED YOGURT,
NORTH INDIAN—STYLE

DAHI KA SAADA RAITA

ᥬᥬᥬᥬᥬᥬᥬᥬᥬᥬᥬᥬᥬᥬᥬᥬᥬᥬᥬᥬᥬᥬᥬᥬᥬᥬᥬᥬᥬᥬᥬ

1 cup plain yogurt

¼ teaspoon salt

½ teaspoon ground roasted
cumin seeds (see page xx),
plus a little extra for
sprinkling

¼ teaspoon nice red chili
powder, plus a little extra
for sprinkling

This is the simplest of generic North Indian yogurt relishes. It is also the base to which you might add vegetables (parboiled and chopped spinach, roasted and mashed eggplant, boiled and diced potatoes, chopped tomatoes, grated cucumbers, etc.) and cooked legumes (chickpeas, urad dal dumplings, etc.). It can be served with all Indian meals, especially northern ones.   SERVES 4

ᥬᥬᥬᥬᥬᥬᥬᥬᥬᥬᥬᥬᥬᥬᥬᥬᥬᥬᥬᥬᥬᥬᥬᥬᥬᥬᥬᥬᥬᥬᥬ

Put the yogurt, salt, cumin, and chili powder in a serving bowl. Beat lightly with a whisk or fork until smooth, creamy, and thoroughly mixed. Sprinkle a generous pinch each of cumin and chili powder lightly over the top.

SIMPLE SEASONED YOGURT, TELENGANA-STYLE

PERUGU PACHADI

ພພພພພພພພພພພພພພພພພພພພພພພພ

1 cup plain yogurt

¼ teaspoon salt

2 tablespoons peeled and finely chopped shallots

1–2 fresh hot green chilies, finely chopped

Generous pinch of ground turmeric

1 tablespoon oil

¼ teaspoon whole brown mustard seeds

¼ teaspoon whole cumin seeds

Generous pinch of ground asafetida

2 dried hot red chilies, one broken in half

6–8 fresh curry leaves, lightly crushed in your hand

From Andhra Pradesh, this dish was part of a meal that S. Sampoorna cooked for me (see page 162).

Here the yogurt is left in a rough state, not whisked until smooth. It can be served with Toovar Dal with Spinach and Sorrel (see page 162), some rice, and Stir-fried Carrots (see page 69).

SERVES 4

ພພພພພພພພພພພພພພພພພພພພພພພພ

From S. Sampoorna

1. Put the yogurt in a bowl. Add the salt, shallots, and green chilies. Stir roughly to mix, then place the turmeric on top of the yogurt, right in the center.

2. Put the oil in a small pan and set over medium-high heat. When it is very hot, add the mustard seeds, cumin seeds, and asafetida. As soon as the mustard seeds pop, add the red chilies and stir for a few seconds, until they darken. Add the curry leaves (take care, as these will splutter), then quickly pour the contents of the pan over the yogurt, aiming to cover the turmeric so that it gets "cooked." Mix and serve.

SIMPLE YOGURT DIPPING SAUCE

DAHI KI CHUTNEY

၁ cup plain yogurt

¼ teaspoon salt

Freshly ground black pepper

Generous pinch of nice red
chili powder

A simple yogurt sauce, this is particularly good with spicy or stuffed Indian flatbreads and pancakes. It can also be served with a meal. SERVES 2–4

Put the yogurt in a bowl and beat lightly with a fork or whisk until smooth and creamy. Add all the other ingredients and mix well.

MY YOGURT DRESSING

DAHI KI DRESSING

꒰ꕤ꒱ꕤ꒱ꕤ꒱ꕤ꒱ꕤ꒱ꕤ꒱ꕤ꒱ꕤ꒱ꕤ꒱ꕤ꒱ꕤ꒱ꕤ꒱ꕤ꒱ꕤ꒱ꕤ꒱ꕤ꒱

1½ cups plain yogurt

½ teaspoon salt, or to taste

Freshly ground black pepper

Generous pinch of nice red
chili powder (optional)

½ teaspoon ground roasted
cumin seeds (see page xx,
optional)

1½ teaspoons white wine
vinegar

2 tablespoons extra-virgin
olive oil

Yogurt (and other dairy foods) often completes the nutritional balance of vegetarian Indian meals, but sometimes I just want a "wrap" made with an Indian pancake or bread and a crunchy green salad to accompany it, an East-West mixture that seems to have become part of my repertoire. I still need some dairy in the meal for its food value, so I have taken to dressing salads of crisp greens with this yogurt dressing that I have created. Use just enough to coat the leaves lightly. The dressing can also be used as a dip. MAKES ENOUGH TO DRESS A SALAD FOR 4

꒰ꕤ꒱ꕤ꒱ꕤ꒱ꕤ꒱ꕤ꒱ꕤ꒱ꕤ꒱ꕤ꒱ꕤ꒱ꕤ꒱ꕤ꒱ꕤ꒱ꕤ꒱ꕤ꒱ꕤ꒱ꕤ꒱

Place the yogurt in a bowl. Add the salt, black pepper, chili powder, and cumin (if using). Beat lightly with a fork or whisk until smooth and creamy. Beat in the vinegar and olive oil, then taste for balance of seasonings and adjust as necessary.

SPINACH RAITA

SAAG KA RAITA

2 well-packed cups raw
spinach

2 cups plain yogurt

¼ teaspoon salt, or to taste

¼ teaspoon nice red chili
powder

1 or 2 generous pinches of
ground roasted cumin
seeds (see page xx), plus a
little extra for sprinkling

Here is a simple northern raita that can be served with nearly all Indian meals. You could also make a light meal for two people by adding two handfuls of drained cooked chickpeas to it.

SERVES 4–6

1. Drop the spinach into a small pan of boiling water and let it wilt. Drain and refresh under cold running water. Squeeze out the water and chop the spinach.

2. Put the yogurt in a bowl. Add the salt, chili powder, and cumin. Beat with a fork or whisk until smooth and creamy. Stir in the spinach, then sprinkle a little roasted cumin over the top.

YOGURT WITH CUCUMBER, KODAVA-STYLE

CHAUTHE PACHADI

అఅఅఅఅఅఅఅఅఅఅఅఅఅఅఅఅఅఅఅఅఅఅఅఅఅఅఅఅఅఅ

3 tablespoons fresh grated
   coconut, or defrosted if
   frozen

1–2 fresh hot green chilies,
   finely chopped

Generous pinch of English
   mustard powder

½ cup peeled cucumber, cut
   into ¼ inch dice

1 teaspoon olive or peanut oil

¼ teaspoon whole brown
   mustard seeds

1 dried hot red chili

5–6 fresh curry leaves, lightly
   crushed in your hand

1 cup plain yogurt

¼ teaspoon salt, or to taste

2 tablespoons finely chopped
   fresh cilantro

Mynah lives in Siddapur in southern Coorg, Karnataka. The front of her house faces miles of open fields—she raises her guinea hens there—and at the back are the forests where she forages for mushrooms, wild fruit, and wild greens, as all people in Coorg seem to love to do. She made a magnificent meal for me in her outdoor kitchen. This is the yogurt relish she served, along with Simple Kodava Mushroom Curry (see page 90), fiddlehead ferns, young colocasia leaves (still furled up), the lightest of rice flatbreads, and egg curry. For more on the people of Coorg, see the introduction to Kodava Mushroom Curry with Coconut (page 86).

SERVES 4

అఅఅఅఅఅఅఅఅఅఅఅఅఅఅఅఅఅఅఅఅఅఅఅఅఅఅఅఅఅఅ

From Mynah Pemmaiah

1. Put the coconut, green chilies, and mustard powder into a mortar and pound with the pestle until you have a coarse paste. Alternatively, whiz these ingredients in a small grinder.

2. Place the cucumber in a bowl. Add the coconut mixture and mix thoroughly.

3. Pour the oil into a small pan and set over medium-high heat. When hot, add the mustard seeds. As soon as they start to pop, a matter of seconds, add the red chili. When it darkens, add the curry leaves (take care, as these will splutter). Quickly pour the contents of the pan over the cucumber.

4. Put the yogurt into a serving bowl. Add the salt and whisk until the yogurt is smooth and creamy. Stir in the cilantro, then fold in the cucumber mixture. Taste for balance of seasonings, and adjust as necessary.

CARROT RAITA

GAJAR KA RAITA

⌣⌣⌣⌣⌣⌣⌣⌣⌣⌣⌣⌣⌣⌣⌣⌣⌣⌣⌣⌣⌣⌣⌣⌣⌣⌣⌣

1½ cups plain yogurt

½ teaspoon salt

Freshly ground black pepper

2 teaspoons sugar

1 fresh hot green chili, finely
chopped, or ¼ teaspoon
nice red chili powder

1–2 tablespoons chopped fresh
cilantro

2–3 medium carrots, peeled
and coarsely grated

2 teaspoons olive or peanut oil

½ teaspoon whole brown
mustard seeds

½ teaspoon whole cumin
seeds

This raita has a slightly sweet-and-sour taste. If you wish, you can add a tablespoon of golden raisins, but soak them first in boiling water for thirty minutes and drain them. Add them at the same time as the carrots. SERVES 6

⌣⌣⌣⌣⌣⌣⌣⌣⌣⌣⌣⌣⌣⌣⌣⌣⌣⌣⌣⌣⌣⌣⌣⌣⌣⌣⌣

1. Put the yogurt in a bowl. Add the salt, pepper, sugar, and green chilies or chili powder. Mix with a small whisk or fork until creamy. Add the cilantro and carrots and mix well.

2. Set a small frying pan over medium-high heat and add the oil. When hot, add the mustard seeds. When they start to pop, a matter of seconds, add the cumin seeds. Let them sizzle for 5 seconds, then pour the contents of the pan over the yogurt. Stir to mix.

YOGURT RAITA WITH TOMATOES, SHALLOTS, AND CUCUMBERS

TAMATAR AUR KHEERAY KA RAITA

꙳꙳꙳꙳꙳꙳꙳꙳꙳꙳꙳꙳꙳꙳꙳꙳꙳꙳꙳꙳꙳꙳꙳꙳꙳꙳꙳꙳꙳꙳

2 cups plain yogurt

½ teaspoon salt

¼ teaspoon nice red chili powder or 1 fresh hot green chili, finely chopped (add more if desired)

¾ teaspoon ground roasted cumin seeds (see page xx)

2 large cherry tomatoes, each cut into 8 pieces, or 4 smaller ones, quartered

2 tablespoons peeled and finely chopped shallots

4 tablespoons finely diced cucumber

2 tablespoons chopped fresh cilantro leaves

Here is a raita that is almost a salad. You can eat it all by itself or as part of a meal. SERVES 6

꙳꙳꙳꙳꙳꙳꙳꙳꙳꙳꙳꙳꙳꙳꙳꙳꙳꙳꙳꙳꙳꙳꙳꙳꙳꙳꙳꙳꙳꙳

Put the yogurt in a bowl. Beat lightly with a fork or whisk until smooth and creamy. Add the salt, chili powder, and cumin and mix well. Fold in all the other ingredients, then taste for salt and adjust as necessary.

YOGURT AND PINEAPPLE SALAD, KERALA-STYLE

PINEAPPLE PACHADI

ᏋᏋᏋᏋᏋᏋᏋᏋᏋᏋᏋᏋᏋᏋᏋᏋᏋᏋᏋᏋᏋᏋᏋᏋᏋᏋ

1 well-packed cup fresh
    pineapple chunks, cut into
    ⅓ inch dice (save any juice)
2–3 fresh hot green chilies,
    finely chopped
Generous pinch of ground
    turmeric
¼–½ teaspoon nice red chili
    powder
Salt
1 tablespoon unsweetened
    coconut powder
2 teaspoons sugar
1 cup plain yogurt
2 teaspoons olive or peanut oil
¼ teaspoon whole brown
    mustard seeds
1–2 dried hot red chilies
5–6 fresh curry leaves, lightly
    crushed in your hand
1 medium shallot, peeled and
    cut into fine slivers

Pineapples came to India in the late fifteenth century with Portuguese traders. They first landed in Kerala, where locals disdainfully declared them to be "the jackfruit of the donkey." They traveled all over the country, going as far north as the Moghul court in Delhi, where they were considered a wondrous curiosity. The British in India began to grow them, along with bananas and mangoes, on the lower reaches of their coffee and tea plantations. For their Sunday club lunches, they loved to combine hot curries with sweet fruit chutneys and relishes. The people of Kerala too began to use them in the same manner, as they did with some of their other fruit, either eating them fresh or incorporating them into their everyday foods. The pineapple yogurt salad or relish is one such dish. Southern pachadis, rather like northern raitas, can be served with most meals.   SERVES 4

ᏋᏋᏋᏋᏋᏋᏋᏋᏋᏋᏋᏋᏋᏋᏋᏋᏋᏋᏋᏋᏋᏋᏋᏋᏋᏋ

1. Put the pineapple and its juice into a medium, preferably nonstick frying pan set over medium-high heat. Add the green chilies, turmeric, chili powder, ¼ teaspoon of salt, coconut powder, sugar, and ½ cup water. Stir, bring to a simmer, and cook until all the liquid has been absorbed. Set aside to cool.

2. Place the yogurt in a bowl. Add ¼ teaspoon of salt and whisk until smooth and creamy. Stir in the cooled pineapple.

3. Put the oil into a small frying pan set over medium-high heat. When hot, add the mustard seeds. As soon as they pop, a matter of seconds, add the red chilies. When they darken, add the curry leaves (take care, as these will splutter). A second later, add the shallots. Stir and fry over medium heat until they start to brown at the edges.

4. Empty the contents of the pan over the pineapple salad. Leave the spices on top, like a decoration, and stir them in at the table.

YOGURT WITH FRESH MANGO

MANGO PAJJI

⌇⌇

1 cup plain yogurt

¼ teaspoon salt

2 teaspoons sugar, or to taste

¼ teaspoon tamarind concentrate (sold in bottles)

2 packed tablespoons fresh grated coconut, or defrosted if frozen

1–3 fresh hot green chilies, finely chopped

2 teaspoons olive or peanut oil

¼ teaspoon whole brown mustard seeds

5–6 fresh curry leaves, lightly crushed in your hand

½ medium onion, peeled and finely chopped

1 clove garlic, peeled and finely chopped

1 ripe mango, peeled, sliced neatly, and cut into ½ inch dice

In the north we call yogurt relishes "raita." In the south, a yogurt "pachadi" or "pajji" is very similar. This is a Kodava recipe from Coorg. (For more about that area, see Kodava Mushroom Curry with Coconut, page 86.) Naturally, this delicious sweet-and-sour relish has southern flavors, such as those that come from coconut and curry leaves.

Usha served this dish to us in her grand ancestral home, known as Chamaraja Villa, in Coorg's capital city, Madikeri (also called Mercara), filled with handsome Anglo-Indian furniture and objects. Coorg was an independent state until it merged with Karnataka in 1956. The British, who went on to build large coffee plantations here and who loved the area's hills, mists, and hunting and fishing traditions, could not pronounce the name of the land, Kodagu, so they began calling it Coorg. Now both names are used.

You can eat this yogurt dish by itself as a snack, but it is normally served with meals, as a relish. It is good with both North Indian and South Indian foods.　　SERVES 4

⌇⌇

From Usha Machaiah

1. Put the yogurt in a medium bowl and add the salt, sugar, and tamarind. Beat lightly with a whisk until smooth and creamy, and well mixed.

2. Put the coconut and chilies into a mortar. Pound with the pestle until you have a rough paste.

3. Put the oil in a medium frying pan set over medium heat. When hot, add the mustard seeds. As soon as they pop, a matter

of seconds, throw in the curry leaves (take care, as these will splutter). Add the onions a second later and fry for about 2 minutes.

4. Reduce the heat to low, add the garlic, and cook for another 2 minutes. Add the coconut paste from the mortar and stir for a minute. Now tip the contents of the pan into the bowl of yogurt and mix well. Add the mango and mix again. Taste to check the balance of seasonings and add whatever you think is needed. Cover and refrigerate until you are ready to serve.

A NOTE ON THE MAHARASHTRIAN/NORTH KANNADA SALAD KNOWN AS KOSAMBIR, KOSHAMBIR, KOSMIR, KOSAMBARI, OR KOSHAMBARI

I first had this salad in a Saraswat Brahmin home in Maharashtra at a formal meal served on a silver thali (platter), which contained all the dishes for our lunch. It had its special place, which was on the left. If it were to be served in a village on a banana leaf, it would still be on the left.

There are hundreds of versions of this salad (it is often eaten as a snack as well), which can be found all over Maharashtra and northern Kannada. It may be prepared with raw vegetables, such as carrots, cucumbers, and tomatoes, or cooked vegetables, such as green beans, beets, and potatoes. It can also include roasted nuts, such as peanuts, for added protein. It is always sour, made so with lime juice, though it could be tamarind water.

It could have a slight sweetness from adding grated coconut. When it is served at weddings and festivals, it always has either soaked moong dal or sprouted mung beans in it. These are offered to God in the morning, then combined with the salad at mealtime for everyone to share the holy blessings.

What most of these salads have in common is a tarka (see page xxii). Once the major ingredients have all been put together, oil is heated in a small pan and seasonings, such as whole mustard seeds, a bit of urad dal, asafetida, and curry leaves, are allowed to splutter for a few seconds before being emptied over the salad. It is this that gives each salad its regional flavor.

GREEN BEAN SALAD

KOSAMBARI

⅌⅌⅌⅌⅌⅌⅌⅌⅌⅌⅌⅌⅌⅌⅌⅌⅌⅌⅌⅌⅌

2¼ cups green beans (round or flat), cut crosswise into ¼ inch pieces

3 tablespoons peeled and finely chopped shallots

1–3 fresh hot green chilies, very finely chopped

4 tablespoons fresh grated coconut, or defrosted if frozen

2 tablespoons chopped fresh cilantro

½ teaspoon salt, or to taste

1 teaspoon olive or peanut oil

½ teaspoon whole brown mustard seeds

1 tablespoon lime juice

Here the beans are cut and steamed before being dressed. Every home in western and southern India has at least one steamer in the kitchen. They used to be made out of wood and bamboo, but those are now for collectors to find and marvel at. The best of today's steamers are made of stainless steel and are used for rice noodles, rice cakes, split pea savories, and vegetables.

This salad is generally served at room temperature, though it could be refrigerated and served cold. Add the lime juice at the last minute so that the beans do not lose their color.   SERVES 4

⅌⅌⅌⅌⅌⅌⅌⅌⅌⅌⅌⅌⅌⅌⅌⅌⅌⅌⅌⅌⅌

From Nina Chandavarkar

1. Steam the beans for about 10 minutes, until tender but with a hint of crispness. (You could also parboil and then drain them.) Refresh with cold water, then pat dry. Place in a bowl, then mix in the shallots, green chilies, coconut, cilantro, and salt.

2. Put the oil in a small frying pan and set over medium-high heat. When hot, add the mustard seeds. As soon as they pop, a matter of seconds, pour the oil and seeds over the beans. Stir to mix.

3. Add the lime juice just before serving and toss again.

CARROT SALAD WITH PEANUTS

KOSHAMBIR

೧೪೧೪೧೪೧೪೧೪೧೪೧೪೧೪೧೪೧೪೧೪೧೪೧೪೧೪೧೪೧೪೧೪೧೪೧೪

Here we have a light salad that can be served with most meals.

SERVES 4–6

೧೪೧೪೧೪೧೪೧೪೧೪೧೪೧೪೧೪೧೪೧೪೧೪೧೪೧೪೧೪೧೪೧೪೧೪೧೪

3 large carrots (about 15 oz in all), peeled and grated

1 tablespoon lime or lemon juice

½ teaspoon sugar

½ teaspoon salt

1 fresh hot green chili, finely chopped

3 tablespoons chopped fresh cilantro

4–5 tablespoons roasted peanuts, crushed

1 teaspoon olive or peanut oil

½ teaspoon whole brown mustard seeds

2 tablespoons golden raisins (optional)

1. Combine the carrots, lime juice, sugar, salt, green chilies, cilantro, and peanuts in a bowl.

2. Put the oil in a small frying pan and set over medium-high heat. When hot, add the mustard seeds. As soon as they pop, a matter of seconds, add the golden raisins (if using). Immediately pour the contents of the pan over the carrots and stir well. Taste for balance of seasonings, adding whatever you think is needed.

TOMATO, ONION, AND CUCUMBER KOSHAMBARI

KOSHAMBARI

꿍꿍꿍꿍꿍꿍꿍꿍꿍꿍꿍꿍꿍꿍꿍꿍꿍꿍꿍꿍꿍꿍

1 medium tomato, diced

1 medium onion, peeled and
    diced

1 small cucumber, peeled and
    diced

1 teaspoon olive or peanut oil

½ teaspoon whole brown
    mustard seeds

1–1¼ teaspoons salt

1 or 2 generous pinches of
    nice red chili powder

1–1½ tablespoons lemon juice

Adjust the salt and lemon juice in the recipe according to the tartness of the tomatoes. It is best to combine all the vegetables in a bowl but add the seasonings shortly before you serve. SERVES 4

꿍꿍꿍꿍꿍꿍꿍꿍꿍꿍꿍꿍꿍꿍꿍꿍꿍꿍꿍꿍꿍꿍

1. Put the tomatoes, onions, and cucumbers into a bowl.

2. Pour the oil into a small pan and set over medium-high heat. When hot, add the mustard seeds. As soon as they pop, a matter of seconds, pour the contents of the pan over the salad. Toss to mix.

3. Just before serving, add the salt, chili powder, and lemon juice and toss well. Taste to check the balance of flavorings, and adjust as necessary.

SALAD WITH INDIAN-STYLE BEAN SPROUTS

KOSHAMBIR/KOSAMBARI

About 10 oz medium cherry
tomatoes, cut into ¼ inch
dice
2 medium cucumbers with
small seeds (about 7 oz in
all), cut into ¼ inch dice
1 medium carrot, peeled and
coarsely grated
½ cup Indian-style mung bean
sprouts (see page 142)
½–2 fresh hot green chilies,
chopped, or 1–2 generous
pinches of nice red chili
powder
Freshly ground black pepper
2 teaspoons olive or peanut oil
1 teaspoon whole brown
mustard seeds
1 teaspoon salt
1½ tablespoons lemon juice
2 tablespoons chopped fresh
cilantro

There are many possible variations of this nutritious, everyday salad from Maharashtra in western India. This version is the first one I ever ate, and I still love it.

The salad can be served with most meals, or by itself as a light lunch. You can add some plain yogurt to it if you wish.

It is best to use small, firm cherry tomatoes here as they hold their shape best when cut.   SERVES 4

1. Combine the tomatoes, cucumbers, carrots, bean sprouts, chilies, and black pepper in a bowl.

2. Put the oil in a small frying pan and set over medium-high heat. When hot, add the mustard seeds. As soon as they start to pop, a matter of seconds, pour the contents of the pan over the salad ingredients. Toss well.

3. Just before eating, add the salt, lemon juice, and fresh cilantro. Toss again.

NEPALESE "PICKLED" POTATOES

ALOO ACHAAR

୧୬

1 lb 2 oz waxy potatoes,
 boiled and cooled, but not
 refrigerated

3 tablespoons tahini (sesame
 paste)

¼ teaspoon nice red chili
 powder

Generous pinch of ground
 turmeric

½–2 fresh hot green chilies,
 finely chopped

2 tablespoons mustard oil

1½ tablespoons lemon juice

2–3 tablespoons chopped
 fresh cilantro

¾–1 teaspoon salt

More a salad than a pickle, albeit a very spicy one, this recipe comes from Nepal. It is traditionally made with mustard oil, which gives it a unique pungency that I just love, but if you find that a bit strong, use a very good virgin olive oil instead. Serve it as you would any potato salad.

In Nepal, this salad is made with sesame seeds that are roasted and ground. You can do so by adding 3 tablespoons of them, in which case you might need to use more oil later on. I have taken the easy way out and used tahini.   SERVES 4

୧୬

1. Peel the potatoes and cut them into 1 inch pieces.

2. Put the tahini in a good-sized bowl. Slowly add 4 tablespoons of very hot water, mixing to a smooth paste as you go. Add the chili powder, turmeric, green chilies, mustard oil, lemon juice, cilantro, and salt (starting with ¾ teaspoon). Mix well so you have a smooth paste. Taste for balance of seasonings, adding more salt if you wish.

3. Add the potatoes and gently mix them in. Serve at room temperature or cold.

SIMPLE SOUTH INDIAN TOMATO SAUCE

TAMATAR PACCHADI

ଔଓଔଓଔଓଔଓଔଓଔଓଔଓଔଓଔଓଔଓଔଓଔଓଔଓଔଓ

1¾ lbs ripe tomatoes, chopped

1 onion (2½ oz), peeled and chopped

1–2 fresh hot green chilies, sliced crosswise into thin rounds

Generous handful of fresh cilantro tops, chopped

1 teaspoon salt

½ teaspoon tamarind concentrate (sold in bottles)

¼–½ teaspoon nice red chili powder

¼ teaspoon ground turmeric

2 teaspoons olive or peanut oil

½ teaspoon urad dal

¼ teaspoon whole mustard seeds

¼ teaspoon whole cumin seeds

8–10 fresh curry leaves, lightly crushed in your hand

This is a wonderfully spicy sauce that can be thrown over pasta or rice noodles, spread over grilled eggplant or zucchini slices, or used as a dip for a variety of crisp and crunchy Indian fritters, chips, and pancakes.

As I use this sauce so often, I like to freeze it and always have it on hand. This way I can defrost it whenever the need arises.

MAKES ABOUT 2 ¾ CUPS

ଔଓଔଓଔଓଔଓଔଓଔଓଔଓଔଓଔଓଔଓଔଓଔଓଔଓଔଓ

1. Put the tomatoes into a bowl and crush them as much as you can with your hand to release their moisture. Add the onions, green chilies, cilantro, ½ teaspoon of the salt, the tamarind, chili powder, and turmeric.

2. Set a medium pan over medium heat and add the oil. When really hot, add the urad dal. As soon as it starts to turn reddish, add the mustard seeds. When they start to pop, a matter of seconds, add the cumin seeds. Let them sizzle for a few seconds, then throw in the curry leaves (take care, as these will splutter). Add the tomato mixture, reduce the heat to medium low, and bring to a gentle simmer. Simmer uncovered, stirring now and then, until the sauce has thickened, about 20–25 minutes. Taste, adding the other ½ teaspoon of salt if needed. Cool a bit, then blend to a thick sauce and serve.

FRESH PEACH SALAD

ARU KA SALAAD

2 ripe peaches, peeled and
each cut into 10–12 slices
⅓ teaspoon salt
Freshly ground black pepper
½ teaspoon roasted and
ground cumin seeds (see
page xx)
⅛ teaspoon chili powder, or
more as desired
1 teaspoon lime or lemon juice
2 teaspoons finely chopped
fresh cilantro

Somewhere between a salad and chaat (spicy snack food), this dish and others like it always remind me of my mother, who made them for us as a treat. In the bazaars of Delhi, similar salads were served in bowls made of large leaves stitched together with twigs. Simple wooden toothpicks took the place of cutlery. At home we had the salad on plates, though my mother always added the toothpicks to get some of the feel of the wild bazaar.

Peaches were never used in the bazaar, as they were expensive. Starfruit, bananas, roasted white yams, and guavas were much more common.

Serve this salad with lunch or as a snack. It should be made just before being eaten because it gets very watery as it sits.

SERVES 2–3

Combine all the ingredients in a bowl. Taste for the balance of seasonings, adding more of anything you wish.

DRINKS, SWEETS, AND DESSERTS

A POMEGRANATE AND MINT DRINK

ANAAR KA RAS

ೞೞೞೞೞೞೞೞೞೞೞೞೞೞೞೞೞೞೞೞೞೞೞೞೞೞೞೞೞೞ

1 cup pomegranate juice

15 fresh mint leaves, crushed,
    plus a mint sprig for
    garnish

2 teaspoons lime juice

4–5 teaspoons honey, or to
    taste

5–6 ice cubes, plus extra for
    serving

When I arrived at the Falaknuma Palace Hotel in Hyderabad recently, they offered me a pomegranate mojito. I wasn't quite ready for a proper drink, so I asked if I could just have the pomegranate juice. This is how they serve it. You could try it with a gin or vodka if you like.

This recipe may easily be doubled. I used organic, pure pomegranate juice that is easily available in health-food stores. At the hotel, they simply squeeze out fresh juice. If you have a juicer, you could do the same.

SERVES 1

ೞೞೞೞೞೞೞೞೞೞೞೞೞೞೞೞೞೞೞೞೞೞೞೞೞೞೞೞೞೞ

From the Taj Falaknuma Palace hotel in Hyderabad

Combine the pomegranate juice, mint leaves, lime juice, honey, and ice cubes in a shaker or jug. Shake or stir well and strain into a glass. Serve garnished with the mint sprig and with a few extra cubes of ice.

SRI LANKAN LEMONADE FLAVORED WITH GINGER AND LEMONGRASS

SRI LANKA KI LEMONADE

᭼᭼᭼᭼᭼᭼᭼᭼᭼᭼᭼᭼᭼᭼᭼᭼᭼᭼᭼᭼᭼᭼᭼᭼

2 sticks of lemongrass

An 8-inch piece of fresh ginger, peeled and chopped

1 cup sugar

1⅛ cups fresh lime juice

Ice cubes

I had this drink in Sri Lanka, at a very elegant ladies' lunch in Colombo, where they also served a marvelous ginger beer. Both were offered before the grand multi-course lunch. SERVES 6

᭼᭼᭼᭼᭼᭼᭼᭼᭼᭼᭼᭼᭼᭼᭼᭼᭼᭼᭼᭼᭼᭼᭼᭼

1. Cut off the very top of the lemongrass sticks, retaining the bottom 8 inches. Lightly smash the bulbous end. Now cut the lemongrass crosswise into very fine slices. Place ends in a medium pan with the ginger, sugar, and 1 cup water and bring to a boil. Reduce the heat and simmer, uncovered, for 15 minutes. Strain and set aside to cool, then store the syrup in a small jug or screw-top jar.

2. Whenever you wish to make a glass of lemonade, put 4 tablespoons of the flavored syrup into a glass followed by 3 tablespoons of fresh lime juice and ½ cup water. Stir to mix, then drop in 6–7 ice cubes and stir again. Taste and adjust the sweetness or sourness as needed. The syrup will make up to 6 glasses in this way.

GINGER MINT TEA

ADRAK KI CHAI

◡◡◡◡◡◡◡◡◡◡◡◡◡◡◡◡◡◡◡◡◡◡◡◡◡◡◡◡◡◡◡◡◡◡◡◡

A 3-inch piece of fresh ginger,
   peeled and cut into thin
   round slices
20 fresh mint leaves
Honey, preferably unboiled, to
   serve (unboiled honey is
   available from health-food
   stores)

A wonderful tea to have on a cold day, or when you have a cold.

SERVES 4

◡◡◡◡◡◡◡◡◡◡◡◡◡◡◡◡◡◡◡◡◡◡◡◡◡◡◡◡◡◡◡◡◡◡◡◡

1. Put the ginger and 4 cups water into a saucepan and bring to a boil. Lower the heat and simmer gently for 15–20 minutes, then strain into a warmed teapot. Discard the ginger.

2. Crush the mint leaves lightly in your hand and throw them into the teapot. Cover and leave to steep for 5 minutes. Serve the tea with honey.

YOGURT AND CUCUMBER DRINK

SOUTHEKAI MAJJIGE

ᘓᘓᘓᘓᘓᘓᘓᘓᘓᘓᘓᘓᘓᘓᘓᘓᘓᘓᘓᘓᘓᘓᘓᘓᘓᘓ

This is a very cooling and refreshing drink.   SERVES 1–2

ᘓᘓᘓᘓᘓᘓᘓᘓᘓᘓᘓᘓᘓᘓᘓᘓᘓᘓᘓᘓᘓᘓᘓᘓᘓᘓ

From Heera Nandi

1 cup plain yogurt, nice and
  cold
7 oz cucumbers (3 smallish
  ones), peeled and chopped
  (I like the seedless Persian
  or Armenian ones)
1 teaspoon peeled and finely
  chopped fresh ginger
2 teaspoons lime juice
½ fresh hot green chili,
  chopped (optional)
¼ teaspoon salt, or to taste
2 tablespoons chopped fresh
  cilantro or 1 tablespoon
  chopped fresh mint
Ice cubes (optional)

Put all the ingredients in a blender in the order listed and blend
until smooth. Strain through a fine sieve, pushing out all the
liquid, and pour into a glass. Add an ice cube or two if you wish.

CURRY LEAF—FLAVORED YOGURT DRINK

CHAAS

2 cups plain yogurt

About 30 fresh curry leaves

1 fresh hot green chili,
    chopped

½ teaspoon salt, or to taste

Ice cubes

༄༄༄༄༄༄༄༄༄༄༄༄༄༄༄༄༄༄༄༄༄༄༄

**A simple, nutritious, and cooling drink that can be served with
meals or by itself.** SERVES 2

༄༄༄༄༄༄༄༄༄༄༄༄༄༄༄༄༄༄༄༄༄༄༄

From the Chinmaya Mission in Delhi

1. Put all the ingredients into a blender along with 1 cup water.
Blend thoroughly. Strain into a jug through a fine sieve, pushing out as much liquid as possible. Refrigerate until needed.

2. To serve, pour into two glasses, adding a few ice cubes to each
one.

YOGURT DRINK WITH CURRY LEAVES, FRESH CILANTRO, AND CUMIN

CHAAS

‿‿‿‿‿‿‿‿‿‿‿‿‿‿‿‿‿‿‿‿‿‿‿‿‿‿‿‿‿‿‿‿‿‿‿‿

4 tablespoons chopped fresh
    cilantro

About 30 fresh curry leaves

1 fresh hot green chili,
    chopped

2 cups plain yogurt

½ teaspoon salt, or to taste

1 teaspoon ground roasted
    cumin seeds (see page xx),
    plus extra for serving

Rohit's family believes that curry leaves help to lower cholesterol. This is another simple, nutritious, and cooling drink that can be served with meals or by itself. "Chaas" is a common North Indian name for yogurt and buttermilk drinks. It is only in the state of Punjab that these drinks are known as lassi, a name that seems to have taken over. SERVES 2

‿‿‿‿‿‿‿‿‿‿‿‿‿‿‿‿‿‿‿‿‿‿‿‿‿‿‿‿‿‿‿‿‿‿‿‿

From Rohit Gandhi in Bombay

1. Put 1 cup water into a blender, add the cilantro, curry leaves, and green chilies and blend thoroughly. Add the yogurt, salt, and cumin and blend again. Strain into a jug through a fine sieve, pushing out as much liquid as possible. Refrigerate until needed.

2. To serve, pour into two glasses, adding a few ice cubes to each one, and dust with a little extra ground cumin seeds.

SWEET CARDAMOM-FLAVORED YOGURT DRINK

MEETHI CHAAS

~~~~~~

2 cups plain yogurt

3 tablespoons sugar, or to taste

1 teaspoon ground cardamom
    seeds

A sweet, cooling drink that can be served with meals or by itself.

SERVES 2

~~~~~~

1. Put all the ingredients into a blender, add 1 cup water, and blend thoroughly. Refrigerate until needed.

2. To serve, pour into two glasses, adding a few ice cubes to each one.

A NOTE ON RASAM

"Rasam" is the Tamil name for a watery, soupy dish that is eaten all over South India. It is known as "saaru" in Kannada and "chaaru" in Telegu, but it also has numerous other names, including "pulusu," "pulichaar," and "satamudhu." Most of the names imply a juice, an essence, or an infusion of some sort.

A rasam is always sour and hot, and those characteristics initially came from tamarind and black pepper. But since India was introduced to tomatoes and red chilies in the fifteenth century, these have happily been added to the earlier ingredients. Stock can also be used in a rasam. The water comes not from meat but from cooked split peas, and is utterly delicious.

At a traditional meal in Tamil Nadu, where all courses are served with rice, prayers come first, then rice with ghee, followed by rice with sambar (see page 166) and assorted vegetables, then rice with rasam, and, finally, rice with yogurt, pickles, and so forth. Everything is eaten with the right hand. No utensils are used, even for the soupiest of dishes.

If you have ever eaten a mulligatawny soup, you should know that its origins lie centuries back in a rasam. The British perhaps mispronounced the words "milagu tannir," which mean "black pepper water." Milagu tannir was just one kind of rasam made with an infusion of black pepper and tamarind. And, of course, the British wanted to eat the "soup" with a spoon, so the rasam was thickened, a little rice was added (instead of the rasam being added to the rice), and a spoon was provided.

And that brings me to the question of serving and eating rasams in the West. It has now become quite customary, even in India, to serve rasam in a small glass or cup or even a wineglass (if the liquid is at room temperature) as a drink. The only problem is that there are all manner of bits and bobs in a rasam. Some float to the top, others sink to the bottom, some hover in the middle. So, ideally, a small spoon has to be offered for stirring. You should stir the rasam from the bottom as you serve it, and stir it before you take a sip. Any curry leaves, chilies, etc., that float up should be put to the side as elegantly as you can. You could also try removing them before you serve.

I have yet another way to serve my rasams. I ladle them into old-fashioned soup plates and put an ice cream scoop of hot rice in the center. And yes, I offer soup spoons.

You will find four very different rasams in this chapter—one made with tamarind, another with yogurt, a third with tomatoes, and a fourth with the stock from toovar dal and tamarind water. Serve them as a small drink or a soup, however you wish.

TAMARIND RASAM

PACHI PULUSU

1 ball of tamarind, about
    1½ inches in diameter

½ teaspoon salt

3 tablespoons peeled and very
    finely chopped onion

1–2 fresh hot green chilies,
    lightly roasted, then
    mashed

2 tablespoons finely chopped
    fresh cilantro leaves

1 teaspoon sugar

2 teaspoons olive or peanut oil

1 teaspoon whole brown
    mustard seeds

½ teaspoon whole cumin
    seeds

1–2 dried hot red chilies,
    broken in half

1 clove garlic, peeled and
    crushed

6–7 fresh curry leaves, lightly
    crushed in your hand

Like most rasams, this can be served in a glass as a drink, and often is, but its main function is to be eaten with rice (see note on page 359). In the Telengana region of Andhra Pradesh, where this dish originates, it is often combined with roasted and ground sesame seeds that thicken it slightly. If you wish to do that, roast 2 teaspoons of sesame seeds in a small cast-iron frying pan set over medium heat, stirring them until they are a shade darker and emit a roasted aroma. Allow to cool, then grind them and stir into the rasam. Also, some people like to roast the green chilies over a fire or in a hot cast-iron pan and crush them into the tamarind juice. I have done that here, but it is not essential.

There are many types of tamarind available. It is best to buy the kind that comes packed in blocks with most of the seeds removed. I like the blocks from Thailand best, as they are much softer and easier to handle.

In the summer this dish can be served cold, either in a small glass or cup. You could also serve it in a soup plate with a scoop of hot Rice with Moong Dal and Potatoes (see page 175) in the center. In Andhra Pradesh they serve this combination with Simple Hard-boiled Egg Curry (see page 282) and some crisp popadams as a light meal.   SERVES 3–4

From Shobhana and Padma Reddy in Hyderabad

1. Break the tamarind into small pieces and place in a medium bowl. Add 3 cups boiling water and set aside for 30 minutes. Rub the tamarind pieces with your fingers to release all the pulp. Strain into another bowl and add the salt, onions, green chilies (one at a time to gauge the heat), cilantro, and sugar. Stir to mix and taste for balance of seasonings.

2. Put the oil in a small frying pan and set over medium heat. When hot, add the mustard seeds. As soon as they pop, a matter of seconds, add the cumin and red chilies. When the chilies darken, add the garlic and stir once or twice. Add the curry leaves (take care, as they will splutter) and quickly pour the contents of the pan over the tamarind mixture. Stir and set aside for 30 minutes. Serve at room temperature.

A toddy tapper in Andhra Pradesh

YOGURT RASAM

MOR RASAM

ભળભળભળભળભળભળભળભળભળભળભળભળભળભળભળભળભળભળ

1 cup sour plain yogurt (see
  introduction)
Pinch of ground turmeric
½ teaspoon salt
2 teaspoons plain toovar dal
½ teaspoon whole black
  peppercorns
1 teaspoon whole cumin seeds
2 teaspoons olive or peanut oil
½ teaspoon whole brown
  mustard seeds
2–3 hot dried red chilies
Pinch of ground asafetida
6–7 fresh curry leaves, lightly
  crushed in your hand

The yogurt used in this South Indian dish needs to be quite sour. Some of the acidophilus yogurts sold by health-food stores are perfect for this dish. Indian grocers also sell good yogurt, often calling it "dahi," its North Indian name. Try to get as natural a yogurt as you can, then leave it unrefrigerated for twenty-four hours: that should sour it.

The dry red chilies in the tarka (see page xxii) may be broken in half before dropping them into the oil. This will make the rasam hotter.

Serve with plain rice or as a drink with the meal or before it. Stir as you drink it.   SERVES 2–3

ભળભળભળભળભળભળભળભળભળભળભળભળભળભળભળભળભળભળ

1. Put the yogurt in a medium pan and beat lightly with a whisk until smooth and creamy. Slowly add 1 cup water, whisking as you go. Add the turmeric and salt and whisk them in too.

2. Put a small cast-iron frying pan over medium heat. When hot, add the toovar dal, peppercorns, and cumin seeds. Stir and roast until the dal is a shade darker and the cumin smells roasted. Transfer to a plate to cool, then grind to as fine a powder as you can manage. Whisk this powder into the yogurt mixture. Set the yogurt over medium-low heat, whisking lightly. Just before it comes to a boil, take it off the heat.

3. Put the oil in the frying pan used for roasting the spices and set over medium heat. When hot, add the mustard seeds and red chilies. As soon as the seeds start to pop, a matter of seconds, add the asafetida and curry leaves (take care, as they will splutter). Quickly pour this mixture over the yogurt, then stir together. Serve warm or at room temperature, always stirring from the bottom first.

TOMATO RASAM

THAKAALI RASAM

Made mainly with tomatoes, this is a lovely rasam (see note on page 359) that can be served hot, warm, or at room temperature. If you wish it to remain only as spicy as it is just after you make it, remove all the chilies when you finish cooking. In South India this dish is always very hot, making a perfect contrast with bland rice.

SERVES 4

1 ball of tamarind, about 1 inch in diameter (for the best type, see page 360)

3 tomatoes (about 13–14 oz in all), peeled and finely chopped

3 cloves garlic, peeled, crushed, and finely chopped

2–3 fresh hot green chilies, slit open lengthwise

1¼ teaspoons salt

1¼ teaspoons sugar

¼ teaspoon ground turmeric

1 teaspoon ground cumin

1 teaspoon ground coriander

1 teaspoon freshly ground black pepper

2 teaspoons olive or peanut oil

½ teaspoon whole brown mustard seeds

2 dried hot red chilies, broken in half if you want the dish really hot

Pinch of ground asafetida

7–8 fresh curry leaves, lightly crushed in your hand

2 tablespoons fresh cilantro leaves

1. Break the tamarind into several pieces and soak in 1 cup boiling water for 30 minutes. Rub the tamarind with your fingers to release all the pulp, then strain the tamarind water into a medium pan. Add the tomatoes, garlic, green chilies, salt, sugar, turmeric, cumin, coriander, black pepper, and 4 cups water. Stir and bring to a boil, then lower the heat and simmer very gently for 30 minutes. Taste for balance of sugar and salt, adding whatever is needed.

2. Put the oil in a small frying pan and set over medium heat. When hot, add the mustard seeds. As soon as they pop, a matter of seconds, add the red chilies and asafetida. When the chilies darken, add the curry leaves (take care, as they will splutter). Stir once and pour this mixture over the rasam. Stir again, then sprinkle the fresh cilantro over the top.

RASAM

SAARU OR CHAARU OR RASAM

½ cup plain toovar dal

1 ball of tamarind, about
    1 inch in diameter (for the
    best type, see page 360)

1 medium tomato, peeled and
    finely chopped

1 medium onion, peeled and
    finely chopped

1 fresh hot green chili, finely
    chopped

1 clove garlic, peeled and
    crushed

¼ teaspoon nice red chili
    powder

1 teaspoon ground coriander

¼ teaspoon ground turmeric

1 teaspoon salt

½ teaspoon sugar

1 tablespoon plain toovar dal

½ teaspoon black peppercorns

1 teaspoon whole cumin seeds

FOR THE TARKA

2 teaspoons ghee (clarified
    butter) or olive or peanut
    oil

½ teaspoon urad dal

½ teaspoon whole brown
    mustard seeds

1–2 dried hot red chilies

Pinch of ground asafetida

5–6 fenugreek seeds

7–9 fresh curry leaves, lightly
    crushed in your hand

1 clove garlic, peeled and
    crushed

This is the most traditional rasam served, with slight variations, in many South Indian homes in Tamil Nadu, Andhra Pradesh, and Karnataka (see note on page 359). The base of this drink is the water that comes from boiling toovar dal. This is the "stock." There are several little steps involved in getting this rasam right. None of them is hard to do, and the results are most gratifying.

SERVES 4–5

1. Wash the dal in several changes of water, then drain and place in a medium pan. Add 6 cups water and bring to a boil. Skim off the froth, then cover partially and simmer for 1 hour. Strain into a large pan, getting at least 4 cups of liquid. If there is not enough, add a little water. Save the cooked dal for other purposes.

2. While the dal is cooking, break the tamarind ball into pieces and soak in 1 cup boiling water for at least 30 minutes. Rub the tamarind with your fingers to release all the pulp, then strain the tamarind water into the pan of dal stock. Add the tomatoes, onions, green chilies, garlic, chili powder, ground coriander, turmeric, salt, and sugar.

3. Put a small cast-iron frying pan over medium heat. When hot, add the toovar dal, black peppercorns, and cumin seeds. Stir and roast until the dal is a shade darker and the cumin smells roasted. Transfer to a plate to cool, then grind to as fine a powder as you can manage. Add this powder to the pan of rasam and bring to a boil. Reduce the heat to medium low and simmer vigorously for 30 minutes or until reduced by about 20 percent. Taste for balance of seasonings, making adjustments as needed.

4. To make the tarka (see page xxii), put the ghee into a small cast-iron frying and set over medium heat. When hot, add the urad dal. As soon as it starts to color, add the mustard seeds, red chilies, and asafetida. When the seeds pop and the chilies darken, a matter of seconds, add the fenugreek seeds, curry leaves (take care, as they will splutter), and garlic. Stir once or twice, then empty the contents of the frying pan into the rasam. Simmer gently for another 10 minutes. Stir from the bottom before serving.

5. I like to serve this hot, in an old-fashioned soup plate with a scoop of hot, plain rice in the center.

A NOTE ON JAGGERY

Jaggery is a form of raw sugar. My father once managed a sugar factory that made refined sugar and candy. Our house at that time was set in the middle of acres upon acres of sugar cane. The cane was cut, juiced, and then boiled. As the juice solidified, it was called jaggery. You could get it fairly molten in the early stages, but then it got harder. As India has always had sugar cane, jaggery has been used since ancient times and is as popular today as it ever was. It is used in many sweet dishes and brittles.

There are really two types of jaggery in India. Along the coast it is made from both palm sugar and sugar cane, but inland only sugar cane jaggery is available.

Indian grocers in the West sell jaggery in various shapes—cones, pebbles, or big rocks—and in colors ranging from dark brown to light brown and everything in between. Sometimes it is crumbly and at other times it is very hard. For the recipes in this book, look for light-colored jaggery that is soft and crumbly. You can use light brown sugar as a substitute, but it will not have the true jaggery flavor.

MELON PAYASAM

KHARBOOJA PAYASAM

~~~~~~

4 cups very finely chopped melon (green or orange flesh)

2 lightly packed cups pale-colored jaggery, grated

¾ cup coconut milk, from a well-shaken can

½ teaspoon ground cardamom seeds, plus a little extra for sprinkling

Meera Prasad cooked what can best be described as a banquet for us in Bangalore, at the end of which she presented this melon payasam. Nothing could have been nicer. Payasam, in South India, is a pudding, generally made with grains or beans and sometimes with fruit. I love fruit desserts, as they tend to be lighter and somehow perfect after a spicy Indian meal. This is served cold, so for me it is doubly perfect—cooling and refreshing. I have been serving it frequently, and now you can do the same. I like to serve this in an ice cream dish with a spoon, as it is fairly watery.

I have used jaggery, a raw Indian sugar here (see note on page 366). I buy the palest variety and grate it on the coarsest part of the grater. You can use light brown sugar instead, but taste as you go because you will need much less of it.

I bought a large melon that weighed about 3¾ lbs. After removing the skin and seeds and chopping it, I got 2 lbs finely chopped flesh. For chopping the melon into a kind of mush just short of pulverization, I use a large knife. I am careful to preserve all the juices and then add them to the melon. You could also put larger pieces of melon into a food processor and chop them very small by pulsing in short bursts.   SERVES 4–5

~~~~~~

From Meera Prasad

Place all the ingredients in a bowl and stir together. Cover and chill in the refrigerator. Dust with a little ground cardamom before serving.

MELON BALLS WITH MINT

PUDINA KHARBOOJA

∽∾∽∾∽∾∽∾∽∾∽∾∽∾∽∾∽∾∽∾∽∾∽∾∽∾∽∾∽∾∽∾∽∾

1 large melon, about 3¾ lbs

1 teaspoon ground cardamom
seeds

6 tablespoons sugar

About 35 fresh mint leaves,
very finely chopped

2 tablespoons lime juice

2–3 teaspoons kewra water,
rose water, or orange
blossom water

A lovely summery dessert, this needs to be made ahead of time and refrigerated.

The melon should be very sweet. If you have a double-ended melon baller, use the larger end of the scoop.

Kewra water has an aroma very similar to that of the Southeast Asian paandaan leaf, a lovely tropical fragrance. Rose water or orange blossom water may be substituted.   SERVES 4–5

∽∾∽∾∽∾∽∾∽∾∽∾∽∾∽∾∽∾∽∾∽∾∽∾∽∾∽∾∽∾∽∾∽∾

1. Cut the melon in half and discard all the seeds. Using a melon baller, scoop out the flesh and place in a serving bowl. Sprinkle with the cardamom and mix well.

2. Put the sugar in a small bowl. Add the mint leaves and rub them into the sugar with your fingers. Add the lime juice and your choice of fragrant water. Mix well and pour over the melon balls. Mix, cover, and refrigerate, stirring every now and then. Serve cold in small dishes with the juices.

CARDAMOM-FLAVORED BUTTER BISCUITS

NAAN KHATAI

⌘⌘⌘⌘⌘⌘⌘⌘⌘⌘⌘⌘⌘⌘⌘⌘⌘⌘⌘⌘⌘⌘⌘⌘⌘⌘⌘⌘⌘

⅓ cup flour

⅓ cup sooji (Indian semolina, see page 197)

⅓ cup chickpea flour (besan or gram flour)

¼ teaspoon baking powder

½ teaspoon ground cardamom seeds

½ cup soft unsalted butter, plus a little extra for greasing

⅔ cup sugar

1 tablespoon chopped flaked almonds

1 tablespoon chopped raw pistachios

These are my favorite Indian biscuits, and very easy to put together. I have loved naan khatai since I was a child. They are light and crumbly and also slightly chewy, with a texture somewhere between that of shortbread and a macaroon. MAKES 24

⌘⌘⌘⌘⌘⌘⌘⌘⌘⌘⌘⌘⌘⌘⌘⌘⌘⌘⌘⌘⌘⌘⌘⌘⌘⌘⌘⌘⌘

1. Preheat the oven to 375°F.

2. Combine the flour, sooji, chickpea flour, baking powder, and cardamom in a medium bowl. Mix together with a fork or dry whisk.

3. Put the butter and sugar in a large bowl. Using an electric beater, cream the two together until light and frothy. Add the flour mixture, then use your hands and a light touch to combine them and form a ball of dough. Break the ball into 24 equal parts and roll each into a ball. Make sure there are no cracks in the balls. Flatten the balls very slightly between your palms.

4. Grease a baking sheet with butter. Lay the slightly flattened balls on it about 1½ inches apart. Cut shallow lines in the pattern of a tic-tac-toe grid on top of each biscuit without going right to the edge. Place a mixture of the nuts in the central square, pushing them down a bit so they do not roll off. Bake for 12–14 minutes (they will still be very soft), then set aside to cool on the sheet for 5 minutes. Using a fine spatula, carefully transfer them to a wire rack to cool completely. Store in a flat, airtight container.

FRIED STUFFED DATES

KHAJOOR KA MEETHA

℣℥℣℥℣℥℣℥℣℥℣℥℣℥℣℥℣℥℣℥℣℥℣℥℣℥

16 medium-sized dates, stoned

About 3 tablespoons chopped raw pistachios and walnuts

3 tablespoons ghee (clarified butter)

1 cup heavy cream, whipped to a soft foam

A long time ago, when I was working on my very first cookbook, I wrote a recipe for simple fried dates that I had learned from my sister, Kamal, who had learned it from her Gujarati Bohra in-laws. It was a sticky, chewy, and easy-to-make sweetmeat, and I just loved it. So, apparently, did Elizabeth David. When my book was published, she wrote me a little note to say so. That made my day! I have been cooking those dates for several decades, but over time I have added this or that to them. Here is my newest variation. I serve it at the end of the meal with coffee, along with Cardamom-Flavored Butter Biscuits (see page 370), and squares of Sooji Halva (see page 376), both of which I make in advance. The dates, though, have to be made at the last minute, but they could be stuffed well ahead of time and kept covered.

Note that the nuts need to be chopped to a fairly small size so they can be stuffed into a date, but not so small that they turn into crumbs.

MAKES 16 DATES

℣℥℣℥℣℥℣℥℣℥℣℥℣℥℣℥℣℥℣℥℣℥℣℥℣℥

1. If the dates have been stoned by making a slit down one side, open them up slightly, one at a time, and stuff about ½ teaspoon of the nuts inside them. If the stones have been pulled out from the top, you will have to push the nuts in from the top and bottom of the date. Cover the stuffed dates with plastic wrap and set aside until you are ready to eat them.

2. Put the ghee in a medium nonstick frying pan and set over medium heat. When hot, add the dates and stir them around for 10–20 seconds. Using a slotted spoon, quickly transfer them to a dish and serve immediately. Offer the cream separately to put on top of the dates.

CARAMELIZED BANANAS WITH SESAME SEEDS

KELAY KA MEETHA

1 teaspoon sesame seeds

2 tablespoons ghee (clarified butter) or ordinary butter

2 tablespoons sugar

2 ripe but very firm bananas

½ cup heavy cream, lightly whipped to soft peaks (optional)

A simple sweet or dessert that could be made hastily for a hungry child or grown-up.   SERVES 2–4

1. Put a small cast-iron frying pan over medium heat. When hot, add the sesame seeds and roast them for a minute or so, stirring until they are a shade darker and smell roasted. They might fly about, in which case, cover loosely but keep stirring. Transfer to a small bowl when done. (This can be done ahead of time.)

2. Put the ghee or butter in a medium nonstick frying pan and set over low heat. When it has melted, sprinkle in the sugar evenly. Stir and let the sugar start to caramelize. Peel the bananas and cut them in half crosswise, then lengthwise. Place them in the pan in a single layer and cook over medium-low heat for about 1½ minutes on each side or until they are golden and coated with the caramel.

3. Transfer the bananas to a serving dish and sprinkle the sesame seeds over the top. Serve hot, offering the whipped cream separately (if using).

SOOJI PUDDING WITH COCONUT MILK

SOOJI KHEER

༄ ༄

4 tablespoons ghee (clarified
butter)

4 tablespoons coarsely
chopped raw cashews

4 tablespoons golden raisins

3½ oz sooji (Indian semolina,
see page 197)

1½ cups light brown sugar
(taste and add more, if
desired, when the kheer
thickens)

½ teaspoon ground cardamom
seeds

A 14-fl-oz can coconut milk,
well shaken

From the Goa region of western India, this dish is one of those
soothing, calming puddings that would make toddlers as happy
as grown-ups. It is similar to rice pudding, except it is made with
sooji, not rice. It is somewhat like the next recipe for halva, but
kheers are less dense and a bit more flowing. This also has the
lovely coastal taste of coconut and cashews.

In India, some fresh coconut, ground so it is satiny smooth, is
added to the kheer. I can never get mine to the right texture, so
I have just left it out and used only coconut milk, which is also
called for. This kheer gets thicker as it sits, so you might need to
thin it with water or coconut milk if you do not eat it immediately.

SERVES 6

༄ ༄

From the Highway Gomantak restaurant in Bombay

1. Put the ghee in a medium nonstick deep frying pan and set
over medium-low heat. When hot, add the cashews and stir
until they turn golden. Using a slotted spoon, quickly transfer
the nuts to a plate.

2. Add the golden raisins to the ghee remaining in the pan.
They will plump up almost immediately. Remove them with the
slotted spoon and put next to the cashews.

3. Put the sooji into the remaining ghee and fry over low heat
for 6–7 minutes, stirring now and then, until it is golden. Add
the sugar and mix well. Add 2½ cups water, the ground cardamom, and most of the reserved nuts and golden raisins (save
some for the decoration). Bring to a simmer over medium-low
heat, then stir and cook over low heat for 4 minutes. Add the

coconut milk, stir, and cook for 5–6 minutes, until the kheer has thickened. Turn off the heat and keep stirring gently until the kheer has cooled a bit. It will also get thicker. Cover the kheer with plastic wrap in such a way that it touches the whole surface of it. This will prevent a skin forming on the top.

4. Serve hot, warm, or at room temperature, decorated with the remaining nuts and golden raisins.

SOOJI HALVA

~~~~~~

4 tablespoons ghee (clarified
butter)

2 tablespoons flaked almonds

2 tablespoons raw, shelled
pistachios, cut into slivers
lengthwise

½ cup sooji (Indian semolina,
see page 197)

⅓ cup sugar

¼ teaspoon ground cardamom
seeds

Sooji, an Indian semolina made with soft wheat, may be used to make quick savory dishes, but it makes equally quick sweet dishes as well. The most popular among them is probably this halva, enjoyed equally by the poorest villager and the richest industrialist in North India. As it is always offered to the gods at temples on religious occasions, then given back to people praying at the temples as prashad (blessed food), it carries with it an air of holiness even when it is cooked at home.

Sooji halva is cooked in ghee and very easy to prepare. It is often eaten by itself as a sweet dish or dessert. You can eat it just the way it comes out of the frying pan, hot and soft, or you can put it into a square or rectangular cake tin, press down on it, and then cut it into squares. These have a cake-like texture and are perfect with a cup of tea.

But there is another way sooji halva is served. At Sunday breakfasts it is frequently offered, nice and hot, with Pooris (see page 235) and spicy potatoes, such as Potatoes Cooked in a Banarasi Style (see page 107). The combination of something sweet and something spicy is quite enticing.

My halva is lightly sweetened, just the way I like it. If you want it sweeter, add another 1–2 tablespoons of sugar.   SERVES 4–5

~~~~~~

1. Put the ghee in a medium nonstick frying pan and set over medium-low heat. When hot, add the almonds and pistachios, and stir just until the almonds turn golden. Using a slotted spoon, quickly transfer the nuts to a plate.

2. Put the sooji into the ghee remaining in the pan and fry over low heat for 6–7 minutes, stirring now and then, until it is golden. Add the sugar and mix well. Add 1½ cups water, the ground cardamom, and the reserved nuts, and bring to a sim-

mer over medium-low heat. Stir and cook over very low heat for 2–3 minutes, then turn off the heat and stir for another minute. Serve hot.

3. If you prefer, you could put the halva into a 7 x 7 inch cake pan or similarly shaped dish. Press down lightly and flatten the surface, then cut into 1½ inch squares. When it has cooled to room temperature, place plastic wrap directly on the surface of the cake to stop a skin forming. Serve immediately or later, as you would any cake.

SOOJI CRÊPES STUFFED WITH CARAMELIZED APPLES, COCONUT, AND WALNUTS

SOOJI KI BHARVA PANCAKE

½ cup plain yogurt

1 cup sooji (Indian semolina, see page 197)

½ cup rice flour (also called rice powder)

2 tablespoons flour

¼ teaspoon salt

1 tablespoon sugar

About 2 tablespoons olive or peanut oil

FOR THE STUFFING

8 tablespoons/1 stick unsalted butter

4 large Granny Smith or other sour, firm apples

½ teaspoon ground cardamom

2 tablespoons chopped walnuts

2 tablespoons chopped raw pistachios

2 tablespoons chopped flaked almonds

½ cup finely shredded fresh coconut, or defrosted if frozen

½ cup sugar

FOR SERVING

1 cup heavy cream

1 tablespoon sugar

¼ teaspoon ground cardamom

In Goa, pancakes are often stuffed with a sweetened coconut and nut mixture. I have added apples to it to make a stuffing of my own. The crêpes are very similar to the Sooji Pancakes on page 239, but instead of spices, they have a bit of sugar in them.

The filling and the crêpes may be made a few hours ahead of time, but do not refrigerate them. Put the filling in a covered dish, then stack the crêpes, interleaved with sheets of waxed paper or parchment paper, and wrap the bundle in foil. Shortly before serving, put the dish of stuffing and the foil bundle into a warming oven to reheat. Serve warm, not hot.　SERVES 6

1. Place the yogurt in a bowl and beat lightly with a fork or whisk until smooth and creamy. Slowly add 2½ cups water, mixing well as you go.

2. Put the sooji, rice flour, flour, salt, and sugar in a large bowl. Slowly add the yogurt combination, mixing until thoroughly blended and you have a batter free of lumps. Set aside for at least 1 hour.

3. To make the stuffing, put the butter into a medium nonstick frying pan and set over very low heat to melt. Meanwhile, peel and core the apples and slice them straight into the butter, folding them in as you do so. I get about 6 thinnish slices from each apple quarter. Add the cardamom, all the nuts, the coconut, and sugar. Stir gently and cook over medium-low heat for about 4 minutes, until the sugar has completely dissolved. Increase the heat to medium high and continue cooking, stirring gently now and then, until the mixture has caramelized a bit, about 7–8 minutes. Turn off the heat and set aside, covered.

4. Put the oil in a small bowl and stick a teaspoon in it. Have two plates nearby to hold the pancakes as they are made. Measure ⅓ cup water into a ladle and mentally note the level to get an idea of how much batter you will need each time.

5. Place a nonstick frying pan over medium heat and add 1 teaspoon of oil to it. When hot, stir the batter from the bottom and slowly pour a ladleful into the pan in an expanding circle about 6 inches in diameter. This batter is very forgiving, so you can fill up any holes and round off the pancake to get the shape you want. Let the pancake sit for a minute or so, until the underside is golden red.

6. Slide a spatula underneath and flip the pancake over. Cook for another minute or so, until the other side is also golden red. Transfer to a plate.

7. Make at least another 6 pancakes in the same way; the first one rarely turns out perfectly, so you might be making 7 or 8. Remember to stir the batter thoroughly each time from the bottom. Place a sheet of waxed paper or parchment paper between each pancake and cover the stack with an upside-down plate. Leftover batter can be stored in the refrigerator for several days.

8. Whip the cream into soft peaks, adding the sugar and the cardamom. Refrigerate until needed.

9. To serve, lay a pancake, best side down, on a plate. Place as much stuffing as will fit easily on half of it, then fold the uncovered half over it. Put a good-sized dollop of cream on top. (Leftover stuffing can be refrigerated and used later.)

MANGOES MUMTAZ

AAM MUMTAZ

ഇഇഇഇഇഇഇഇഇഇഇഇഇഇഇഇഇഇഇഇഇഇഇഇ

FOR THE PRALINE

Olive or peanut oil, for
    greasing
½ cup chopped unsalted, raw
    pistachios
½ cup sugar
½ teaspoon ground cardamom
    seeds

FOR THE MANGOES

1 cup heavy cream
3 tablespoons sugar
½ teaspoon ground cardamom
    seeds
½ cup chopped unsalted, raw
    pistachios
¾ cup canned, sweetened
    Alphonso mango purée
1 cup fresh mango flesh,
    preferably from an Indian
    Alphonso or other good
    ripe mango, neatly diced

It has never been easy for me to decide what the dessert should be after one of my more formal Indian dinners. I like light, fruity desserts, but India seems to have a shortage of them (we tend to eat fresh fruit instead), so I have taken to creating my own. This is one of them. I have been serving it in different versions over the last twenty years, and this is the latest incarnation.

I was to attend the Mango Festival in Florida one year, and shortly before it a reporter from the *Miami Herald* came to interview me in New York. She turned out to be an old friend, Maricel Presilla, the most knowledgeable wizard of Latin American cooking. I made a lunch for her that ended with this dessert. "What is it called?" she asked as she took notes. "I don't know," I answered. "It is just something I make." "You can't have no name for it. Let's call it . . ." And so Maricel named it "Mangoes Mumtaz."

The best mango purée you can use is one that comes from canned, sweetened Alphonso mangoes. Indian grocers sell them.

SERVES 4

ഇഇഇഇഇഇഇഇഇഇഇഇഇഇഇഇഇഇഇഇഇഇഇഇ

1. First make the praline. Preheat the oven to 350°F. Grease a small baking sheet with oil.

2. Spread the pistachios on another baking sheet and put them into the oven. Stir every few minutes until lightly toasted. Set aside.

3. Put the sugar into a small, heavy-based saucepan and set over medium-high heat. Keep swirling the pan as the sugar melts and then starts to caramelize. As soon as it becomes light brown, add the toasted pistachios and the ground cardamom seeds. Let the mixture bubble for a few seconds as you stir. Quickly take the pan off the heat and spread the praline on the oiled baking sheet. Allow 10 minutes for it to cool and harden, then break

into pieces and either crush in a mortar or whiz in a blender. Keep it in a screw-top jar and use as needed.

4. The rest of the dessert should be made just before serving. Whip the cream with the sugar until it forms soft peaks. Add the ground cardamom and pistachios, plus 1–2 tablespoons of the praline, and fold together. Pour in the mango purée and fold lightly so you can see swirls of both white and orange.

5. Scoop the mixture into four serving bowls. Divide the diced mango between the bowls, mixing it in lightly. Decorate each bowl with a teaspoon of the praline and serve immediately.

ഔഔഔഔഔഔഔഔഔഔഔഔഔഔഔഔഔഔഔഔഔഔഔഔഔഔഔഔഔ

CHAPTER RECIPE LISTS

ഔഔഔഔഔഔഔഔഔഔഔഔഔഔഔഔഔഔഔഔഔഔഔഔഔഔഔഔഔ

SOUPS, APPETIZERS, AND SNACKS

DALS:
DRIED BEANS AND LEGUMES

EGGS AND DAIRY

CHUTNEYS, RELISHES, AND SALADS

DRINKS, SWEETS, AND DESSERTS

ೞೞೞೞೞೞೞೞೞೞೞೞೞೞೞೞೞೞೞೞೞೞೞೞೞೞೞೞೞೞ

ACKNOWLEDGMENTS

ೞೞೞೞೞೞೞೞೞೞೞೞೞೞೞೞೞೞೞೞೞೞೞೞೞೞೞೞ

I would like to thank the following for helping me to make this book possible: Vikram Doctor, Rita D'Souza, Fatma Zakaria, Sunita Nair, the Taj Hotel in Bombay, Shashikala Potnis and Sanjali Potnis at the Highway Gomantak restaurant in Bombay, Rajul Gandhi, Boman Kohinoor at Britannia and Company, Usha Subramaniam, Rohit, Sarita, Kapil, and Yogesh Malhotra at Dell' Arte Inde, Ravi Gandhi at Gazdar, Aziz Javeri at Joy Shoes, Kalini Kodial, Suman Kodial, Simran Lal, and Anita Lal from Good Earth, Meera Kumar, Cecelia Kerketta, Mugdha Savkar, Janaki Shirgaonkar, Tarini Bahadur, the Chinmaya Mission in Delhi, the Aurobindo Ashram in Delhi, Saraswathy Ganapathy and Girish Karnad, Geetha Rao, Malathi Srinivasan, Nina Bopiah, Kaveri Ponnapa, Nina Chandavarkar, Tara Chandavarkar, Shantha Gersappe, Sarvanna, Dr. Meera Prasad, Chef Selveraju at Vivanta by Taj in Bangalore, Varukaranam Usha Rani, K. P. Uthappa and Vani Uthappa, Chhoti and Kiran Machaiah, Mynah Pemmaiah, Heera Nandi, Zubeda Vagh, Chef Srinivasan at the Windflower Resort and Spa in Mysore, Swarnalatha and Rajalaxshmi, Andrew, our driver, Usha Ramakrishna, Vinita Pittie, Geeta Devi, Falaknuma Palace Hotel, Rehana, Anwar Alikhan and his family, Sanjeeda Shareef, D. Lalitha, Smita Kulkarni, Shobhana Reddy, Padma Reddy, the Babai Hotel in Vijaywada, S. Sampoorna, the Taj Gateway Hotels in Vijaywada and Vishakapatnam, P. Posaiah and P. Ramanna, fisherfolk on Edilamma Lanka in the Godavari River, Jayanti Rajagopalan and her mother, Hotel Vasavi in Rajahmundry, Sayi Rani, Kaveri Kaul, Yasmeen Tayebbhai, Mehreen Khosla, Juji and Viru Dayal, Bhargavi Menon.

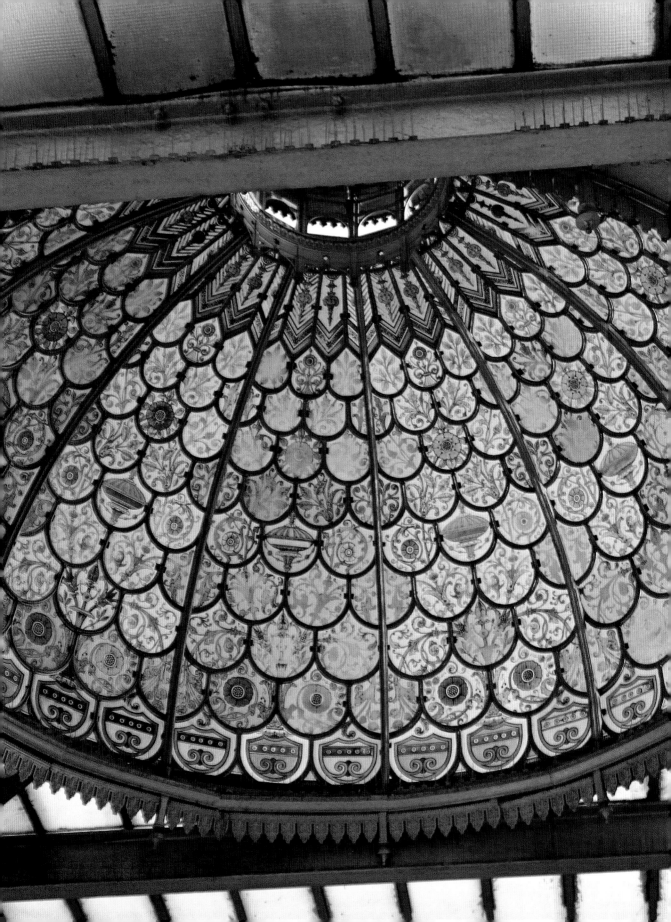

INDEX

chickpea flour (besan or gram flour)
(continued)
    Hot Yogurt Sauce from Southern
        India, 136–7
    and Tomato Pancakes, 248–9
    and Yogurt Sauce, Okra in, 138–9
chickpeas, 121
    in Fresh Coriander Sauce, 134
    in a Simple Northern Style, 132, 133
    Spinach Raita with, 330
chili(es):
    -Fried Eggs from Sri Lanka, 275
    green, fresh, xix–xx
    heat of, xix
    powder, heat of, xix
    red, dried, xix, xx
    tarka, xxiii
Chinese-inspired Indian dish: Stir-
        Fried Indian Cheese with Green
        Peppers, 294, 295
Chinmaya Mission, Delhi, 9, 355
Chitrapur Saraswat Brahmins of
        Coastal Kannada, Simple Toovar
        Dal from, 160–1
chutneys, 304–20
    Cilantro, Fresh, and Yogurt), 307
    Coconut, Simple, 306
    Dry, Made with Three Dals, 313
    Eggplant "Gojju" on Toast, 31–2
    Fresh Cilantro, Ginger, and Coconut,
        310
    Gingery Cranberry, with Mustard
        Seeds, 320, 321
    Green, 304, 305
    Green Mango, Sweet, 319
    Peanut and Garlic Crumble, Spicy, 312
    Peanut Crumble, Spicy, 311
    Red, 318
    Tamarind, Simple, 308, 309

Tomato and Ginger, 317
Yogurt and Pickle, Quick, 316
Yogurt Dipping Sauce, Simple, 328
Yogurt Sauce, 5
cilantro:
    Black-Eyed Peas with Green Chilies
        and, 122, 123
    Ginger, and Coconut Chutney, 310
    Green Chutney, 304, 305
    Sauce, Chickpeas in, 134
    and Yogurt Chutney, 307
    Yogurt Drink with Curry Leaves,
        Cumin and, 356, 357
coconut:
    Chutney, Simple, 306
    Fresh Cilantro, and Ginger Chutney,
        310
    Goan Black-Eyed Peas with, 124–5
    Kodava Mushroom Curry with, 86–8
    Milk, Sooji Pudding with, 374–5
    Red Chutney from Konkan Coast, 318
    Sauce, Wild Mushroom Stew with,
        26–7
    Sooji Crêpes Stuffed with
        Caramelized Apples, Walnuts and,
        379–80
    Steamed Green Beans with Mustard
        and, 60–1
Coorg (Kodagu), Coorg-style cooking,
    86, 336
    Broiled Portobello Mushrooms,
        28–30, 29
    Egg Curry with Potatoes, 285
    Kodava Mushroom Curry with
        Coconut, 86–8
    Simple Kodava Mushroom Curry, 90
    Yogurt with Cucumber, Kodava-Style,
        332
    Yogurt with Fresh Mango, 336–7

A NOTE ABOUT THE AUTHOR

Madhur Jaffrey is the author of many previous cookbooks—seven of which have won James Beard Awards—and was named to the Who's Who of Food and Beverage in America by the James Beard Foundation. She is the recipient of an honorary CBE from Queen Elizabeth II for her services to drama and promoting the appreciation of Indian food and culture. She is also an award-winning actress, having won the Silver Bear for Best Actress at the Berlin Film Festival, with numerous major motion pictures to her credit. She lives in New York City.

A NOTE ON THE TYPE

This book was set in Scala, a typeface designed by the Dutch designer Martin Majoor (b. 1960) in 1988 and released by the FontFont foundry in 1990. While designed as a fully modern family of fonts containing both a serif and a sans serif alphabet, Scala retains many refinements normally associated with traditional fonts.

Composed by North Market Street Graphics
Lancaster, Pennsylvania

Printed and bound by Toppan Leefung Printing
China

Designed by Soonyoung Kwon